Policing Euro^ ^s are to
^

Also by Bill Hebenton and Terry Thomas

B. Hebenton and T. Thomas, *Criminal Records: State, Citizen and the Politics of Protection*

T. Thomas, *The Police and Social Workers*

Policing Europe

Co-operation, Conflict and Control

Bill Hebenton

and

Terry Thomas

M

St. Martin's Press

First published in Great Britain 1995 by
MACMILLAN PRESS LTD
Houndmills, Basingstoke, Hampshire RG21 2XS
and London
Companies and representatives
throughout the world

A catalogue record for this book is available
from the British Library.

ISBN 0–333–60006–1 hardcover
ISBN 0–333–60007–X paperback

10   9   8   7   6   5   4   3   2   1
04   03   02   01   00   99   98   97   96   95

Printed in Malaysia

First published in the United States of America 1995 by
Scholarly and Reference Division,
ST. MARTIN'S PRESS, INC.,
175 Fifth Avenue,
New York, N.Y. 10010

ISBN 0–312–12423–6

Library of Congress Cataloging-in-Publication Data
Hebenton, Bill, 1955–
Policing Europe : co-operation, conflict, and control / Bill
Hebenton, Terry Thomas.
p. cm.
Includes bibliographical references and index.
ISBN 0–312–12423–6
1. Police—European Union countries—International cooperation.
I. Thomas, Terry, 1946–   . II. Title.
HV8194.5.A3H43   1995
363.2'094—dc20   94–27003
                                                       CIP

To all our loved ones – past, present and future

'It must be considered that there is nothing more difficult to carry out, nor more doubtful of success, nor more dangerous to handle, than to initiate a new order of things. For the reformer has enemies in all those who profit by the older order, and only lukewarm defenders in all those who would profit by the new order.'

Niccolò Machiavelli, *The Prince*

Contents

Contents

List of Figures

List of Tables

Acknowledgements

In the writing of this work we have accumulated numerous intellectual debts. Ken Pease, in his typical way, has always given more than he ever receives and the School of Social Policy at Manchester University continues to provide a reassuring and stimulating environment in which to work. Jon Spencer deserves a special 'thank you' for sharing his illuminating ideas on the situation in Eastern Europe. Also at Manchester, the Henry Fielding Centre for Police Studies and Crime Risk Management responded cheerfully to requests to use their library resources. Martin Baldwin-Edwards, formerly of the University of Manchester (now at the Institute for European Studies, Queen's University Belfast), contributed greatly to our understanding of current immigration debates. Thanks are due to colleagues at Leeds Metropolitan University; Sue Palmer and Paul Schofield for helping create necessary time for writing; Sheila Milner for word processing; Pat Fairfoot, Mary Cousins and Gary Dimmock for offering support in a variety of ways.

Thanks are also due to Alice Mahon MP for helping obtain 'difficult' material and to Eugene McLaughlin for his positive comments at an early stage of this work. At the Home Office we wish to thank Della Cannings.

Next several libraries and their staff deserve mention: the John Rylands University Library of Manchester; Leeds Metropolitan University Library; the Brotherton Library at the University of Leeds; the British Library Document Supply Centre at Boston Spa; and the Research Office of the European Parliament, London. In addition, several networks and their associated publications have contributed to our understanding of policing Europe, principally the Edinburgh University Project Team on European Police Co-operation, the *Statewatch* group; *Platform Fortress Europe* network; and our friends, the ever-youthful and enthusiastic Steve Wright and Pete Abel of the OMEGA Foundation, Manchester. Joanne Morrison helped in the preparation of the index and Denise Austin produced an excellent draft cover design,

We owe a debt of gratitude to Frances Arnold, our commissioning editor, for her faith in the project and her professionalism. Finally, this has been a truly joint transPennine project and we owe each other a special acknowledgement.

Manchester   BILL HEBENTON
Leeds   TERRY THOMAS

List of Abbreviations

ACIU	Analytical Criminal Intelligence Unit
ACPO	Association of Chief Police Officers
AMSS	Automatic Message Switching System
ASF	Automated Search Facility
BKA	Bundeskriminalamnt
BND	Bundesnachrichtendienst
BVD	BinnenlandseVeiligheidsdienst
CCC	Customs Co-ordinating Committee
CELAD	Comité Européen de la Lutte Anti-Drogue
CGI-SIE	Comisaria General de Informacion-Servicio de Informacion Exterior
CIREA	Centre for Information, Discussion and Exchange on Asylum
CIREFI	Centre for Information, Discussion and Exchange on Immigration
CIS	Customs Information System
CNIL	Commission Nationale de l'Informatique et des Libertés
COCOLAF	Community Co-ordination Committee on Fraud Prevention
COREPER	Committee of Permanent Representatives
CRI	Centrale Recherche Informatiedienst
DCPP	Direzione Centrale Della Polizia di Prevenzione
DEA	Drugs Enforcement Agency
DVLC	Driving Vehicle Licensing Centre
EDU	European Drugs Unit
EFTA	European Free Trade Area
EIS	European Information System
ELO	European Liaison Officer
ELS	European Liaison Section
ENP	European Network for Policewomen/men
EPC	European Political Co-operation

xiii

EPI-Centre	European Police Information Centre
FLNC	National Liberation Front of Corsica
FPIP	Fédération Professionelle Indépendente de la Police
HMI	Her Majesty's Inspectors
IACP	International Association of Chiefs of Police
ICAO	International Civil Aviation Organization
ICC	Internal Control Commission
ICPC	International Criminal Police Commission
ICPO	International Criminal Police Organization
ILO	International Labour Office
INADPAX	International Air Transport Association Control Working Group on Inadmissible Passengers
IPEC	International Police Exhibition and Conférence
IRP	Irish Republican Police
MAG	Mutual Assistance Group
MOUs	Memoranda of Understanding
NCB	National Central Bureau
NCIS	National Criminal Intelligence Service
NDIU	National Drugs Intelligence Unit
NFIU	National Football Intelligence Unit
NTSU	National Technical Support Unit
PNC	Police National Computer
POTA	Prevention of Terrorism Act
PRSU	Police Requirements Support Unit
PSDB	Police Scientific Development Branch
PWGOT	Police Working Group on Terrorism
R and D	Research and Development
RCS	Regional Crime Squad
RIC	Royal Irish Constabulary
RIO	Refugees in orbit
RUC	Royal Ulster Constabulary
SCENT	System Customs Enforcement Network
SCODA	Standing Conference on Drug Abuse
SD	Sicherheitsdierst
SEPAT	Stupéfiants Europe Plan d'Action à Terme
SGP	Syndicat Général de la Police

SIRENES	Supplementary Information Request at the National Entries
SIS	Schengen Information System
SOPEMI	Continuous Reporting System on Migration
STAR	Standiage Arbeidsgruppe Rauschgift
STCIP	Service Technique de Coopération Internationale de Police
TSF	Technical Support Function
UCLAF	Unité de la Coordination de la Lutte Anti-Fraude
UISP	Union Internationale des Syndicats de Police
USC	Ulster Special Constabulary
WITS	Working Group on International Technical Support

Introduction

For many of us, it appears that we live in increasingly fragmented times. The features of our lived experience appear to involve institutionalized pluralism, variety, contingency and ambivalence (Bauman 1992). Historically, policing has been viewed as a regalian function of the state. However, this conception of 'the past' of policing is increasingly under challenge (Reiner 1992a). Deeper social processes are transforming the police institution and part of this process is reflected in the complexities of co-operation, conflict and control in the policing of Europe.

To have the luxury of writing a book on Europe and policing at the present time is both opportune and problematic. Opportune in the sense that we appear to have entered a distinct period where European governnments see real benefits in striving towards enhanced practical police cooperation both as a response to perceived threats to order and security and as a means of compensating for removal of border controls. Problematic, since it can be argued at the European level we are on shifting sand – with highly flexible strategic and tactical alliances (and conflicts) between supranational bodies, individual European member states, police organizations and their constituencies. We argue in this book that the emergence of new forms of police co-operation and conflict reflects and itself constitutes what some refer to as the 'unfolding of a transnational policing system' (McLaughlin 1992).

With the increasing political and economic co-operation in the EC, enhanced police co-operation is high on each member state's agenda. Traditionally, commentators have stressed the position of the police as 'a mechanism for the distribution of non-negotiably coercive force' (Bittner 1971) and as the 'specialist repository domestically of the state's monopoly of

legitimate force (Reiner 1992a). In short, police is the label
and policing the means used by the state when asserting its
exclusive title to the use or threat of force against dangers
emanating from within its boundaries. This identification of
police with 'nation-state' (see Giddens 1985), however, begs
one of the central questions underpinning the discussion over
the forms of police co-operation appropriate to Europe in the
1990s, namely the nature of the relationship between Europeanization initiatives in the police sector, and integration
within the EC. This relationship displays a deep complexity.
In trying to understand or 'make sense' of this complexity, we
have found it useful to borrow from the fields of international
relations and political science two concepts not commonly
used in traditional police studies: first, the idea of 'internal
security deficit' and second, the notion of an 'international
regime'.

European Insecurities

In relation to the security dilemma, central to an adequate
understanding, in our view, is the argument that the external,
or international, function of the state is inseparable from the
internal, or societal, one. To put it differently, the state
operates in a complex environment in which policy discussions, process and outcomes cut across state boundaries and in
which the pattern of authority corresponds less and less to
that implied by a system of sovereign states. Here, according
to Nettl, 'the state acts for the society internationally, and
internal matters relating to foreign affairs are a state prerogative . . . In short, the state is the gatekeeper between intra-
societal flows of action' (Nettl 1968). At the general level,
political and strategic ambiguities cut across the sharply
demarcated boundaries implied by a notion of external
sovereignty. These ambiguities, themselves the expression of
a still unfolding process, are altering the significance of
territorial boundaries, and hence of the theoretical division
the domestic (intra-state) and international (inter-state) environment. In this context, power and authority are dispersed
across a far more diverse and complex set of interactions and

institutions than is postulated by the system of sovereign states. This is not to suggest that state sovereignty does not still constitute, at least formally, the dominant vehicle through which authority is exercised but rather to highlight the widening gap between form and substance.

We would argue that the failure of national states to make adaptive responses to an increasingly fragile global environment results in the further delegation of tasks and resources to international and supranational forums and agencies. This institutional outgrowth, even when directly instigated and monitored by states, is likely to give rise to an intricate pattern of co-operation and conflict which imposes yet further constraints on the state's freedom of action. In other words, the greater the need for policy co-ordination the more difficult it will be for governments to go it alone, and the greater the tendency for international institutions to place additional limitations on the practical options available to states. It can further be argued, therefore, that one very likely outcome is a patchwork or 'architecture' of contexts, coalitions and interactions within and between national societies that escape the effective control of the central policy organs of government.

The concept of international security illustrates the continuing penetration of the state's boundaries. To take the simplest case, the concept of security has always been problematic for the EC. This is because security has tended to be seen predominantly in military and defence terms and was therefore inextricably bound up with the national sovereignty of a state. Military and security issues were seen as taboo and certainly not part of the legitimate competence of the EC. Indeed, the 1957 Treaty of Rome was silent on security until the amendments introduced by the Single European Act of 1985. Then, however, security was seen in political and economic terms as part of the EC's wider brief on external relations and European Political Co-operation (EPC). The situation changed notably as a result of the growing cohesion on foreign and security issues among member states. This was mediated not through the Commission of the European Communities but through the EPC, which even today remains a parallel body to the EC even though it has been incorporated into the treaties via the amendments introduced by the Single Act. Enshrined in the EPC and the Single Act is the view that security remains the essential prerogative of the member states. This has had implications for the discussions on internal security. Following the experience of EPC, internal security co-operation has developed on an *ad hoc* basis. It has developed, moreover, within the context of foreign security mechanisms through the process of EPC. For example, EC interior and justice ministers met for the first time in 1976. Then a primary goal was to deal with issues arising out of international terrorism and the desire to apprehend and prosecute fugitive terrorists. EC member states acceded to, and gradually inched towards ratifying, the Council of Europe's Convention on the Suppression of Terrorism (see Lodge 1988). However, as Lodge argues, the operational consequences of this and the move to abolish internal EC borders were not properly appreciated, and neither were they systematically dealt with. Many member states failed to realize that the creation of the Single Market, and the associated strenghtening of its 'external frontier' had important and immediate implications for those in the member states whose job it was to police states' boundaries. The removal of internal borders would affect not just customs and excise officers but police and immigration officers too.

The realization of the 'Four Freedoms' of movement, goods, services and capital underlined this, not least because the removal of internal barriers could be exploited by those engaged in the illicit movement of these goods, services, capital and persons. For some time, in the public arena, the only issue that surfaced was that of the advantages a borderless EC would have for fugitive terrorists. Gradually, this expanded to include fugitive bank robbers, international criminals and those trading in illicit substances and illegal immigration. Writing in 1994, we would argue that it is clear that the EC has developed a role in internal security matters and has begun to confront the operational implications within the Single Market. Linkages between police sectors are being recognized. From one perspective, the overall effect is, of course, to expand the level and scope of integration. However, it can be argued that one specific result has been the construction of an internal security 'ideology', based on the idea of a permanent security deficit as a result of the removal of borders. The production of the security deficit did not emerge as part of a conscious design to promote European union: rather it has emerged from the nexus of 'talk about' (or 'discourse' as the sociologists describe it) a borderless Europe and specific actions such as EC efforts to implement among the Twelve measures to combat drug trafficking and money laundering.

A European Police Co-operation Regime?

In addition to the notion of 'security deficit', attempting to understand the Europeanization of policing requires a framework relating state sovereignty and the implications of 'security-deficit' for European member state co-operation. One framework, borrowed from and developed within international relations work is that of international regimes (see Krasner 1983; Young 1989). Starting from the difficulties of collective-action problems that make co-operation difficult at international level, international regimes can be seen as a response to these problems.

The core concept of regime can be viewed as a social institution governing the actions of those involved in specifiable activities or sets of activities. Like all social institutions, they are perspectives consisting of recognized roles linked together by clusters of rules or conventions governing relations among the occupants of these roles. Like other social institutions, regimes may be more or less formally articulated, and they may or may not be accompanied by explicit organizations. Indeed, Young (1989) points out that in considering 'regimes', it is important to note that even when a regime is articulated formally in a contract or treaty, informal rules typically grow up in conjunction with the resulting institutional arrangement in practice.

International regimes can be viewed as specialized arrangements that pertain to well-defined activities, resources or geographical areas. In considering any international regime Young argues that one needs to consider five questions:

1. *Institutional character.* What are the principal rights, rules, and social choice producers of the regime ? How do they structure the behaviour of individual actors to produce a stream of collective outcomes?
2. *Jurisdictional boundaries.* What is the coverage of the regime in terms of functional scope, areal domain, and membership? Is this coverage appropriate under the prevailing conditions?
3. *Conditions for operation.* What conditions are necessary for the regime to work at all?
4. *Consequences of operation.* What sorts of outcomes (either individual or collective) can the regime be expected to produce?
5. *Regime dynamics.* How did the regime come into existence, and what is the likelihood that it will experience major changes in the foreseeable future? (Young 1983: 29–30)

This agenda is of value in considering police co-operation. This is so because of the very problems of the relationship between policing and wider European macro-political development. The dynamic which powers change in the policing domain can be appropriately 'caught' within the connection of 'security deficit' and the production of an European regime of police co-operation.

In the end, however, we are aware that the development of European policing is a 'complex, multi-layered affair which tends to resist analysis in terms of clear purposes and linear progress.' (den Boer and Walker 1993: 24). In this book, as well as describing the background to current policing arrangements, we have endeavoured to make visible the contextual conditions which have allowed discussion on policing Europe to flourish. For readers keen on definitions, we have taken 'policing' to be a function of existing law enforcement agencies which vary in organization and in relationship to institutions of government, and in their competence to, for example, collect evidence and use force. Police, as Cain (1979) has argued, however, must be defined by their key practice. As of midnight on 31 October 1993, the UK is now a member of a greater European Union. The Treaty on European Union has the theoretical possibility of allowing more coherent policy-making in respect of policing than ever before and will play its part in determining the key practice of European policing. Some argue that the key practice of a transnational policing system can already be known, and that it will entail ever more intense policing of those officially defined as 'enemies' of the Union (see Bunyan, 1991b; McLaughlin 1992). As we indicate throughout the book, there is much to support this view. However, the conjuncture of circumstances that has led to this requires presentation and it is this that we have sought to undertake. This is our attempt at 'embracing contingency' and trying to describe and understand the policing of Europe in the 1990s.

1

Contemporary Structures of European Policing

The history of policing modern Europe has been an area of study marked more by its neglect, until recent years. Although historians have studied incidents of public disorder and riots and revolutions they have tended to stay with the actors and causes behind such disorders rather than the measures of policing brought in to control them. This area of neglect has slowly been corrected as a history of policing and its social and political context in various European states has started to be pieced together.

Brian Chapman's early work on 'police states' and their nature provides us also with an analysis of the word police itself. Derived from the Greek *politeia* and the Latin *politia* Chapman argues that police power has always been at the heart of state authority and that the 'police state' has a more all-encompassing meaning than that attributed to it in more recent years. The police state of the eighteenth century, unlike that of the twentieth century had more enlightened and progressive aspects, rather than being merely repressive. On behalf of the state, police powers were exercised to codify and prescribe in regulations the limits of acceptable behaviour, and in turn the police force could be used to ensure that behaviour was forthcoming. The police acted to ensure the well-being and integrity of the state, but did so in a non-arbitrary and non-repressive manner in trying to achieve a more modern reformist state than some of those that had gone before (Chapman 1970).

Chapman singles out two eighteenth century policing systems as precursors of later developments. The Prussian

8

police state reformed by Frederick William of Prussia (1620–88) provided a tightly organized and rigorously administered state where bureaucratic forms replaced feudal powers. Internal order and discipline was imposed through a dedicated civil service and military. In Austria Joseph II (1741–90) demonstrated an early concern to have, what would later be called a 'high' police capable of dealing with political subversives and secret societies, working alongside an enlightened 'low' police organizing other activities of the state (Brodeur 1983). This 'low' policing of Austria, and also of Prussia took on a multitude of tasks we would not now recognize as policing, including regulating markets, traffic, fire protection and street lighting.

Mid-eighteenth century France was policed by a quasi-military force – *maréchausée* – under the central command of the King. They were assisted by local village constables and a special Parisian police, who again took on the duties of lighting, fire protection, garbage collection and food supply maintenance, amongst other things (Stead 1957: 43–50). The French Revolution in 1789 and the subsequent rise to power of Napoleon Bonaparte saw the concept of state policing move on to a new plane. Local forces were disbanded and replaced in 1791 by a national *Gendarmerie* to be controlled from Paris. Under the command of Joseph Fouché, appointed as the first Minister of General Police of the Directory, centralized Napoleonic policing was to become a model for export to the rest of Napoleon's European empire.

Fouché saw his role as being closely allied to that of the Emperors in order to carry out the will of the state. The form of policing employed was one not averse to using terror and purges to achieve regulation and control from the top down. Fouché developed his own form of 'high' political policing, 'saying he had little time for "whores, thieves and street lamps"' (S. H. Palmer 1988: 13). Ultimately such 'haute policing' was unable to save Napoleon from downfall and Bowden argues that it was the excesses of the police repressive tactics that led to public reaction against it (Bowden 1978: 54–7).

Before his downfall Napoleon had annexed a number of European states into his empire. In Prussia, despite some resistance from the powerful Junkers family, the Napoleonic police state was duly imposed by the French. The Prussians, having already developed their own highly centralized state were able to accommodate the French ideas without too much dissension. Policing was already an accepted part of the power of the state – *Staatsgewalt* – and consisted of a centralized state, police alongside a municipal police. In the south, Napoleon took on the states of Piedmont, Lombardy and Veneglia in what would later become northern Italy. Napoleon saw no reason for him to be involved in any unification exercises as he had been in creating the Helvetic Republic – Switzerland – in 1803. He was happy to work alongside the existing smaller states in Italy rather than create a strong unified neighbour for himself on his southern flank. The repressive Napoleonic code was successfully introduced in the northern states to good effect: 'the fullest tribute to the effectiveness of the French administrative reforms came at the Restoration when the legitimist (Italian) rulers made no serious attempt to undo the work of administrative centralisation' (Davis 1988: 23).

The history of the Italian states both before and after Napoleon is beset with public unrest and disorder. States were in conflict with one another, poverty and food shortages were ever present and wandering brigands and vagrants made large areas unsafe. Eighteenth century policing was poor in quality and numbers. To one observer in 1783: 'Nothing more resembles a brigand than the Roman gendarme. The "shirri" are nothing more than licensed bandits who are entrusted to make war on bandits less privileged than themselves' (Davis 1988: 132).

If the French could make a contribution to improved Italian policing, they would also take their policing ideas to Belgium in 1795, and Luxembourg in 1798. In the Netherlands an existing decentralized system of urban and village policing was replaced with the Napoleonic model during the French annexation of 1811-13. The '*korps marachausee*' – later to be renamed as *gendarmerie* continued to police rural areas for many years alongside the local systems reintroduced by the Dutch when Napoleon departed. Denmark came under the influence of the Prussians but not direct rule and developed its own national police force, covering a much smaller geographic area than the French or Germans.

All this French activity across Europe was watched by Britain with some disdain. Eventually the Napoleonic wars and British success would leave a lingering bitterness between the two countries. Britain's own attempts at policing were more hesitant, but any mention of adopting the continental French system was sure to be met with resistance.

The policing of Britain in the eighteenth century and earlier was carried out by a mix of night watchmen, rural constables and Justices of the Peace (JPs). In London, Henry Fielding, JP, the principal magistrate in Bow Street, arranged for the employment of a group of professional thief-takers to assist in the detection and apprehension of offenders in 1750. These Bow Street Runners have a legendary place in the history of British policing, although their activities 'were never entirely above suspicion' (Emsley 1991: 18–19; see also Lock 1982).

The orthodox view is that the coming of industrialization and its accompanying need for a disciplined work force, led to the formation of more formalized policing. Industrial unrest and public disorder such as the 1780 Gordon riots, made the point to Government that, left unpoliced, crowds can be dangerous. Public opinion, however, was not instantly swayed by the new arguments and the 1785 London and Westminster Police Bill and the 1812 Police Bill both failed through lack of support. The British suspicion of French-style centralized policing and their extensive use of informers is generally cited as the reason why the British held back. In the words of one 1812 pamphleteer: 'The police of France, say some, is admirable. Then go to France and enjoy it, be the reply of every free-born Briton' (quoted in S. H. Palmer 1988: 165)

From 1812 to 1821 British society was characterized by economic recession, high food prices and public unrest. Tens of thousands of demobilized soldiers from the French Wars created havoc in the streets. In the north, Luddites were protesting against the unfair competition of new technology in the textile industry (1811–12) and in Manchester armed yeomanry cut down demonstrators at Peterloo in 1819. The political climate was moving to acceptance of a form of policing. The orthodox view of historians has long held that this new policing brought with it enlightenment and stability to a troubled social order (e.g. Reith 1956; Critchley 1978).

The orthodox view of policing has been challenged more recently by a revisionist school of thought that sees policing in nineteenth-century England as an imposed force to ensure a political stability for the ruling classes. If the first decades of the nineteenth century witnessed nothing less than 'the making of the English working class' (Thompson 1968), then measures were needed to regulate their behaviour and help socialize them into their subordinate position (see, e.g., Philips 1977; Brogden 1982). Even more recently there have been attempts to synthesize the orthodox with the revisionist schools to illustrate the complexities of what was going on in these years. Then as now policing did help working-class people who were victims of working-class crime, and the new bureaucratic policing was a way forward. Evidence does also exist that the ruling class with their own private policing arrangements were not so panicked into creating a police force as some believed. Policing could also be seen as a part of the diffusion of local government administration that tried to bring rational order to many parts of life. To this extent policing 'was not an automatic reflex of urbanisation and industrial capitalism' (Reiner 1992b: 47; see also Emsley 1991).

The 1829 Metropolitan Police Act introduced by Robert Peel, the Home Secretary, saw the first acceptance of modern policing in England. Under the guidance of two police commissioners, Colonel Charles Rowan and Richard Mayne (a barrister), the new police took to the London streets in uniforms of blue, swallowtail-coats and top-hats. In London and the provinces the long march to acceptance had begun. Demonstrations, riots and radical politics did not disappear overnight, however, and the 1835 Municipal Corporation Act saw the idea of policing spread to other towns and cities and ultimately to rural areas. The 1856 County and Borough Police Act would later consolidate the law and lay a foundation of permanence for policing that would be supervised by the Home Office, but administered locally. The centralized French ideas of a national police force had been successfully resisted and a 'low' form of policing by an unarmed citizen in uniform set out an Anglo-Saxon tradition of policing to counterpose the continental model. Employment as a police officer eventually offered a security that made it attractive to lowly paid industrial workers.

Although 'low' policing had been successfully incorporated into England, Scotland and Wales by the mid-1850s the same could not be said of Britain's western island, Ireland. Whilst a centralized national police force was resisted vehemently on the mainland it was precisely such a system that was felt necessary for the policing of the Irish. The policing and politics of Ireland, and its relationship with England have been inextricably bound up ever since. The 'problem' for the eighteenth century Englishman was that:

> In Ireland past rebellions, ongoing rural outrages, and deficient Protestant local authorities provided ample reasons for introducing an armed, centralised police. English assumptions of cultural superiority, the belief that Paddy was often feckless and sometimes savage, united to the reality of Protestant political dominance within the British archipelago, ensured that the police would be kept out of the hands of the papist peasantry. (S. H. Palmer 1988: 521-2)

After the 1785 London and Westminster Police Bill had fallen, the Government had successfully introduced the Dublin Police Act 1786. The following year the idea was taken out to Ireland's rural areas. If policing was not yet acceptable for the mainland, it was going to be imposed upon the Irish. The British had, said one commentator at the time, taken the new idea of a police force, and 'in a manner of speaking tried it on the dog. The dog was Ireland' (quoted in S. H. Palmer 1988: 28). Another pamphleteer argued in 1822 that 'England had chosen to police Ireland by a "French gendarmerie"' (S. H. Palmer 1988: 245). Centrally controlled from Dublin, the Royal Irish Constabulary was an armed force to impose order across Ireland and was a police force quite unlike anything the English would tolerate for themselves.

Countries at the edges of the European continent were spared the incursions of Napoleon. Spain had adopted a centralized French model of policing in 1829 when its absolutist Government introduced the *caribineros*. Greece achieved independence from its Turkish oppressors in 1821 and in 1833 established a national *Gendarmerie*. In 1864 a new Greek Constitution was drawn up on the basis of the Code Napoléon. Portugal was overun by the French and only achieved liberty in 1811, by which time the basis of a centralized policing had been laid.

Nineteenth-century Progress

Having made their introduction police systems across Europe developed throughout the nineteenth century. The French police remained as a centralized force – *Gendarmerie Nationale* – after the demise of the Napoleonic regime, but a new form of localized policing for Paris was introduced. Training schools for the police were opened in Paris in 1883 and Bordeaux and Lyons in 1898. The over-reliance on recruiting former soldiers into the *Gendarmerie* was being questioned because although 'the army [was] a school of honour and of courage . . . it [was] not a school for police' (Director of the police technical laboratory at Lyon, quoted in Berlière 1991). Public order remained a priority especially after the 1848 riots and revolutionary attempts that swept across Europe.

In the German states the events of 1848 pushed most states towards constitutional government. The Prussians under Bismarck led the 1870 unification of German States, with each state (or *Land*) becoming responsible for its own policing. The Franco/Prussian model was the preferred model of policing, and each state jealously guarded its policing autonomy. An ill-fated attempt to improve national co-ordination was made in 1897 when no agreement could be reached (Browder 1990: 2). Recruitment was largely from the military but, as in France, civil police training schools began to be opened toward the end of the century (H. Reinke 1991). Policing also began to drop many of its wider responsibilities as other bureaucracies of state were developed to take them over. Law and order policing more in the mode we are familiar with began to appear. Public order policing was still on hand to put down the miners' strike of 1889 in the Ruhrgebiet area, and the German policeman always knew he had the full support of the military should he need it. Three hundred people had been killed in the Berlin riots of 1848.

The Grand Duchy of Luxembourg established by the Congress of Vienna in 1815 was part of the confederation of Germanic States between the years 1815 and 1866 and was duly influenced by the Prussian approach to policing. Records of an earlier form of village policing can be traced back to 1748, and the Municipality Act of 1843 granted wider self-determination to the Communes and their policing. In 1867 the Treaty of London declared Luxembourg a neutral state, it did not become part of the newly unified Germany.

Spain's nineteenth century rulers modelled themselves on the French and Piedmont forms of government, establishing its force of *caribineros* in 1829 and the *Guardia Civil* in 1844. The two were to join forces in the new *Guardia Civil* formed in 1940, under the dictatorship of Franco.

The 1848 riots and public disorder across Europe for various reasons missed out the British Isles. The Irish peasantry were exhausted by the potato famine and in England the working class seemed complacent about events in the midst of their own economic depression (S. H. Palmer 1988: 482).

Public disorder took place in Prague, Vienna and Budapest, while Milan experienced five days of street-fighting and there were uprisings in Palermo, Naples and Venice (S. H. Palmer 1988: 483).

The Italian States reorganized their policing arrangements in the light of the 1848 disturbances. The emphasis was moved from one of negotiating between social groupings to one of reassuring the propertied classes by preventing crime and protecting the social order. Piedmont introduced Public Security Regulations in 1852 and 1854, Tuscany reorganized its police force in 1849 and Rome and Modena did likewise in 1850 and 1854 (Davis 1988: 139).

The unification of Italy in 1859–60 brought with it attendant problems for the police. Sicily and the southern states expressed some dissatisfaction with the union in various forms of public disorder and later in acts of anarchism. At the same time the traditional need for police to deal with marginal groups of itinerants and strangers coming to the cities for work led to a merging of the protesters with the criminal fraternity. It was within this situation that the idea of the 'Mafia' or 'camorra' first arose as evidence of new forms of organizational relationships independent of the state. From a position of openly supporting southern protest they became synonymous with more secretive, criminal activity.

The merging of criminality with legitimate protest on the 'Southern Question' also gave a useful pretext to the state to use repressive measures in the interests of fighting crime generally. When the north threatened to introduce emergency powers in 1874 there is evidence to suggest it turned whole sectors of southern society to the political left in parliamentary elections (Davis 1988: 292–3). Mafia relationships camouflaged criminal activities in corporate solidarities of protest which the police were expected to try to resolve (see Hobsbawm 1959; see also Gallant 1988 for an account of similar social banditry carried out by the Haiduks in rural Greece).

By the close of the nineteenth century the Italian crime problem was considered one of the worst in Europe. Whether or not it actually was is hard to quantify. Certainly it is true that two of the pioneers of the new profession of criminology were Italians. Cesare Beccaria (1734–94) had produced his treatise on 'Crimes and Punishment' which advocated rational approaches to sentencing and punishments designed to rehabilitate and reform the criminal, and later Cesare Lombroso (1835–1909) had developed his medical model of criminality that enabled 'diagnosis' by physical appearance. According to one socialist politician of the time, 'it was only in the miserable matter of crime that Italy had achieved its 'sad primacy' amongst the European nations' (Davis 1988: 314).

In the Netherlands progress was more regulated by the State than by events. The French influence continued to be significant in the creation of the Royal Military Constabulary (*Corps Maréchausée*) which survives to this day. The National Police Decree of 1851 brought the National Police under the Minister of Justice and in 1856 a National Rural Constabulary was created.

The policing of Victorian England has been seen as a period in which the police became an accepted social institution and the working classes in turn needed less policing as they became incorporated into society. Despite initial misgivings at this 'plague of blue locusts' (Storch 1975), the idea of an efficient and effective force was being developed throughout the century, as training and job security made it an increasingly acceptable profession. The myth of local accountability to Watch Committees was already under attack and the use of Inspectors, the amalgamation of small forces and judicious funding by the Home Office started a trend towards centralization that has never been checked (see Emsley 1991: ch. 4).

On an international front Britain was not keen on developing policing links with its European neighbours. Having always been critical of centralized state policing systems, and having made its distinctive stand for local decentralized policing that marked it out from its neighbours across the sea, the British government now placed its faith in an open liberal democracy that insisted all police communications between countries should be made on a diplomatic level. This did not prevent one of the duties of the newly formed CID in 1878 being mysteriously defined as 'Investigations for Governments', and its first appointed head being someone who had made 'a special study of foreign police forces' (Porter 1989: 102–3).

It was this same open liberal democracy in the last quarter of the nineteenth century that also saw Britain become a haven for European radical politicians and anarchists excluded from their own countries. In turn these countries put pressure on Britain to deny these 'troublemakers' access to a country where they seemed not only safe, but able to plot and plan their next moves back on the continent. Between them European countries drew up schemes of police co-operation which ultimately foundered because of 'resistance from Britain; whose participation was obviously vital' (Porter 1987: 40). According to Porter's careful research into these times:

> Other ideas put to Britain were for closer police cooperation across national boundaries, and for the outlawing of anarchist doctrines. Specific proposals along these and similar lines came from France in 1892, from Belgium and Spain in 1893, from Austria in 1894, from Italy in 1898,

from Russia in 1900, and from Russia and Germany in 1901,
1902 and 1904 (Porter 1987: 111)

Britain's initial argument was always that if only the rest of
Europe was as progressive and liberal as Britain they would
not require centralized policing and repressive laws because
they would not spawn radical politics and anarchists in the
first place. It is believed that many European liberals and
reformers did indeed look 'to England for their new constitutional models, and their new police, though often, if they
achieved power, they felt too unsafe to employ their understanding of the English police model on its own' (Emsley 1991:
240).

Britain turned a conveniently blind eye to Ireland and its
other colonies, but such a position was soon to become
untenable. A long Irish resentment of political control being
imposed from London was to break out in the Fenian
bombing campaign of 1883–4 and suddenly Britain had its
own internal terrorist troubles – the Irish 'dynamiters' – that
required a political response. Again Britain avoided a need for
tighter immigration control and co-operation with foreign
police forces, but the response was to institute a form of
'high' political policing in the shape of the newly-created Irish
Special Branch in 1887. Such a move, in conditions of some
secrecy avoided the need for new laws and for international
co-operation because anarchists and Fenians were being dealt
with without recourse to either. When the international anti-
anarchist conference of 1898 was convened in Rome, the
British, although in attendance, could play a minor part
throughout (Jensen 1981).

Twentieth Century

The Great War of 1914–18 provided another watershed in the
policing of Europe. Germany, as the losers of the War, had to
re-think their systems of policing because they could no longer
rely as before on back-up from a large standing army. The
Allies were also determined to ensure the Germans did not

create a *de facto* army by increasing the size of the police force and giving them heavy arms. At the same time the German state was faced with considerable social unrest from a working class who had watched the Russian Revolution unfold in 1917. As Imperial Germany gave way to the Weimar Republic it was still Prussia who took the lead in state organization. The Prussian Interior Minister, Carl Severing, with his new head of police, Wilhelm Abess, embarked on a programme to demilitarize the police and turn them into a professional force using the new technology of cars, telephones and telegraphy. The process was not an overnight one, and ingrained militarism was not easily shaken off. Getting the public to trust them was no easy matter and the police were always ready to be repressive when called on. During the Communist demonstrations of May 1924 in the working-class districts of Wedding and Neukoln in Berlin, the police response resulted in 33 dead and 189 injured in what became known as *Bluitmai*, or 'Bloody May' (Bowlby 1986; Bessel 1991).

Attempts to co-ordinate the German police as a whole were also fraught with difficulty. In 1925 a German police commission was founded with an advisory role, and some states took on specialist functions, such as the Dresden missing persons bureau and the Berlin central fingerprint file (Browder 1990: 38). But, by the time of the 1926 Great Police Exhibition in Berlin, the German police felt able to offer an image of a professional crime-fighting force, using new technology and developing a close relationship with the people (Bessel 1991: 188).

Political unrest continued to break out in the form of public disorder in many parts of Europe. In Holland the government felt it necessary to create a new State Security System (*Centrale Inlichtingdierst*) to monitor political subversion, and a new military division (*Korpspolitietroepen*) to help the civil authorities deal with public disorder. Minor adjustments were also made to improve the effectiveness of central control of the police should it be needed (Fijnaut 1991).

The British General Strike of 1924 saw public order policing stretched to the limits. The British police themselves had gone on strike in 1918 and 1919 leading to the immediate sacking of every police officer involved, none of whom would ever be re-employed as a policeman. The Desborough Committee, which had been appointed to look into the pay and conditions of the police and which had led to the industrial action, decided on the removal of the Police Union altogether and its replacement by a Police Federation, which had no power to call a strike (Desborough Committee 1920; see also Reynolds and Judge 1968).

In Ireland the independence movement found policing and politics inextricably linked. The police were a 'highly visible manifestation of state power, consequently controlling the police . . . became crucial for groups seeking to maintain or to gain power' (Sheills 1991).

The struggle for independence completed in the summer of 1922 also saw the creation of a brand new police force for the new Republic of Ireland. The Royal Irish Constabulary (RIC) was disbanded and parts of it removed to the North to form the Royal Ulster Constabulary (RUC). An embryonic Irish Republican Police (IRP) had been formed by the political party, Sinn Fein, but in the new Government's reorganization the RIC and the Dublin police were to be replaced by the *Garda Siochana*, Guardians of the Peace; the idea of the IRP never took hold. Although the *Garda Siochana* was to be still centrally controlled from Dublin the new police were to be unarmed: 'the day of the militaristic and coercive policeman was at an end in Ireland . . . [police were to be] servants of the people . . . neither militaristic nor coercive, above party and class . . . and responsible to the government alone' (Sheills 1991: 151).

It is interesting to note that many of the disbanded RIC officers found re-employment in the British colonial police overseas including a large number who went to police the Palestinian protectorate. The RIC depot in Dublin had provided a 6-month training course for British colonial police officers from 1907 onwards, with the Irish experience being seen as a better grounding for policing colonies than the Anglo-Saxon model of policing on the mainland. Even after 1922, training continued to take place in Northern Ireland at the RUC depot in Newtownards until it was finally wound up in the 1930s (S. H. Palmer 1988: 542–5).

The RUC commenced operations in Northern Ireland, or Ulster, in 1922. It remained a centralized force and was controlled from Stormont, taking over policing duties from the RIC and Ulster Special Constabulary (USC). In fact the USC continued to co-exist with the RUC, although not without some antagonism between the two. Many RUC men were late of the RIC and there was always the suspicion that their loyalty was questionable. The USC were more likely to be loyalists and in particular formed the part-time 'B' specials. Hostility between the two forces at one point led to an exchange of shots (Shiells 1991).

A concerted attempt was made to improve police co-operation through the meeting of the International Criminal Police Congress in Vienna in September 1923. An earlier inaugural meeting of the Congress in Monaco in 1914 had never been repeated due to the outbreak of war. The 1923 meeting founded the International Criminal Police Commission which would later become the International Criminal Police Organization (ICPO) or Interpol. Seventeen states were represented but not Britain, who joined the following year at what became an annual conference. An attempt to establish an alternative Congress – the International Police Congress – in 1925 failed to get off the ground.

From its inauguration Interpol was never intended as an operational police force but was concerned to see general co-operation achieved between national police systems and to facilitate that co-operation by acting as an information exchange agency. In that role Interpol has stayed the course and, as we shall see, remains today an important player in the activities of police co-operation in Europe.

The severe economic depression of the 1930s saw the resort to political causes of the extreme left and right. The Communist party gained support throughout Europe and ran alongside the new Fascist parties emerging at the same time. For the police it was a time of political policing combined with public order policing. The Greek republic, for example, having been formed in the mid-1920s, saw the rise in 1936 of the Fascist leader, John Metaxas, in an unholy alliance with the monarchy. Italy had witnessed the 1922 Fascist 'March on Rome' and the rise of Mussolini in the 1930s; Portugal had a military rising in 1926 and most famously the Spanish Civil War had seen the overthrow of the Popular Front by Franco's Military Fascist Falange which installed its own nationalist government in 1939 that would remain in power until the late 1970s. Portugal saw the end of its monarchy in 1910 and ultimately the republic taken over by military forces in 1926 that would hold power until the fall of dictatorship in April 1974.

The Weimar Republic's transition to the Fascist party's Third Reich in 1933 in Germany started the long haul to the Second World War. The story of the German police through this period is still being unravelled. Browder has described how the new revolutionary police of the National Socialists were able to manoeuvre themselves into a position to take over elements of the existing police, in particular the Nazis' own security police – the *Sicherheitsdierst* or SD – working with the State Security Police – the *Sicherheitspolizei* or 'Sipo' – and taking in the regular *Kriminalpolizei* (Browder 1990).

The ease with which this new idea of a police-state could be formed has been explained by the party-political sympathies of the police and a perceived need for order which the new structures offered. It has also been put down to the 'professionalism' of the police developed in the Weimar republic by Severing, Abess and others. By concentrating on the techniques of policing, the new officers could effectively ignore the wider political and social context of their work and the direction in which it was taking them (Bessel 1991).

A degree of mystery still surrounds the role of the International Criminal Police Commission (ICPC) during the war years. The Germans moved its physical headquarters from its offices in Vienna to premises in Berlin, but most of its records have disappeared, leaving the allegation that it became an arm of the Nazi State largely unproven. This did not stop the French President, Mitterrand, saying at the opening of the new Lyons Interpol buildings in 1989, that 'the Nazi invasion [of Austria] led to the institution being used for unacceptable ends, against the wishes of its founders and most of its members' (quoted in Bresler 1992: 51).

The journalist Fenton Bresler has tried to resolve the mystery of the ICPC war years, and concluded that business carried on much as normal (Bresler 1992: 75–81). A copy of the ICPC journal for June 1943 has been unearthed with a cover portrait of its German President of that year, Ernst Kaltenbrunner, who was later to be executed for war crimes after the Nuremberg Trials. Also discovered was a booklet by the general secretary, Oskar Dressler, entitled *Die Internationale Kriminal Polizeiliche Kommission und Ihr Werk* dated 1943 and seemingly emphasizing the normality of the international police co-operation being undertaken (Bresler: 50–6).

Following the end of the Second World War in 1945 German policing was the subject of radical restructuring. Not only in Germany but also in other occupied countries where the police had collaborated in the maintenance of public order, 'the whole concept of policing in much of Europe was deeply controversial, and existing police traditions were largely discredited' (Jenkins 1988). In West Germany all internal security police forces were disbanded, along with the much-feared riot police. Individual states, or *Länder*, were to be responsible for policing with no national police forces. The new 1949 West German constitution very specifically detailed the powers of the new police. In fact it was soon found that West Germany was not going to be able to survive without a national police force and the *Bundeskriminalamnt* – or BKA – came into being in 1951, at the same time as the new more heavily-armed federal police troop, the *Bundesgrerzschutz* (or Federal Border Guard).

In the Communist German Democratic Republic (GDR, or East Germany) policing took a different post-war form again. The Government attempted a new civil force, decentralized to *Länder* as in the West and with its role defined in a decree of 1964 to guarantee public order and security in the construction of socialism in the GDR. The *Volkspolizei* were reinforced by the Ministry for State Security (*Ministerium für Staatssicherheit*, or Stasi (Cullen 1992: 6–11).

In the Netherlands a wide ranging inquiry into police powers was instituted in 1945 and 'paramilitary policing was seen as unacceptable per se' (Cullen 1992). The 1945 Police Decree made the National Police the joint responsibility of the Ministers of Justice and the Interior, and greatly reduced the role of the Royal Military Constabulary. The Vichy national police structure in France was retained, but with an extensive purge of personnel. Italy and Greece had more traumatic periods of transition. Italian workers responded to an assassination attempt in 1948 on the Communist leader, Togliatti, by taking over factories and other key strategic points where the police were helpless to stop them. Demonstrations in Rome in 1945 had called for a clean up of the police, and 'the Carabinieri with their Royalist Sympathies were singled out as a force to be purified' (Domenico 1991).

In Greece the civil war of 1944 saw many old grievances aired, and not least against the police. 'Years of right wing dictatorship, occupation and civil war had transformed the Greek army, city police and gendarmerie into the lefts fanatical rivals' (Alexander 1981: 162). Particular hatred was aimed at the wartime Security Battalions, made up of Greeks equipped by Germans. When they were reintegrated into the new Greek National Guard, this 'played a major role in provoking the civil war' (Jenkins 1988). The bitterness remained until the demise of the colonel's dictatorship in 1974.

British policing survived the war with its reputation intact, if not enhanced. Wartime had seen a further centralization take place and the post-war years saw even more amalgamations of small forces into larger ones. The process was enhanced by the 1962 Royal Commission on the Police and the subsequent 1964 Police Act, which led to extensive amalgamations by the end of the decade and the laying down of the present system of accountability. Crucial to the new system was the continuing rise of the Association of Chief Police Officers (ACPO) to a prominent policy-influencing position following its formation from earlier representative bodies in 1948 (Johnson 1992).

Present Policing Arrangements

We are conscious that this has been a very brief run-down of a European policing history that perhaps has still to be written in full. We are also aware that we have largely concentrated on the countries that now comprise the European Union (EU) and not those of the wider Europe of Scandinavia, Austria, Switzerland and Eastern Europe. We would hope to bring them into the discussions as appropriate as we proceed. For the moment we impose the same limitations on ourselves as we consider the present policing arrangements in Europe (see Interpol 1988; Benyon *et al.* 1993: ch. 3; and Bunyan 1993 for more detailed accounts). Table 1.1 presents a recent summary of arrangements.

Belgium

Until quite recently Belgium had a Military State Police, or *Gendarmerie*, accountable to the Department of Defence for organizational matters and the Interior Minister and Justice Minister for operations. On 1 January 1992 this traditional military police force was demilitarized and became accountable only to the Ministry of Justice and Ministry of the Interior. The country is divided into 52 Districts and 427 Brigades and has some 16 000 Gendarmerie officers under the command of a Lieutenant-General for each District. Despite the changes some observers believe the military traditions and *esprit de corps* remain strong within the *Gendarmerie* and 'are sceptical about the real impact of new regulations on day-to-day operations and the traditional modus operandi' (Klerks 1993; see also Judge 1991).

In addition to the *Gendarmerie*, there are also 17 000 municipal police organized in the 589 municipalities and forces are accountable to the local mayor (*Bourgmestre*) through their individual police Commissioners (*Commissaire*). A further 1300 judicial police or detective force operates across the country through 26 Districts, each with its own police Commissioner in Chief and its own Counsel for the Prosecution. At a national level the Commissioners are co-ordinated by the office of the Commissioner-General, which is also responsible for the Interpol National Central Bureau (NCB). In 1988 a national unit of the judicial police was established to concentrate on terrorist activities and organized crime.

Denmark

Denmark has a centralized national police force under the direction of a National Commissioner of Police (*Rigspoliti-*

Table 1.1 *Policing Arrangements of European Union States*

Country	Population (millions)	Major Police Forces and Actual Number in (1989 figures: 1988 in brackets)	Interpol NCB Location	Police Working Group on Terrorism Member Agency	Important Border Control and/or Internal Security Forces (Latest available figures)
Belgium	9.9 (1986)	*Genarmerie* 16 000 (15 839) Municipal Police (589 forces) 17 000 (16 744) Judicial Police 1300 (1256)	Judicial Police	*Group Interforces Anti-Terroriste* (GIA)	Customs Services (7247) Maritime Police (251)
Denmark	5.1 (1987)	*Rigspolitiet* (De-centralised State Police Force) (54 force areas) 10 350 (10 350)	National Commissioner's Office	*Politiets Efterretningstjeneste* (PET) Police Intelligence Service	
France	55.6 (1987)	*Police Nationale* 124 960 (125,225) *Gendarmerie Nationale* 91 827 (91 646) (Municipal Police c. 25 000)	*Police Nationale* – Judicial Police	*Unité de Co-ordination pour la Lutte Anti-Terroriste* (UCLAT)	*Police de L'Air et des Frontières* (PAF) *La Douane*
West Germany	61.1 (1987)	Federal Forces *Bundeskriminalamt* (BKA) and *Bundesgrenzschulz* 26 963 (23 640) 11 *Länder* (State) Forces 171 382 (169 644)	BKA	BKA – Abteilung Terrorismus	*Bundesgrenzschulz* Federal Railway Police
Greece	10.0 (1987)	Hellenic Police 38 783	Criminal Service Directorate	Minstry of Public Order	
Ireland	3.5 (1987)	*Garda Siochanna* 10 472 (10 749)	*Garda* HQ	*Garda* – Crime and Security Branch International Liason Office	

27

Italy	57.2 (1986)	State Police 91 829 (85 280) *Caribinieri* 112 814 (107 698)	State Police	*Direzione Centrale Della Polizia di Prevenzione* (DCPP)	*Guardia di Finanza* 56 700 (54 170)
Luxembourg	0.37 (1984)	Police Corps and *Gendarmerie* 957 (914)	Police Corps	*Gendarmerie (Sureté Publique)*	
Netherlands	14.7 (1988)	*Rijkspolitie* (State Police) 10 850 (10 765) *Gemeentepolitie* (Local) (148 forces) 24 756	*Rijkspolitie– Centrale Recherche Informatiedienst* (24 574) (CRI)	(CRI)	*Koninklijke Maréchaussee*
Portugal	10.2 (1985)	*Guarda Nacional Republicana and Policia de Seguranca* 38 783 (*Policia Judiciara –* c. 15 000)	*Policia Judiciara*	*Direccao Central de Combate ao Banditismo* (DCCB)	*Guarda Fiscal* (c. 8200)
Spain	38.8 (1986)	*Cuerpo Nacional de Policia* (CNP) 53,462 *Guardia Civil* (64,000) (GC) *Policia Autonomica* (Autonomous Regions) 35 000	CNP – Judicial Police	*Comisaria General de Informacion– Serviciode Informacion Exterior* (CGI-SIE)	Customs Service and GC's *Servicio Fiscal*
UK	55.8 (1981)	52 separate police forces 148 182 (146 504) (as well as over a dozen specialist national or local forces responsible to government departments, especially the British Transport Police and Ministry of Defence police)	Within HQ of Metropolitan Police at New Scotland Yard but funded from common police services	Metropolitan Police Special Branch	HM Immigration Service, HM Customs & Excise, British

Source: House of Commons (1990), p. xvii.

chef) who is accountable to the Minister of Justice. Fifty-four police districts cover the whole nation, each with its own Chief of Police (*Politimester*), except for Copenhagen whose size warrants a Commissioner (*Politidirektor*). For operational matters including both public order and criminal investigations the Chiefs and the Copenhagen Commissioner are directly accountable to the Ministry of Justice, and together have some 14 000 officers under their command. Uniformed officers number 7400, and there are some 2000 detectives and 3000 civilian employees. The police employ their own attorneys to conduct prosecutions and generally act in accordance with Chapter 11 of their Administration of Justice Act. Other legal references to policing are attached to various Acts and are known as 'stipulations'.

The National Commissioner of Police is responsible for central administration, recruitment and personnel matters as well as for centralized functions like the Police National Computer (PNC) and the Interpol NCB. The 54 police districts are grouped into seven regions to offer mutual aid across district boundaries in times of emergencies or as required. One of the district Chiefs of Police is designated as the head of the region.

Republic of Ireland

Another single national police force operates in the Republic of Ireland. The Minister of Justice as an elected member of the Dáil has oversight of the government-appointed Commissioner of the *Garda Siochana*. The Commissioner works from a central office at Phoenix Park in Dublin directly providing intelligence services, and general support services including the Interpol NCB, and directing the activities of some 11 000 police officers throughout the Republic.

The police are administratively divided into 23 Divisions with 18 of the Divisions working to a Chief Superintendent and the other five comprising the Dublin Metropolitan Area and coming under the command of an Assistant Commissioner. Of the 10 500 total police numbers, some 8500 are uniformed officers, 1500 detectives and approximately 500 are civilians.

Germany

In the period following the Second World War, Germany was anxious to limit any centralization of power and the law gives a primacy to policing being carried out at local state or *Land* level. Today some 170 000 police are deployed throughout 11 *Länder*, compared to only 4000 officers working at a national level. Each Länd has its own uniformed officers (*Schutzpolizei*), criminal investigation units (*Kriminalpolizei*) and police training schools, and each police department has its own clear hierarchical command structure accountable at a political level to the *Land* Minister of the Interior. The *Länder* also provide a standby policing unit to combat public disorder (*Bereitschaftspolizei*), with a system of mutual aid being available between *Länder* and a degree of centralized control, and a river police (*Wasserschutzpolizei*: (Cullen 1992: 17–24).

At a national level the German Federal Border Guard (*Bundesgrenzchutz*) is responsible for policing international drug trafficking or terrorism and general questions of border control. It is accountable to the Federal Minister of the Interior, but is an arm of the Military.

The BKA is the federal criminal police office based in Wiesbaden with the responsibility of offering a co-ordinating role to the *Länder* and other direct help if requested. The BKA also operates as an information and communication centre to all the Federal police services as well as directly working on serious organized crime, drug trafficking, terrorism and international money laundering and fraud. The BKA operates the Interpol NCB (Cullen 1992: 36–47), and overall the German police force is recognised as: 'perhaps the world's most advanced in its use of sophisticated computer, telecommunications and forensic equipment. Its data information system allows local, regional or state police forces to communicate or co-operate through more than 6,500 computer terminals' (Klerks 1993).

The re-unification of Germany in 1991 posed major adjustment and assimilation problems throughout German society and not least in the world of policing. The GDR had to re-think ideas of police accountability and policing for the public

instead of entirely for the State. The dismantling of the East
German security police, the Stasi, revealed an intrusion on
privacy by a police state that was considered unacceptable in
the West (see, e.g., Bridge 1992).

Italy

Italian policing is also established on three levels and shared
primarily between the State Police and the *Carabinieri*. The
Carabinieri are a branch of the Military responsible for public
security, with their 112 000 officers distributed evenly throughout the country, and the State Police are a civil organization
centred on provincial regions and municipalities and comprising around 91 000 officers. The *Guarda di Finanza* provides a
third form of policing as another arm of the military, and
deals with border controls and so-called financial crime.

Responsibility for all policing matters is co-ordinated by the
Minister for Internal Affairs, through the Public Security
Authority (*Amministrazione de Pubblica sicurezza*) that in
turn over-sees the work of the Public Security Department.
The Department comes under the direction of the Chief of the
Italian Police (*Direttore General della Polizia di Stato*). At a
local level accountability rests with the provincial *prefetto* at a
political level and the local Head of State Police (*Questore*).
Judicial authorities direct police investigative work on criminal inquiries.

In October 1991 the Italian government adopted proposals
to help the fight against organized crime. The *Direzione
Nazionale Antimafia* co-ordinates efforts to combat organized
criminal activity under the authority of a national procurator-
general, and a *Direzione Investigativa Antimafia* was created to
co-ordinate police and customs investigations.

Luxembourg

A dual system of policing also takes place in the Grand Duchy
of Luxembourg. General policing duties are carried out by the
national *Gendarmerie* who number about 600 and cover the
country in three Districts, each commanded by a Major or
Captain. At a national level a Colonel of Police is accountable

to the Minister of Justice and the Ministry for Security Forces. The *Corps de Police*, or police force other than the *Gendarmerie*, number around 500 and are responsible for judicial policing or criminal investigation.

Criminal investigation is also carried out by the *Sûreté Publique*, an arm of the Gendarmerie; the *Sûreté Publique* are also responsible for maintaining the Interpol NCB.

Although both policing arrangements are subject to the civil code there is a strong militaristic element to policing in Luxembourg. Both forces are subject to the military penal code and disciplinary regulations of the army, and recruits to the *Gendarmerie* come only from corporals of the Luxembourg army.

France

Contemporary policing in France is organized on dual lines between the National Police (*La Police Nationale*) and the *Gendarmerie* (*Gendarmerie Nationale*). Both are centrally administered for the whole country, with the National Police accountable to the Minister for the Interior as a civil force and the *Gendarmerie* to the Ministry of Defence as a military force. Both provide a service of criminal investigation and ensuring public order.

At a central level the National Police are organized into a number of Directorates concentrating on specialist functions such as inspection and monitoring, personnel and training, logistics and administration, crime investigation, territorial policing, including border control, an intelligence service and the Republican Security Companies. The last named is better known as the CRS (*Compagnies Républicaines de Sécurité*) and is a force to maintain public order. The Directorates in turn break down into component sub-directorates (*sous-directions*). The Central Directorate of Crime Investigation, for example, consists of sub-directorates responsible for forensic and technical support, criminal affairs, economic and financial affairs and resources and liaison which include the Interpol NCB. In all the National Police deploy almost 130 000 police and civil staff.

The French *Gendarmerie* are a military force available nationally and housed in barracks away from the public. Numbering some 91 000 officers, the *Gendarmerie* are an example of policing for the state rather than the community, and have a clear military hierarchy and command structure. As with the National Police the *Gendarmerie* offer criminal and public order policing, with the latter being the province of the *Gendarmerie Mobil*, a force of over 18 000 officers who can be used anywhere in France. Other policing is provided by the *Gendarmerie Départementale*, with small local units sited across the country, reflecting various levels of public administration with *legions* at regional level, *groupements* in the *départements* and *companies* at *arrondissement* level.

The French have added a third form of policing to these two national forces in the shape of the *Police Municipale* introduced in 1983. These new local police forces under civil control were permitted by enactments of the decentralization campaign implemented by President Mitterrand in the early part of his administration. As additional police resources they have proved popular with municipalities and now number over 25 000. Enforcement powers are limited and they have no general investigative powers but can engage in surveillance of suspects and can arrest for violations of national laws, and call in the *Gendarmerie* or National Police as required (see Kania 1989). The policing of Paris was incorporated into the National Police in the mid-1960s, some 21 000 officers are now part of the Paris Prefecture of Police.

Greece

Spain, Portugal and Greece were all later arrivals on the EC stage and all had political changes to make to extricate themselves from varying degrees of totalitarianism and the rule of dictatorships. Such changes inevitably required a rethinking of police attitudes and styles of policing.

The end of the 'Colonels' rule in Greece in 1974 marked their return to democratically accountable government. Since 1985 the Ministry of Public Order has been responsible for a single Hellenic Police Force through the appointed chief of police. A central office provides a security and public order force but the majority of the 39 000 officers are deployed in local services co-terminous with the 51 local Prefectures. Each Prefecture constitutes a police precinct commanded by a Major General and advised by a Police Committee. Slightly different arrangements apply in Attica and Thessalonika where the catchment area is known as a Police Directorate, but still has a committee and a commanding officer. All policing arrangements are subject to a police inspectorate.

A regional level of policing is superimposed on the Prefecture system with each region offering a particular specialism such as public security, drug trafficking and immigration control. A regional Criminal Service Directorate is responsible for the Interpol NCB.

Portugal

In Portugal the Salazar regime lasted from 1932 to 1968 and the subsequent rule of Prime Minister Caetano ended in April 1974 in a bloodless coup, enabling the Portuguese to emerge alongside Europe's parliamentary democracies. A number of separate police forces came into being at differing levels.

A clear line of political accountability was established from the elected Attorney-General through the Minister of Justice to a Director General responsible for the Judicial Police (*Policia Judiciára*). The Judicial Police, focusing on criminal investigation, offer a national and a local service through their 15 000 officers tackling serious crime, drug trafficking and terrorism. At their head office support services are available in the form of communications, administrative support and computerized record systems, and these also cover the maintenance of the Interpol NCB.

Apart from the Judicial Police, Portugal has two other related police forces to counter public disorder. The Public Security Police (*Policia de Siguranca Publica*) deal with urban areas and the National Republican Guard (*Guarda Nacional Republica*) with rural areas. Together they can muster around 39 000 officers and both are accountable to the Ministry of Interior, with the Ministry of National Defence providing uniform, armaments and equipment to the National Republican Guard. A further force, the *Guarda Fiscal* with over 8000

officers, is responsible for policing financial fraud, customs
and border controls, and a Maritime Police (*Policia Maritima*)
has a seaborne policing capacity.

Spain

The demise of the Franco dictatorship in Spain came about in
1977, when the Spanish were able to hold their first democratic elections since 1936. Today Spanish policing is constituted at a national, regional and municipal level.

Policing nationally is provided by the Guardia Civil and the
National Police (Cuerpo Nacional de Policia). The Guardia
Civil is a military based police force numbering some 65 000
officers living in barracks with their families and covering the
whole of Spain. It is accountable to the Minister of the
Interior and the Ministry of Defence and is responsible for
policing frontiers, ports, airports and traffic control across the
country's rural areas. The large urban areas of Spain are
policed by the Civil National Police accountable only to the
Minister of the Interior and comprising approximately 55 000
officers. They are responsible for the Spanish ID system,
passports, border control and international co-operation,
including the operation of the Interpol NCB for Spain.

The regional police and the municipal police are accountable to local civil governors and have responsibility for traffic
control, protection of municipal property and the enforcement
of local laws. Being accountable to autonomous regions these
policia autonomica deploy around 35 000 officers.

Both national and local forces have had to adjust from a
perspective of serving the state to one of service to the people
and are guided by a written Code of Ethics expounding
respect for the Constitution and for human honour and
dignity.

The Netherlands

Until recently the police of the Netherlands were subject to the
1957 Police Act and locally organized into 148 municipal
forces (the *Gemeentepolitie*). A separate state police (*Rijk-
spolitie*) acted as a national police incorporating specialist

functions, such as the National Criminal Intelligence Service and the Interpol NCB as part of the *Centrale Recherche Informatiedienst* (CRI). The Royal Constabulary, a branch of the military policed the borders (*Koninklijke Maréchausee*).

A dissatisfaction with these arrangements led the Dutch to consider alternatives. After administrative attempts to rationalize the numerous local forces came to nothing (Wiebrens 1990), political action was taken to legislate for a new structure. The 148 municipal forces were re-ordered into just 25 regional police units made up of the former 25 000 municipal officers but with the addition of many former state police bringing them up to 32 000. A much smaller national police unit remained with about 3000 officers maintaining specialist functions like the CRI. Border policing remained unchanged.

It remains to be seen how this restructuring will work out in practice. From 1992 each of the 25 regional police units became accountable to the *burgomaster* of the largest town in the region and under daily operational command of a Chief of Police. Accountability was to both the Ministry of Justice for operational matters and the Ministry of the Interior for organization and administration. The smaller national police unit became the responsibility of the Ministry of Justice. The Dutch hope that the new larger regions will improve efficiency, allow for better policy planning and improve the fight against crime where a falling 'clear-up' rate has been conspicuous in recent years (den Boer 1991: 9–12).

The United Kingdom

The United Kingdom currently organizes its police on a decentralized model with some 52 forces throughout England, Wales, Scotland and Northern Ireland. Following the Police Act 1964, formal accountability is 'shared' between the local authorities, the Home Office and the Chief Constable of each force. Certain national services, such as the PNC or the Interpol NCB based in London at Scotland Yard, are funded jointly by the national forces and the Home Office as 'common police services'.

Recent changes and speculation about the police, suggest a movement away from the 'traditional' Anglo-Saxon policing based on local communities towards a more centralized structure. Suggestions for the creation of a new National Criminal Intelligence Service (NCIS) for the police in April 1992, and the search for effectiveness and efficiency by possible amalgamations, have been put forward (Home Office 1993a). Regional crime squads were reduced in number to cover larger areas in 1992, and there was widespread talk of reducing the already marginalized role of local authorities in the tripartite structures of accountability; according to one observer: 'Legal change and political practice have eroded to virtual impotence the local police authorities who are supposed to be the crucial leg of the tripartite system for police governance instituted by the Police Act 1964' (Reiner 1992b: 207).

The British police force is made up of over 150 000 officers employed in the 52 separate police forces as well as with the British Transport Police and Ministry of Defence Police. We will return to look at British policing in more detail in the context of greater police co-operation in Europe in Chapters 4 and 5.

Conclusions

Present policing arrangements in the nation states of Europe have evolved slowly over the last 200 years. The original idea of a 'police-state' regulating all kinds of civic activities has given way to the idea of policing being directed at more specific anti-social criminal activities.

The organization of police forces has moved along a continuum from centralization to decentralization. The former adopted and exported by the Napoleonic regimes of France were based on ideas of a national force controlled at the centre and being imposed across given territories. Such 'high' policing stood in marked contrast to the decentralized 'low' policing of municipal and rural areas espoused by the police of the British Isles, albeit with the exception of Ireland.

By the twentieth century, police forces had over-come any major resistance to their existence as essential pillars of the modern state. Apart from the aberrations of the centralized and militarized police forces of Germany in the 1930s and 1940s, which gave a whole new meaning to the idea of a 'police state', policing became a recognized career for both men and women across Europe. Contemporary systems of policing were influenced by local factors and, in more recent years, by the developing exchange of ideas on an international basis.

2
Police Co-operation: A Crowded Policy Space

In the previous chapter we presented an over-view of the development of the police of Europe, and highlighted some early examples of co-operation between nation states. This book, however, is principally concerned with the recent emergence of new forms of police co-operation in Europe in general, and in the EU in particular. From the perspective of the 1990s, European police co-operation is an opaque and complex patchwork of institutions, agreements and structures which aim to promote different forms of co-operation. Bilateral and multilateral agreements and groups exist alongside associations and less formal networks, and 'together they form a complicated, interconnecting mesh of relatively invisible – and sometimes highly secret – channels, through which collaboration and liaison occurs between law enforcement agencies in the European Union; and sometimes with those elsewhere in Europe and beyond' (Benyon *et al.*, 1993: 285).

In looking back over the 1970s and early 1980s, from the perspective of 1993 and the Treaty of European Union, police co-operation appears as a series of *ad hoc* developments. Any analysis of clear purposes and linear progress would, in our view, be inappropriate because of this fragmented history. While the absence of a clearly articulated 'programme' of change and development would be resistant to any such analysis even if attempted, there is no doubt that a number of definite themes have emerged despite, or indeed because of, this fragmented background. Arguably the most pronounced is that of an 'authoritarian European state' (Spencer 1990; Bunyan, 1991b). The final chapter of the book will, among other things, consider the way in which radical critics have drawn out this theme in the developing European policing terrain. However, here we begin with what can best be termed a conceptual mapping exercise: a process moving from interests at state level through a consideration of the primary institutions and forms of agreement that have helped to weave the patchwork and which make up the conceptual space of police co-operation.

The Patchwork

Writing now in late 1994, there is no doubt that the most significant structures for Europe are Interpol, Schengen and the EU's inter-governmental TREVI-derived network. Interpol, whose origins were discussed in the previous chapter, will not feature further here, but will reappear in Chapter 3. However, both Schengen and EC developments will be examined in the context of our analysis.

The structure of current co-operative arrangements can be presented in different ways. In this regard, there are three useful, although slightly contradictory, 'heuristic devices' available for structuring developments in police co-operation. Those of van Reenen (1989a) and Anderson (1989) will be referred to in the next chapter. The third, and probably the most general of the three, was formulated by the University of Leicester's Centre for the Study of Public Order and presented in evidence to the UK House of Commons Select Commmittee on Home Affairs when they were examining police co-operation in Europe (House of Commons 1990b: xvi). The Leicester framework presents police co-operation as operating at three inter-related levels:

- a *macro level*, concerned with constitutional and international legal agreements and harmonization of national laws and regulations
- a *meso level*, concerned with police operational structures, practices, procedures and technology
- a *micro level*, concerned with the prevention and detection of specific offences and crime problems

As Benyon and his Leicester colleagues indicate, this framework does not of itself have explanatory power. The three levels, which are not mutually exclusive, represent an indication of points along a continuum of the degree of political agreement required for the establishment of strategies for police co-operation (Benyon *et al.*, 1993). The House of Commons Home Affairs Committee in their Report concluded that while such an attempt at classification was useful it was also important to 'avoid any straitjacket of tidy structure' (House of Commons, 1990b: xviii), the Committee considered that it was probably equally valid to consider Europe in policing terms as made up of a series of concentric and overlapping circles. Figure 2.1, slightly adapted from the original, is illustrative.

Of course, the complexity is a reflection of the organizational reality, which in other studies of public government has been characterized as a 'crowded policy space'. European police co-operation can profitably be viewed as such a space, with different countries and interest groups responsible for laying emphases on particular areas of co-operation. In essence, until very recently, there has been no systematicity because there has been no central 'programmatic' authority: instead, developments at national and inter-governmental have prevailed. In addition, co-operative emphases have reflected the deep complexities of police organizational interests both *within* nation state policing structures and *between* states.

From our brief over-view of European national police arrangements in Chapter 1, it is easy to draw general, but over-simplistic conclusions about the nature of policing *within* any one state. In European comparative policing terms, Bayley (1985) compares Anglo-Saxon and Continental models of policing. Such a traditional account needs to be revised, not only because it obscures rather than illuminates the full picture, but more pertinently because it does not facilitate the development of an understanding of 'forces-at-work' in police–state relations; an understanding of the geometry of forces at national level is important. Although we do not have space in this book, the national level of discussion and influence is worthy of study, and its relationship with regio-

Figure 2.1 *Europe in Policing Terms*

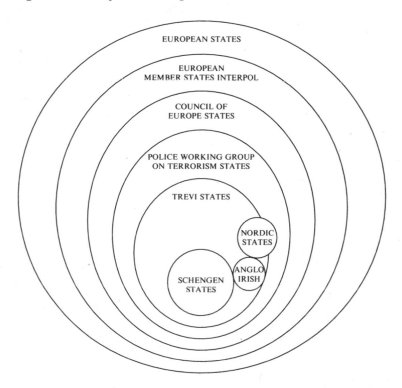

EUROPEAN STATES

EUROPEAN
MEMBER STATES INTERPOL

COUNCIL OF
EUROPE STATES

POLICE WORKING GROUP
ON TERRORISM STATES

TREVI STATES

NORDIC
STATES

ANGLO
IRISH

SCHENGEN
STATES

Source: House of Commons (1990b), p. xix.

nal and local levels varies from state to state, depending on whether the national policing model is centralized or decentralized.

France is an interesting case in point. Traditionally portrayed as providing sharp contrast with policing in England and Wales, it is often presented as completely centralized (Bayley 1985). However, recent revisionist accounts are more helpful in indicating the complexity of forces at work in France (Gleizal, Gatti-Domenach and Journes 1993). Although not specifically related to examining French police arrangements in Europe, it is clear that such accounts now emphasize that there has always been a plurality of police forces in France, and when centralization and unification of the police system has occurred, it has taken place over a very long period, very slowly, and has been a very uneven process. The decisive break in French police history came in April 1941, under the Vichy regime which established the *Police Nationale*.

Although historians say it was due very largely to the authoritarian political power of Vichy, it is worth noting that much of the 1941 law was kept after the liberation. The real explananation for this was that the *Commissaires* took advantage of the political situation in order to have their own proposals enacted (Gleizal, Gatti-Domenach and Journes 1993). They were able to do this because many of the politicians (most of whom were mayors) were excluded from the political life of Vichy. The police became, as a result, a state police in every town of more than 10 000 people and a National Police College was established near Lyons. The efforts to construct a truly unified police system in France only bore fruit in 1966. Then, the Parisian police lost its individual identity and was put into the National Police system administered by the *Sûreté Nationale*, which became (together with the provincial police) a part of the *Police Nationale*.

The police of France thus became 'centralized and unified' as late as the mid-1960s. The issue of the extent of such unification and centralization remains however. As indicated in Chapter 1, France now has three police systems: the *Police Nationale*, the *Gendarmarie*, and the municipal police. In 1990, 125 000 people worked in the *Police Nationale*. In the Ministry of the Interior, the National Police Department includes a personnel section, a resource section, a criminal police section, a counter-espionage section and since 1992, a central territorial section made up of urban police, political police (*Renseignement Génereaux*) and air police. The National Police Department also includes a central CRS (riot police) and the general police inspectorate. Locally, we find a diversity of structures; these include some eleven sections made responsible for resources, and nineteen for criminal investigation. Counter-espionage and the riot police have been organized regionally, as have the political police which operate both on a regional and a departmental basis. The 90 000 *gendarmes* who provide the police service in rural areas are part of the army and therefore belong to the Ministry of Defence. They are, however, headed by a civilian. Their structure is based on military regions and companies and brigades are devolved to departments. In the third arm, the municipal police, there are currently some 10000 officers. Diversity abounds in the municipal police: in terms of numbers, forces vary from as few as two to three officers to 250, working in nearly 3000 localities. Their numbers have grown substantially in recent years, reflecting a view at a local level that mayors wish to be able to implement local policing policies, including the ability to carry firearms.

Any assessment of France, therefore, must ask to what extent there is a co-ordinated police system as a consequence of these three police forces and to what extent the jurisdiction of the forces actually overlaps. As the *Gendarmerie* is no longer a solely rural police force and as each organization acts according to its own strategy and interest, the conflicts between the National Police and the *Gendarmerie* have been numerous (Guyomarch 1991). This is the case even though they are supposed to co-operate in criminal investigations. The *Gendarmerie* has often been used to check alleged corruption in the National Police force, and this in turn has obviously inhibited the co-operation which government has sometimes argued for. The vector of forces and interests are complex, particularly as to their impact on how national and sub-national police understand and relate to calls for greater European co-operation. One significant factor may be the extent to which national and sub-national forces have 'equivalents' or not at European level. The *Gendarmerie*, dependent as they are on the Ministry of Defence, do not present an easy 'fit' within a developing European police terrain, and have often been portrayed as 'opposed' to European co-operative developments (Bigo 1992). The *realpolitik* of where a national or sub- national force fits or, more importantly, can 'potentially' fit into European co-operative structures is important. The question of 'structural fit' together with perceived concomitant rivalries on budget reallocations, structural and personnel arrangements all play their part in constructing such oppositional interests.

In the UK, one should also examine the interplay of the development of interests. While any full and adequate analysis must await detailed research, one can obtain an insight by looking at evidence given to government inquiries. Evidence to the House of Lords Select Committee on the European Communities '1992: Border Control of People' (House of Lords 1989), the House of Commons Home Affairs Committee (House of Commons 1990b), and finally, the Home Affairs Committee, 'Migration Control at External Borders of the European Community' (House of Commons 1992) can serve as examples.

The formation of 'bureaucratic' interest is well exemplified in Gregory's (1990) case study of the police response to a borderless Europe. As Gregory indicates, an understanding of the very limited police service response in the summer of 1989 to the House of Lords inquiry (only some four pages) compared with the much fuller 32-page response to the March 1990 Home Affairs Committee investigation depends on awareness of new policy developments both in forces and at ACPO level. First, the ACPO International Committee, established in the summer of 1989, was a unique ACPO Specialist Committee in that it was composed of representatives of all the other ACPO Committees such as Crime, Training and Traffic. Second, a small increase in the Common Police Service allocation to the ACPO General Secretariat gave that body a greater support facility. Third, the Metropolitan Police agreed that its European Monitoring Unit should become a joint ACPO/Met European Unit thus providing a resource for the entire police service of England and Wales. Fourth, the ACPO International Committee had requested all forces to appoint a European Liaison Officer (ELO) as point of contact and action on Europe. Fifth, there was added stimulus through, for example the Home Office Police Requirements Support Unit (PRSU) award to allow an officer of the Devon and Cornwall police to travel and complete a '1992' project; and indeed, that same officer was later to comment that the bibliography on European policing matters at the Bramshill Police Staff College consisted of less than two pages (see Devon and Cornwall Constabulary, 1990: 1).

By the end of 1989, the level of police awareness on Europe was growing appreciably and the ACPO/Met Unit of some four dedicated officers was producing a series of briefing papers (Gregory 1990: 28). The Devon and Cornwall force also produced early in 1990 a number of researched background papers, and at ACPO level, there was a small but growing amount of visits to European forces and police conferences, together with of course an increase in level and frequency of ACPO's involvement with the EC TREVI forum through the TREVI 1992 Working Group headed by the Chief Constable of Devon and Cornwall, Mr J. Evans (see TREVI, described later in this chapter).

While it is important to understand, the development of interests in the UK context the interplay between police, HM Customs and Excise and the Home Office HM Immigration Service is equally important. Again, a brief look at the evidence to Government Committees can be illustrative. In relation to border controls and checks at entry points, government committees were concerned to explore the possibility of a single multi-functional unified 'Border Control Service', of the kind common in other European countries. What if the HM Customs and Immigration presence was significantly reduced? This point relates to any consideration that there might be of changing the current system of three separate services with distinct functional responsibilities (immigration, police and customs) carrying out separate controls or checks at ports and airports, two of the services (immigration and customs) being locally organized and nationally organized and the third – the police – being geographically deployed. Of course, the extent to which the three services can argue their interests and 'make their case known' differs. Customs and Excise is in quite a strong position to defend its role at borders: first in positional terms it is under a key ministry, the Treasury; second, it is a national organization with both functional and regional sub-structures; third, it has been able to demonstrate that it plays an important role in controlling a politically significant and socially alarming area of criminal activity, namely drug trafficking. On this point, the Customs and Excise told the House of Lords inquiry that information from the ports of Dover and Felixstowe and Heathrow airport showed that around 90 per cent of drugs finds were 'cold': that is, the result of proactive work by a trained Customs officer (House of Lords 1989: 135). In the same evidence, the Home Office also backed up this position by pointing out that in the government's view, Customs and Excise checks provide a significant deterrent to smuggling (House of Lords 1989: 140). Interestingly, while the Home Affairs Committee inquiry focused on police, and its terms of reference excluded Customs and Excise and immigration, it is noticeable that Customs and Excise sent in a detailed Memorandum of Evidence (House of Commons 1990b, Appendix 3) setting out the value and breadth of their role.

The Immigration Service operates from within the Home Office and is a non-uniformed body of civil servants. In comparison with police and HM Customs and Excise, it is quite small in personnel terms (around 2000 people). However, it could be argued that this small group of specialists has certain advantages in putting its case: it is a national service with a simple hierarchy, and during the late 1980s its head of department was the national policy response co-ordinator for all border-control agencies, input to EC fora for developing border control systems. Additionally, one may suggest that the task of integration and focusing of the service's interests is a much less complex task.

The interplay of interests must, we would argue, be visible in relation to any proposals for a structural change in arrangements. Here, it is interesting to examine the mix of evidence to the Home Affairs Committee inquiry on practical police co-operation in 1990, and the later migration control inquiry in 1992. In the 1990 inquiry, the Home Office's observation to the Committee was to the effect that: 'The immigration service, the police and the H.M. Customs and Excise have distinct and specific tasks to perform in relation to work at the ports and airports. The Government does not see a need for changes in the roles of these services' (House of Commons 1990b: 77). The police evidence was rather more mixed. At one point, the British police service memorandum seems to complain of the effects of the lack of co-ordination, stating that 'The effectiveness of the working arrangements was greatly reduced in 1989 when, without prior notification to police, new policies were introduced by HMIs to facilitate passenger flow and to streamline procedures in anticipation of post 1992 requirements' (House of Commons 1990b: memorandum 2). Yet in other parts of their evidence the police said 'a unified port control authority combining police, customs and HMIS could be viable . . . but . . . There is only limited support within the Police Service for unified authority' (House of Commons 1990b: memo 2).

In the 1992 inquiry on migration control, the ACPO representatives' response to the matter of a unified service develops similar points but also mentions other competing themes: one representative notes the caveat:

> one of them would be sharing of information and intelligence. We do not have a commonality of purpose there. There may be a clouding of issues. The second one would most certainly be training and I would rest uneasy with very specialized training of specialized Customs officers who are also police officers but cannot leave ports, and similarly police officers (House of Commons 1992: 22–3).

Another ACPO representative develops yet another theme: 'Accountability . . . You are creating a further enforcement agency within the United Kingdom and so you would have to develop some accountability structures . . . My own feeling is that to make the leap in constitutional and accountability terms and perhaps in cost terms may be a big one' (House of Commons 1992: 23). A final theme which emerged was community relations. The Police Federation representative noted that:

> the policing function at ports has a sensitivity with the community aspect and the needs of the community. The police function at the ports at the moment needs to be very sensitive to the feelings of the community because if it is done incorrectly and done insensitively it could cause horrendous problems elsewhere in the country. I query whether the projected service would have the knowledge of the policies of the police force and the problems of the police force and the training and expertise of the police in community relations (House of Commons 1992: 23).

Structural change was rejected in the police evidence to these inquiries; instead greater co-operation and an extension of powers from one service to another was advocated. Of course, in this example of border checks, in the final analysis the police do not have to advance their particular case at entry-points, since they have a general duty to prevent crime. HM Customs and Immigration Service would perhaps have a greater need to argue their respective roles in terms of a positional politics.

To conclude, any conceptualization needs to begin by trying to understand how, within the national level, moves to greater co-operation create and are created by 'actors' establishing a bureaucratic position for themselves in this 'crowded policy space'; we have given a very brief sketch of two examples from France and the UK, and there are other useful starting points provided by Greer (n.d.) in relation to Spain, and Galeotti (1993) on post-Soviet Russia. Trying to map out the vector of forces here is very difficult, since organizational values are not one directional and change with contextual conditions. For example, it could be argued that *some* specialisms, particularly those having an 'intelligence' role (like drug squads within the UK police), have and will continue to benefit from developments in Europe; others, the 'bread and butter' of crime prevention departments, for example, are less likely to because of (a) the relational topography of bureaucratic structure and (b) because of the way the threat facing law enforcement in a borderless Europe has been presented, as we will try to show in Chapter 6.

Institutional Structures

Figure 2.1 presents the policing of Europe from a territorial perspective, with concentric (and sometimes overlapping) circles mapping the institutional and functional with the geographic. Policing Europe is a moving target, and as commentators trying in this chapter to illustrate 'the map' we are acutely aware of the limiting conditions of the exercise; there are overlapping institutional sources, territorial remits, functional specialisms and strategic emphases. There are several options for presenting the current policing of Europe's 'policy space'. First, one could draw two axes: locating arrangements on a national/international continuum on one axis, and at the same time an axis which presents a continuum of function with, at one end, the general, and at the other the particular or specialist forum or arrangement. Second, one may wish to emphasize criteria that account for the 'achievements' of practical police work: from operations through to legal infra-structure. Finally, one could consider territorial sectors, crime area and degree of institutionalization. In the end, none of these are wholly satisfactory, for as with Benyon *et al.*'s (1993) three-level (macro, meso, micro) classification, they fail to capture the complexity of the situation and, perhaps more importantly, the process. The process in sociological terms, we would argue, negates a search for settled meaning to the arrangements, in reality, any such meaning is in the end 'derived' since at any given moment individual actors, bureaucracies or states promote such (varied and variable) meanings because it helps to resolve internal or bilateral problems (Bourdieu 1989). However, putting this caveat to one side by necessity, we can still fruitfully proceed.

The European Community/Union

In considering police co-operation, one could argue that closer co-operation arises directly from the functional needs of policing contemporary society: in other words, the mobility of large numbers of people in the EC requires that policing is closely co-ordinated across internal frontiers in order to maintain adequate levels of crime control: functions which will generally be displaced to the external frontiers. In the EC context, for many purposes, including policing, member states continue to view the European level as a legitimate arena for action and decision. However, while this functional requirement is 'stated', we would also argue that the actors (here member states) are engaged in a process of bargaining within the framework of medium- (and perhaps longer-) term strategic goals, from which both the scope of co-operation as well as the institutional form of co-operation will emerge.

Of course, since November 1993 and the coming into force of the 'Maastricht' Treaty (Treaty on European Union 1992), we have an emergent structure. For convenience, we have diagrammatically set this out in an Appendix to this chapter. Essentially, the EU's Council of Interior and Justice Ministers now co-ordinates a number of once distinct EC fora; these fora will be described in the next chapter but will simply be mentioned now. The fora include the TREVI forum, the Customs Mutual Assistance Group (MAG), the *Comité Européen de la Lutte Anti-Drogue* (CELAD), the Horizontal Group, and the Ad Hoc Group on Immigration. The Council has a Committee of Permanent Representatives from each Union state (COREPER) who negotiate and agree agendas for the Ministers, and this is serviced by a committee known as K4 (taken from the relevant Article of the Treaty of European Union). The K4 Committee, composed of one official from each member state plus the European Commission, has three steering groups (each with a number of working parties):

- *immigration and asylum* with working parties on migration, asylum, visas, external frontiers and clearing houses on asylum (CIREA Centre for Information, Discussion and Exchange on asylum) and immigration (CIREFI Centre for Information, Discussion and Exchange on immigration)
- *security, law enforcement, police and customs* with working parties on terrorism, police co-operation, organized crime and drugs, customs and Europol.
- *judicial co-operation* with working parties on criminal justice issues and civil matters

K4 Committee also has over-sight of the development of two computerized systems: the European Information System (EIS) and the Customs Information System (CIS) (*Statewatch*, 3, 6, 1993).

This edifice has its basis in the Treaty of European Union (principally TITLE VI Articles K1, K2 and K4), which establishes a new EU extending beyond the traditional institutions and jurisdiction of the EC and brings policing and home affairs into its ambit. In addition to a Political Declaration which commits member states to co-operate in a number of practical areas, member states are also directed to regard as 'of common interest' policies on:

- asylum
- rules governing crossing of external borders
- immigration and nationals of third countries
- drug addiction
- combating fraud
- judicial co-operation in criminal and civil matters
- customs co-operation

Most importantly, Article K1.9 stipulates police co-operation for the purposes of preventing and combating terrorism, unlawful drug trafficking and other serious forms of international crime, including if necessary certain aspects of customs co-operation, in connection with the organization of a Union-wide system for exchanging information within a European Police Office (Europol). It can be argued that Europol is the centrepiece of this EU framework, at least from a law enforcement perspective.

However, while at one level it can be argued that the Treaty presents a qualitative shift in at least the politics of police co-operation, with a general agreement on the need to pursue co-operation in justice and home affairs, it may be a mistake to view the shift as unproblematic or 'determining' in a any broad sense. N. Walker (1993) points to uncertainties regarding Europol establishing a hegemonic position in the policing of Europe. The Treaty text leaves much scope for alternative interpretations, together with the fact that its list of commitments also allows for wide interpretation and fails to indicate either a particular order of priorities or a definite timescale on progress. Europol is left as an information exchange without any attempt to address whether, still less how, it may develop into an operational office, comprising 'normal' powers of arrest, detention and questioning. Uncertainty also surrounds how the Europol initiative relates to the broader regulatory framework under the Treaty; although (as mentioned above) the Council of Ministers, through the K4 Committee, provides an umbrella role covering asylum, immigration, external borders' policies and international crime fighting, just how in practice discrete policy sectors will be co-ordinated with each other is unclear. Finally, there is the peculiar hybrid position that policing occupies within the Community's legal system, being neither merely inter-governmental nor suprana- tional. While there appears a significant executive role, the EC does not have a legislative competence, and neither does the competence extend to core areas of judicial co-operation in criminal matters (Nugent 1991).

Of course, one could argue that the propensity of the whole may prove greater than its parts, and the cumulative effect of various factors may provide the conditions for the transfor- mation of the authoritative base for policing Europe. As Bulmer (1993) points out in his analysis of EC development, the Community's governing structure has the 'ability' to develop into new areas despite the absence of strong political initiatives from member states. However, even where the Community has developed its own 'policing capacity' against fraud through the establishment of UCLAF (*Unite de la Coordination de la Lutte Anti-Fraude*) this has not been unproblematic.

UCLAF as a case study is interesting and illustrates quite nicely both the non-determining nature of current arrange- ments in the EC and the essential tension, at the moment, between specialist agencies and *potential* central policing capacities like Europol (see S. Reinke 1992 for a concise review of UCLAF's role and functions). Recent analyses of the EC criminal policy on fraud have concluded that UCLAF has failed. In general, formal organizations like the EC have to try to harmonize legal and policy responsibilities with broader economic power interests of member states. On fraud, the Commission has tried to compensate for the drawbacks that stem from the fundamental competence– interest conflict. It has striven for a large increase in its direct and indirect control powers by having the Council accept regulations that include the right to carry out independent or co-operative controls in member states (Ruimschotel 1993). It has also pushed for (and obtained) more explicit supervisory powers by imposing a duty on member states to report not only cases of fraud in the area, but also to provide other additional information. Thus, national law enforcement systems are put under pressure when we look at the most recent EC legislation that can be described alternatively as 'operationalizing' their law enforcement obligations or diminishing their overall responsibility. Recent EC regulations try to incorporate increasing powers for the Commission in the area of information gathering, autonomous controls in the member states and joint controls and thereby an increase of evaluative possibilities on member states' law enforcement activities.

However, analyses of this particular criminal policy point to a challenging issue: the lack of political will to combat fraud (see Sherlock and Harding 1991) which characterizes efforts by member states. After all, for the member states, exposure of the overall amount of fraud may imply a duty to reduce it further, so more money would have to be spent on law enforcement of Community regulations, although national interests may be deemed to have a higher priority. In financial terms, the only effect for a member state in exposing more fraud is that less Community money will be channelled to economic actors within that state, and there would be an increased risk of having to reimburse EC funds. In addition, 'national pride' may be at stake; what if huge national differences are revealed either in the amounts or in law enforcement effectiveness?

Even within the EC, the hegemony of the Community in police co-operation is not fully 'determined'. The Schengen arrangements, which will be fully described in Chapter 3, present a direct challenge (at least a prima facie challenge). The Schengen Agreement of 1985 was signed by five EC states and acknowledged the need to abolish obstacles to the free movement of goods and persons, notably border controls. It authorized the detailed discussion of a number of issues concerned with police and criminal justice co-operation, including drugs, firearms, frontier controls, surveillance, mutual assistance, visas and asylum. An Implementing Convention of 1990 set out detailed measures, and by the end of 1992 nine of the twelve members of the EC were in Schengen. While, as we discuss in next chapter, there have been a number of difficulties in maintaining the momentum of the Schengen initiative, it is clear that it has far greater political and resource 'capital' from member states and opinion-forming police officers than the EC Europol concept.

The above examples illustrate the uneven characterization of police co-operative developments in the EC. However, one should not downplay the significance of the formation of the K4 arrangements. As we discussed in the introductory preface to the book, the notion of a permanent security deficit has acted as catalyst to both Schengen and the EU's K4 (Bigo 1992). The Council of Ministers under the EU now has oversight of a number of previously discrete policy areas; these are linked so that there is a continuum of immigration and asylum with organized crime, drugs and terrorism. The ideology of this security deficit has encouraged not only certain arrangements but has focused on the specific order at EC level and has acted to differentiate this from specific interests of other territorial areas. This may be important in the long run for an enhanced EC supranational law enforcement capacity. We return to this issue in Chapters 6 and 7.

Beyond the European Community/Union

In the opening paragraphs of this chapter we emphasized that European police co-operation remains under a number of spheres of active influence, of which the European Community/Union is one such sphere. TREVI has now been incorporated into the workings of K4, but the other highly significant institution has been and is the Council of Europe.

The Council of Europe now has 26 member states, and all 12 EC states are members. Although founded in 1949, since 1989 it has been revitalized and it has recently been suggested that the EC itself may join as a member. Over the last 35 years the Council has been responsible for a number of measures covering extradition, mutual legal assistance, and more recently measures to encourage suppression of terrorism and confiscation of proceeds of crime (money-laundering). A disadvantage of this organization has been its size, which hampers negotiations and makes it more difficult to come to 'quick and unanimous' decisions. However, the work of the Council is illustrative of other, deeper problems in the relationship between legislative arrangements and the European policing terrain.

Often it has been said that the national criminal law systems have to become harmonized, in order to combat crime effectively. Attempts to do this, however, have produced documents that partly overlap and partly differ in emphasis (Schutte 1990): again, a patchwork quilt effect. Let us illustrate this with an example: confiscation of proceeds of crime (see Keyser-Ringnalda 1992). There are at least three relevant international conventions on confiscation, which have recently been formulated: the United Nations Convention against illicit traffic in narcotic drugs and psychotropic substances ('Vienna Convention') of 1988, the G-7 (Seven Major Western Countries) Report of the Financial Action Task Force on Money Laundering of 1990, and the Council of Europe's own 1990 Convention on Laundering, Search, Seizure and Confiscation of the Proceeds from Crime. Formulated from different institutional bases, all three present different scope for co-operation. The Council of Europe's is the most all encompassing and has the strictest member state obligations. In addition, while for the most part national laws have to be brought in line with these international agreements, it is still not clear how this would be given effect in practice.

Conclusions

Developments and proposals at the supranational or multilateral level exist in this 'crowded policy space' alongside a plethora of bilateral agreements and initiatives on a continuum of formality. We have, in this chapter, tried to argue that there is no readily available way to make sense of this patchwork. Clearly, the pursuit and justification of a broad range of security stances by European member states and constituent police forces has had a catalytic effect, with the developing notion of an internal security deficit gaining momentum and serving as a kind of 'structuration ideology' (we analyse this further in Chapter 6). In addition, there are foci and 'achievements' of practical co-operation that must be covered, and we do that in the next chapter. However, in the end, it appears to us that the most appropriate way is not to look for simple structure(s), but to take this field of European police co-operation as a site for struggle and influence at all levels with no definite, immutable trajectories for development.

Appendix

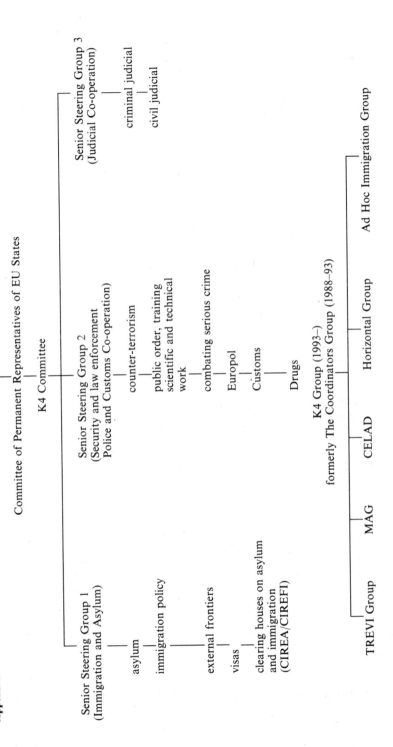

Council of Interior and Justice Ministers

Committee of Permanent Representatives of EU States

K4 Committee

Senior Steering Group 1
(Immigration and Asylum)

asylum

immigration policy

external frontiers

visas

clearing houses on asylum
and immigration
(CIREA/CIREFI)

Senior Steering Group 2
(Security and law enforcement
Police and Customs Co-operation)

counter-terrorism

public order, training
scientific and technical
work

combating serious crime

Europol

Customs

Drugs

Senior Steering Group 3
(Judicial Co-operation)

criminal judicial

civil judicial

K4 Group (1993–)
formerly The Coordinators Group (1988–93)

TREVI Group   MAG   CELAD   Horizontal Group   Ad Hoc Immigration Group

...tical Police Co-operation: Possible Models (1) The Big Three

On a practical level we have seen from Chapter 1 that some degree of European police co-operation has been attempted for the last 100 years. Today we are presented with a number of up-and-running models of co-operation that have been entered into by European police forces, from formalized projects to abandon frontier controls altogether through to various informal mechanisms of direct cross border co-operation.

Van Reenen has argued that police co-operation is only one form of internationalization that the police can enter into. Co-operation is the most common form and the one we are most familiar with, as it leaves existing national police powers and structures untouched. It incorporates information exchange, co-operation in training and the field of observation.

Two other forms of internationalization are identified by van Reenen. Where 'horizontal integration' has taken place police officers of one national force are authorized to act in another country, or government officials get authority over the police or officers of another country. 'Vertical integration' occurs when a police organization is created with central authority over several countries. Both these forms of inter-nationalization, involving a degree of integration are uncommon in policing terms compared to straightforward co-operation. Examples do exist, such as a right of 'hot pursuit' by police to track a criminal across a national border (horizontal) and the creation of an EU policy system

(UCLAF: see below) to track down fraud concerning EU funds (vertical) (see van Reenen 1989a).

The examples of co-operation we cite could also be arraigned along a continuum of models as suggested by Anderson. Anderson places the 'centralized-state' model and the 'decentralized-state' model of international police co-operation at each end of his continuum, with the former allowing communication and meetings in accordance with codified rules strictly adhered to, usually through the medium of a national body. The 'decentralized-state' model, on the other hand, permits direct contact between the police at different levels within a country with their counterparts, with national offices reduced to an advisory role. In between these two points on the continuum are what Anderson calls the 'qualified centralization' and 'qualified decentralization' models, where qualifications are placed on the pure models in special circumstances, such as urgency or the seriousness of the crime being investigated (Anderson 1989: 171–8).

In this chapter we examine the three most formalized arrangements that exist for police co-operation: the Schengen Convention, Interpol and the so-called TREVI group. In Chapter 4 we look at the more informal cross-Channel arrangements that exist in the south of England with France, Belgium and Holland, and various other fora that have been devised for police to talk to each other across borders, including the meeting of police trade unionists and other associations. We also consider some very specific bilateral models of policing borders presented by the building of the Channel Tunnel, and the Anglo-Irish Agreement and its impact on policing for the RUC and the *Garda Siochana*, as well as some other specific responses made within and between police forces to particular crimes such as drug trafficking, public order and terrorism.

The Schengen Convention

 The Schengen Convention provides us with the most complete model we have of international police co-operation within

Europe. The Convention was signed on 19 June 1990 by France, Germany and the Benelux countries (Belgium, the Netherlands and Luxembourg). At this time Spain and Portugal had observer status at meetings leading to the signing, but became full signatories to the Convention on 24 June 1991. Italy had signed the Convention in November 1990 and Greece on 6 November 1992. Nine countries are now signatories to the Schengen Convention with only the UK, the Republic of Ireland and Denmark standing outside it (Schengen Convention 1990).

The origins of the Convention can be traced back to an earlier Convention signed by the Benelux countries on 1 July 1960, which put passport controls at external Benelux frontiers, and recognized national identity documents for their own citizens moving between the countries. The closeness of these countries and their common borders as well as earlier economic collaboration clearly lent itself to this police co-operation. In February 1977 the German and French governments had reached an agreement on localized police co-operation in the south west regions of Germany and on 13 July 1984 the two countries signed a more comprehensive Agreement – the Saarbrüken Agreement – lifting many bilateral frontier controls, and 'strengthening cooperation between French and German customs and police authorities' (see Cullen 1992: 66, 74).

On a Dutch initiative discussions were opened to bring the Benelux countries and Germany and France into a multi-lateral Agreement. The five countries were able to sign the original Schengen Agreement at the Luxembourg village of Schengen on 14 June 1985. Other EC members were not prepared to accede to this agreement, although others were to add their signatures later. In 1985 the events 'went almost unreported in the British press and . . . it took some considerable time for the implications of this agreement *à cinq* to be appreciated' (Butt Philip 1991a).

The Agreement of 1985 eventually became the Convention of 1990, designed to implement the original Agreement. The Convention has sometimes been referred to as Schengen II, or the 'Implementing Convention'. The intervening five years were not blessed with the easiest of discussions and became a focus for some of the multiplicity of views we have seen in Chapter 2. The document itself expanded from an original 33 Articles to a 1990 total of 143 Articles as well as a Final Act with six joint statements *a proces*: verbal with one joint statement and two unilateral declarations, and a Joint Statement by the Ministers and State Secretaries. There was also a failure to meet an agreed deadline of December 1989 for final signatures to be put to the Convention; in public the blame was put primarily on the fall of the Berlin Wall and the new borders created by a unified Germany (Butt Philip 1991a).

The Convention entered into force for France, Germany, Luxembourg and Italy on 1 May 1991. It also entered into force for Poland when the then six Schengen states signed an Agreement to re-admit persons in an irregular position, on the request of any party. The mutual re-admission obligations will in fact fall only in respect of Polish nationals, the obligation being 'accepted by that State (Poland) because of the abolition of visa requirements for Polish citizens' (O'Keeffe 1992).

The aim of the Schengen Convention is to remove all internal frontiers between the 'contracting parties' – the nine signatory countries – to create a free travel area for all EU citizens, but to ensure external borders are strengthened with a view to controlling the entry of external 'aliens' who will not have such freedom of movement. Non-EU citizens will need a visa to secure entry which will normally be for just three months. Individual national visas may admit for longer periods but the aim is to 'harmonize' all visa criteria and the list of countries from whose nationals a visa will be demanded. The onus will be put on airlines and shipping companies to ensure the visas and papers of travellers are in order and, if they are not, 'carrier sanctions' will be incurred.

Asylum seekers will not require visas but their applications for asylum are to be on a 'one-chance' only basis, with the state responsible for admitting the person to their territory being the same state that will examine the request for asylum. The other Schengen states will abide by the admitting state's decision, and asylum seekers will not be subject to the phenomena known as RIO – 'refugees in orbit' – whereby application is made to a succession of countries until someone agrees to grant asylum status.

Integral to building this free travel area are the compensatory measures felt necessary to police a frontier-free terrain, and in particular increased police co-operation between countries within the secure ring fence. The police foresee increased border surveillance and the right of 'hot pursuit' across the borders to follow known criminals they need to arrest. At the heart of the policing arrangements is the perceived need for comprehensive exchange of information between police forces in order to carry out collaborative work and also the establishing of a discrete Schengen Information System (SIS) to enable contracting parties to have automatic cross border data transmission on known criminals or from a collated 'undesirable aliens' list. The Convention goes into some detail on the mechanisms of the SIS and its data protection provisions, and it has been pointed out that such a mix of detailed rules on a computerized information system, together with equally detailed rules on asylum and immigration rules, is really quite unique (O'Keefe 1992).

The SIS would comprise of a central data base in Strasbourg servicing initially the five contracting parties, and to be known as the Technical Support Function (TSF). Each country would also have its own national data base known as SIRENES – Supplementary Information Request at the National Entries – linked to Strasbourg, and each one following a similar format. An information report by the police on an individual is to include only:

- name
- any identifying physical feature
- date and place of birth
- sex
- nationality
- whether violent
- whether armed
- reason for the report
- action to be taken

The Convention specifically excludes collection of information solely on the basis of someone's racial origin, religious convictions, sexual behaviour or membership of an organization which is not itself illegal. We will look at the data protection implications later. Two regions of the Dutch police – Rotterdam and Arnhem – were reportedly using a test version of the SIS in October 1992 (*Statewatch*, 2, 5, 1992).

Discussions on the Schengen Convention have been very much wrapped up in secrecy and have not had the benefit of any public contributions. The EC has always considered policing matters to be outside its 'competence'. Of the original five 'Schengenland' countries, only the Dutch Parliament openly discussed the text of the Agreement in 1986; in France, for example, its existence allegedly only came to light when '"Le Figaro" first reported . . . "Le Secret de Schengen" as late as 14 May 1989' (Pastore 1991). The Director of the Netherlands police academy has described breaking the news of Schengen to some senior British police officers in 1989 and watching them turn pale (van Reenan 1992). Added to the lack of 'competency' is the perceived need to treat all police matters as somehow 'operational' and therefore as confidential from the public. An 'opaque screen' is thrown around the deliberations (McLaughlin 1992) and 'conclusions will eventually be presented to national Parliaments as faits accomplis' (J. Palmer 1990).

In fact, as we explored in Chapter 2, differences are voiced and examples are emerging of national governments and Parliaments not accepting *faits accomplis* when they do emerge. Portugal, one of the later countries to join the Schengen arrangements, drew back at the eleventh hour from signing a bilateral 'hot pursuit' agreement with Spain due to be effective on 1st January 1993, having previously gone along with the proposal for a 50 km limit across the border. The bilateral arrangement was intended to hasten the introduction of Schengen II, but it was blocked by President Mario Soares who questioned its legality (*Platform Fortress Europe?* February 1993).

An even more symbolic blow to the Schengen Convention came when France, once one of the initial driving forces behind the idea, indefinitely suspended introduction of the Convention following a change of government in 1993. An unspoken factor was believed to be the new government's desire to clamp down on illegal immigration and to avoid France being 'at the mercy of the inefficiency of other countries if proper policing were not maintained at the Community's external frontiers' (Nundy and Doyle 1993). This decision by such a prominent member of the original group of five Schengen counries left the future of the Convention very much in the balance. In fact within a few months the French had changed their minds again and agreed to implement the Schengen provisions (Smart 1993; see also Benyon *et al.* 1993: ch. 4.2 for an overview of Schengen).

Interpol

The early history of Interpol has been touched on in our opening chapter with its origins for some observers being traceable back to the 1898 Anti-anarchist Conference in Rome and its more formal beginnings from the inaugural meeting of the ICPC in Vienna in 1923. After its rather uncertain wartime history the Commission's offices in Berlin were moved to Paris, where in 1946 its first post-war General Secretary, Louis Ducloux, started a French ascendancy that would last until the mid-1980s. In 1956 the Commission's statutes formally changed its name to ICPO, although it still remains far better known as simply Interpol.

Today Interpol's aims are summarized in Article 2 of its constitution:

  (a) to ensure and promote the widest possible mutual assistance between all criminal police authorities within the limits of the laws existing in the different countries and in the spirit of the 'Universal Declaration of Human Rights';
  (b) to establish and develop all institutions likely to contribute effectively to the prevention and suppression of ordinary law crimes. (Quoted in House of Commons 1990b: Vol.2, p. 30)

In practice it is a police information and intelligence exchange system that also advises police officers having to visit other countries, and carries out research and analysis of international crime patterns. Although its permanent General Secretariat is based in Lyons, its operations are not confined to Europe and Interpol is a global organization for over 170 participating police forces around the world.

The supreme governing body of Interpol is its General Assembly which meets annually in different parts of the world, and which takes all major policy decisions and decisions concerning working methods, finances and budgeting. An executive committee meets three times a year to monitor the policy decisions and prepare the annual Assembly's agenda. A president is elected for four-year terms of office.

The General Secretariat of Interpol is its permanent presence, and since 1989 it has been located in Lyon, having moved in that year from its previous office in St Cloud, Paris. The Secretariat is divided into four Divisions covering general administration, police matters, research and technical support. The Secretariat produces its own bi-monthly journal, the *International Criminal Police Review*, published in the four main languages used by Interpol: English, French, Spanish and Arabic. The General Secretary is elected by the General Assembly to serve for five-year terms of office.

Each member country of Interpol is required to nominate an office for communications with Lyons. These NCBs are usually located in 'high-level' centralized police offices and act as a focal point for international communications for the country concerned. In the UK the NCB has traditionally been within the Metropolitan Police at New Scotland Yard, London. It is funded as a common police service available to all 52 provincial police forces throughout the country (see also Home Office 1989a: paras 7–12). Moves have now been made to tie the UK NCB in with the NCIS formed in April 1992 (see Home Office 1991a; and Chapter 4). In the Netherlands the NCB is an integral part of their NCIS or CRI housed in the same office in The Hague, and accountable to the same Director.

Interpol's bread and butter is the circulation of police information between NCBs on what are known as 'international notices'. An individual notice gives identity particulars

as well as photographs, fingerprints and a physical description. The notices are categorized and colour-coded as:

- wanted (red) for arrest and extradition
- inquiry (blue) for the collection of additional information
  on a person
- warning (green) about 'professional' criminals who
  operate in more than one country
- missing person (yellow) to assist in their location
- unidentified body (black), with fingerprints if available
  (see House of Commons 1990b: Vol.2, p. 32)

Interpol has been dogged by a poor image in police circles
for many years. It has been seen as remote and distant from
'on-the-ground' policing, as well as being bureaucratic and
cumbersome when it is called upon. The House of Commons
Home Affairs Committee, when looking at police co-operation in Europe, found 'Interpol's performance was subject to
considerable criticism in evidence and in the course of our
visits' (House of Commons 1990b: Vol.1, para. 69). Even
more damning than its slowness and remoteness was the
belief that it was not a secure communications system with
regard to terrorism.

Article 3 of Interpol's constitution had long been held to
prevent it getting involved with terrorist acts, as being
'activities of a political, military, religious or racial character'. The 1984 General Assembly in Luxembourg chose to
reinterpret the reading of Article 3 to declare terrorist acts as
crimes when innocent people were involved and acts took
place in countries declared to be outside the original 'conflict
area'. By 1986 the General Assembly was approving an
Interpol 'Guide for Combatting International Terrorism'
(Anderson 1989: 142).

Even with Interpol moving more directly into tackling
terrorism, however, doubts have remained due to a feeling
that its world-wide membership could still lead to information
in the Interpol network getting into the wrong hands. The
Metropolitan Police Special Branch has indicated that it
expresses a view held by other European Special Branch-type

agencies that 'Interpol staff are not experienced in affording the proper protection to classified material . . . and the politics and motives of some of its member agencies are to say the least, questionable in this context' (House of Commons 1990b: Vol.2, p. 43). Interpol rejects the criticism as 'simply not true' (House of Commons 1990b: 39) but came in for some defamatory comment when it was alleged to have withheld information on a Palestinian 'guerilla chief' who visited France for medical treatment (Doyle 1992).

In 1985 the election of Englishman Raymond Kendall to the position of Interpol General Secretary broke a long sequence of French General Secretaries. Kendall was re-elected for a further five years in 1990 and is widely attributed as being the man who has revived Interpol's fortunes during his time at St Cloud and Lyons (see, e.g., Bresler 1992). In particular Kendall has over-seen a move to new purpose built offices in 1989 and has brought in a degree of computerization and information technology not seen in Interpol before. The average time to process a message sent by a country has dropped from 24 hours to 1½ hours (House of Commons 1990b: Vol.2, p. 33).

In February 1987 Interpol disbanded its largely manual record system and introduced its present computerized Criminal Information System. The move was made in order to:

- improve methods of storing and retrieving information on crimes and criminals
- speed up replies to NCB inquiries
- give the Interpol Police Division immediate, direct access to the computerized files

The Criminal Information System currently comprises the following files:

- names
- drug seizures
- case
- counterfeit currency
- property

A 'back record conversion' exercise was undertaken to weed out old manual files and to decide what would go on the new computerized data base. The process was completed in 1989 and some 60 terminals are now linked to the computer memory and available to staff at the General Secretariat. A group of staff were selected in 1993 to initiate an Analytical Criminal Intelligence Unit and were given awareness training on the benefits of analysis.

A new Electronic Archive system was developed between 1987 and 1990 to preserve electronically on optical disks the criminal record files remaining in paper form. The aim was to make maintenance and retrieval much easier and faster. Similarly, the development of an Automated Search Facility (ASF) was being got under way to offer a data base that contained selected images, photographs, fingerprints and other information and which was available by electronic linkage to NCBs. The 1990 General Assembly adopted a document entitled 'Rules Governing a data base of selected information at the ICPO-Interpol General Secretariat and direct access by NCBs to that data base' (see also Kendall 1989; Abel *et al.* 1991).

Like any global organization there are pressures within Interpol to see its programme on a regionalised basis (Anderson 1989: 101–3). An estimated 80 per cent of communications traffic going through Lyons is between European countries both inside and outside the EU. In recognition of this, European countries have since 1971 made a bigger financial contribution to Interpol through the *Stupéfiants Europe Plan d'Action à Terme*, known as SEPAT (Anderson 1989: 118); the UK's own contribution runs annually at some £500 000 (*Hansard*, 18 February 1992, cols 91–2). Of some 70 police officers from member countries working in Lyons on secondment from their national forces some 54 are from European countries (House of Commons 1990b: Vol.2, p. 34; see also Benyon *et al.* 1993: ch.4.1 for an overview of Interpol).

At an Interpol operational level to assist communications in the European region, Interpol has hosted an annual European Drugs Conference since the mid-1970s in parallel with the work of the Pompidou Group (see below; House of Commons

1990b: 113), a European Fraud Conference every two years (House of Commons 1990b: Vol.2, p. 34), and a European Regional Conference every year for European NCB staff to meet each other (House of Commons 1990b). A Technical Committee on Co-operation in Europe is a permanent arrangement brought into being by pressure from the Germans and a resolution of the 1985 European Regional Conference to make recommendations on improving co-operation. In 1993 it was chaired by Bill Taylor, an Assistant Commissioner from the Metropolitan Police. In turn it has duly recommended the European Contact Officers System whereby each NCB in Europe nominates an officer to take care of the interests of the other Interpol European members in his or her NCB (House of Commons 1990b: Vol.2, p. 35).

The Technical Committee has also been responsible for recommending the European Secretariat which started work in Paris in 1987 with the brief of supporting and carrying out tasks for both the Regional Conference and the Committee, ensuring liaison with the General Secretariat and identifying shortcomings or weaknesses in European co-operation. In due course the Secretariat's role was expanded into its successor, the European Liaison Bureau (ELB), consisting of specialist staff from various European countries, with linguistic and legal training to co-ordinate work on complex investigations. In full, the role of the ELB includes:

(1) advice on the legal and technical implications of assistance sought;
(2) assisting the acquisition and exchange of information;
(3) monitoring and coordinating complex investigations; and
(4) organising and supporting ad hoc working groups on specific cases. (House of Commons 1990b)

The ELB is divided into three teams to cover the European region, and its officers are encouraged to build as many contacts as possible. Officers of the ELB are also reminded not to bypass the NCBs of each country and of the need for mutual assistance and reciprocity (see also ICPO-General Secretariat 1990; *Hansard*, 18 February 1992, cols 91–2).

The TREVI Group

TREVI has been a European intergovernmental forum holding regular meetings at ministerial and officer level to discuss
cooperation on the policing of drugs and serious crime,
terrorism, football hooliganism, public order, police equipment, training and forensic science. TREVI has also been
looking at a frontier free Europe and the pragmatics of
cooperation post-1992. The forum was established in 1976
on the initiative of the British, and involved all EC member
states; although falling outside of the formal EC constitution.
A number of other countries with observer status are known
colloquially as the 'friends of TREVI' and include Austria,
Canada, Morocco, Norway, Sweden, Switzerland and the
United States of America (House of Commons 1990b:
para.64). At the TREVI Group meeting of 12 June 1992 in
Lisbon it was agreed that in future Spain would 'brief'
Argentina on TREVI proceedings, and Denmark should
'brief' Finland; it was stated that Germany already 'briefed'
Hungary (*Statewatch*, 2, 4, 1992).

The original remit of TREVI was to look at issues relating
solely to the policing of terrorism following the rise of terrorist
incidents from the 'sky-jackings' of the late 1960s through to
the early 1970s, and in particular the 1972 hostage taking
off the Israeli competitors at the Munich Olympic Games. As
we have seen Interpol's constitution had in the past left it open
to criticisms of 'softness' on terrorist acts. Fijnaut cites a
German police conference in 1974 as 'the first occasion on
which this criticism was expressed in plain terms' (Fijnaut
1987), and it has been suggested that the TREVI initiative
followed the refusal of the Interpol General Assembly of 1975
in Buenos Aires, to take on the terrorist question. According
to Interpol's General Secretary, Raymond Kendall, this
refusal was:

> . . . largely responsible for the fact that today other
> initiatives have developed, particularly in such things as a
> certain type of anti-terrorist activity coordinated by the
> Interior Ministers of the Common Market countries, which
> I personally think would not have needed to happen if

[Interpol] had taken the stand that it should have done in the early seventies (quoted in Bresler 1992: 161).

As we have seen, the TREVI remit slowly expanded from its original concern with terrorism and 'led TREVI to look increasingly at the mechanics of police cooperation in the European Community across the whole range of crime, the use of liaison officers and the creation of a common information system' (House of Commons 1990b: 5). The TREVI method of operation has been to shadow that of the EC Council of Ministers and to make itself manifest on three levels. As the Council Presidency rotates between the member states every six months, so too has the Presidency of TREVI between Interior Ministers, with meetings of Ministers held every June and December. Senior officials have met every May and November and work is also allocated to the TREVI Working Groups which involve officials and senior police officers (see *Hansard*, 19 October 1992, cols 45–6, for a sample schedule of meetings). Emergency meetings of TREVI have also taken place and one was organised in Luxembourg on 22 January 1991 to consider possible terrorist repercussions of the Gulf War (*Hansard*, 24 January 1991, col.300).

TREVI has had no permanent secretariat or office, although the idea has been put forward. A permanent base will be required if the European Information system proposed by TREVI comes to fruition (see below). To date secretarial support has been provided by the Presidency country and the immediate past two Presidencies and future Presidency countries – the so-called TREVI 'piatnika'. The UK Government believed that 'TREVI's distinctive strength lies in the informal, spontaneous and practical character of its discussions' (ibid: 5); at the same time the Government has supported moves toward a permanent secretariat (Home Office 1991c: 3). Whether 'spontaneous' or not, the accountability of TREVI has been a subject of some debate (see below); in 1988 TREVI came under the auspices of the newly created Coordinators Group.

The Coordinators Group was yet another inter-governmental body made up of high-ranking officials and senior civil servants to oversee not just TREVI, but other groups like the *ad hoc* Working Group on Immigration, the Mutual Assistance Group of EC Customs Officers and the European Committee to Combat Drugs (CELAD). The idea was to try to sort out delays amongst the member states and clarify responsibilities, but not necessarily to make TREVI and the other groups any more accountable. Following the Maastricht Agreement in December 1991 TREVI's constitutional position underwent further changes (see below; see also Benyon *et al.* 1993: ch.4.3).

Accountability and Legal Standing

Having considered the three main organizational forms of police co-operation in Europe we need to consider their legal standing and political accountability. We have already noted some of the Agreements and Conventions underlying Interpol and Schengen and the political co-operation behind the TREVI group. What other problems and questions arise when a state seeks to go beyond its immediate terrain of sovereignty on questions of law enforcement?

The normal conventions of state sovereignty are that a state has effective jurisdiction of its own law enforcement agents that extends to its territorial borders. In practice this means that a Spanish police officer, for example, has no power to arrest anyone beyond the Spanish borders and indeed no powers to compel anyone to do anything. Nadelmann has summarized the position: 'The sovereign power of states forecloses unilateral police action by one state in the territory of another. Sovereignty requires that most international law enforcement efforts be bi-lateral, cooperative ventures' (Nadelmann 1990).

Nadelmann cites the concept of a continuum of law enforcement principles moving from the sovereign state into the rest of the world:

- the territorial principle: jurisdiction within a state's territory over persons or things;
- the nationality principle: allows a state to assert jurisdiction over the conduct of its nationals anywhere;

- the protective principle: under which a state can claim jurisdiction over acts beyond its borders that threaten its security;
- the passive personality principle: whereby a state can claim jurisdiction over conduct that harms its nationals outside of its territory;
- the universality principle: under which a state can claim jurisdiction over 'international crimes' such as piracy, slave trading or aircraft hijacking. (Nadelmann 1990)

In moving beyond the initial territorial principle the sovereign state is going to require some form of Agreement for action in law enforcement either with one other country (bilateral) or a number of countries (multilateral). The multilateral form of Agreement lends itself to a collection of countries in close proximity to each other such as in Europe, and the bilateral arrangements, although not exclusively so, to the more physically distant countries. In looking at the origin of the Schengen Convention, for example, we detailed the earlier multilateral Benelux Convention of 1961 and the bilateral French–German agreements of 1977 and 1984.

The Council of Europe has been an important focus of multilateral agreements in the European context. Of particular note from the point of view of international police co-operation are the following Conventions agreed by the member states of the Council:

1950   Convention for the Protection of Human Rights and Fundamental Freedoms

1957   Convention on Extradition

1959   Convention on Mutual Assistance in Criminal Matters

1977   Convention on the Suppression of Terrorism

1981   Convention for the Protection of Individuals with regard to Automatic Processing of Personal Data

The 1950 Convention on Human Rights is required to underpin legislation passed in any of the Member States who are signatories, and judicial appeal can be made to the Strasbourg based European Court of Human Rights. The

European Court of Justice in Luxembourg is not primarily a means of enforcing the 1950 Convention, although it has frequently made reference to the provisions of the Convention. The Court of Justice sees its role in relation to Community Law and refers questions of human rights to national jurisdictions or Strasbourg. The President of the EC has indicated that he would like to see the Court of Justice turn its attention more to criminal matters, and that may be a future development for that court (speech at the European Court of Justice, 4 December 1992; Sage 1992).

The European Convention on Extradition has more direct applications to policing, and although it was originally agreed in 1957 it was only ratified by the UK Government in May 1991. The British had until then preferred to rely on their own bilateral treaties with various countries and their own procedures which included a requirement that other states present prima facie evidence to a UK court before an extradition could be granted. The removal of the prima facie rule was made by means of the Criminal Justice Act 1988 and consolidated later in the Extradition Act 1989, but not without some protests by legal and other organizations. Removal enabled the UK to sign and ratify the Convention and it is now only necessary for another state to demonstrate that the offence for which extradition is requested is one falling within the scope of the Convention, is common to both states and is punishable in both with imprisonment for 12 months or more. The intent is to make it much easier to bring criminals to book in any of the EC member states, who have now all ratified the Convention.

The European Convention on Mutual Assistance in Criminal Matters has also been described as 'a fairly venerable treaty' (House of Commons 1990b: Vol.1, para.95), but it too has now been ratified by the UK after the passing of the Criminal Justice (International Cooperation) Act 1990. A Home Office discussion had previously had to admit that:

The United Kingdom's failure to participate in formal mutual legal assistance arrangements has earned us a poor reputation for co-operation, even in the event of entirely reasonable and proper requests. It has also caused serious problems for our own prosecution authorities as other states may refuse to render assistance because of lack of reciprocity. (Home Office 1988)

The UK was the last EC member country to sign and ratify the Convention which entered into force here on 27 November 1991 and eases the movement between countries, of writs and records of judicial verdicts, the appearance of witnesses, experts and prosecuted persons as well as criminal record histories (Foreign and Commonwealth Affairs Office 1992).

A central feature of mutual assistance both before and after the UK ratification of the 1959 Convention is the *Commission Rogatoire*, which is a letter of request from one judicial authority to another. Most European countries expect a formally worded *Commission Rogatoire* to be presented before any inquiry or operational visit can be made by the police of one state to another. The request is made by a magistrate with power of jurisdiction to another magistrate or a police officer who has the same power to make similar inquiries in the receiving country.

In the UK assistance to the police to complete a *Commission Rogatoire* is offered by the Crown Prosecution Service and a translation must be made into the language of the country concerned. Copies have to be deposited with the Foreign and Commonwealth Office for onward transmission through diplomatic channels, and the police officers' visit cannot commence until authority is granted from the country in question. The Interpol NCB in London offers consultation to police officers on the execution of *Commission Rogatoires*, and presumably other European NCBs offer a similar service to their national forces (see Home Office 1989a: paras 17–27; and Foreign and Commonwealth Affairs Office 1992: 3–4).

The idea of some kind of legal harmonization across Europe or even a freely operating police officer with executive powers is clearly some way off. The former French President, Giscard d'Estaing, once envisaged a degree of harmonization he could describe as *Espace judiciaire européen* (see also Chapter 4). At present countries are unwilling to cede their criminal justice sovereignty, and Conventions, Protocols and devices such as *Commission Rogatoires* are a means of reach-

ing out beyond national frontiers in the interests of criminal
law enforcement.

The ratification of the 1957 and 1959 Conventions in a
short space of time by a government that had delayed signing
and ratification for almost 30 years must tell us something
about the momentum that is building up in certain quarters to
ensure police co-operation in Europe is as smooth as possible.
As Spencer comments, the UK Government has never had
any reluctance before to appear an 'odd man out' in Europe,
but presumably does not wish to be seen as 'soft' on crime
(Spencer 1990: 93). It is all in marked contrast to the UK
initiated 1977 Convention on the Suppression of Terrorism
which was signed and ratified by the British Government by
the following year. The 1981 Data Protection Convention will
be considered separately later.

Interpol has managed to achieve its pre-eminence in
international policing matters without reference to any major
Convention. Having incrementally developed over the years as
an international police organization it has achieved recognition internationally by 'passing references' in Conventions
concerned primarily with other things. The 1957 European
Convention on Extradition, for example, makes reference to
Interpol in its Article 16 and the 1959 European Convention
on Mutual Assistance in Criminal Matters 1959 in its Article
15(5), the latter Convention citing Interpol as a recognized
organization through which requests for mutual assistance
may be passed.

The two Conventions mentioned above are both Council of
Europe initiated multilateral Conventions and the Council
gave further formal recognition to Interpol through a diplomatic 'exchange of letters' in 1960 (Council of Europe 1960).
Interpol is a member of the Council's Committee on Crime
Problems and has been responsible for drafting possible
conventions for the Council of Europe; something that has
been suggested as going somewhat beyond its brief (see
Anderson 1989: 69).

In 1947 Interpol applied to the United Nations for recognition as an international non-governmental organization, but
the application was unsuccessful. A 1955 United Nations
resolution on narcotics included a reference to Interpol as

being the international organization best qualified to circulate information on drug trafficking, and by 1971 Interpol was recognized by the United Nations as an inter-governmental organization. United Nations funds have subsequently been made available to Interpol to establish a telecommunications network in the Caribbean (Anderson 1989: 70).

Other international bodies have 'recognized' Interpol in a similar vein, such as the Customs Co-ordinating Committee (CCC), the International Civil Aviation Organization (ICAO) and for personnel purposes the International Labour Office (ILO). The sheer size of its world-wide membership must also have helped Interpol's claims for recognition.

On the domestic front Interpol HQ has had to come to some agreements with its host country, France. In 1972 a Headquarters Agreement between France and Interpol recognized Interpol's right to engage in property and financial transactions and to be exempt from taxation. A further Headquarters Agreement made in 1982 resolved some data protection issues for the French (see below) and ultimately gave Interpol 'the independence, autonomy and legal personality characteristic of inter-governmental organisations in general' (Anderson 1989: 66) but without any specific Conventions on the organization ever having been signed.

We have also described the evolution of TREVI as an inter-governmental organization; an evolution made in conditions of some secrecy. No international Conventions or Agreements have recognized the existence of TREVI, and the UK Government expresses the view of other participating governments that the respective Interior Ministers report back to their national Parliaments, and not to the European Parliament or European Commission (*Hansard*, 23 January 1992, col. 478–9). The UK Government has never been persuaded that anything more than a written answer to a Parliamentary Question was needed to keep the UK Parliament informed of TREVI deliberations (Home Office 1991c: 3). In fact, the first such written answer concerning a body that had been meeting since 1976 only appeared in June 1990 (*Hansard*, 27 June 1990, col. 220). The Government has refused to give Parliament the minutes of TREVI meetings (*Hansard*, 3 June 1991, col. 77) or to disclose the cost of British participation

(*Hansard*, 19 March 1991, col. 70). Even a Home Office circular to Chief Constables, advising them of TREVI's structure and issued on 2 September 1977 (Circular 153/77), remains a classified document to this day (personal correspondence, 14 April 1993). The Circular contained descriptions of the working groups and summarized their initial deliberations as reported to the next meeting of EC Ministers of the Interior held in London in May 1977. Chief Constables were invited to submit agenda items for future discussion and the circular outlined practical arrangements to facilitate co-operation to counter terrorism.

The secrecy surrounding TREVI has some resonance with that we have already looked at in relation to Schengen's early development. As one commentator describes it: 'The extent of public information about TREVI seems to be in inverse proportion to the importance attached to it by governments and police officers' (Cullen 1992: 71).

The EC had no direct police competence and TREVI was always designated as independent of the EC. The Commission has had an interest in its deliberations but has 'not sought a formal role' and has had 'no wish to be given competence in policing matters' (House of Commons 1990b: Vol.1, para. 52). The European Parliament, on the other hand, did express its concern in December 1989:

> that the secret discussion, without democratic control by parliamentary supervision, on matters of police action, internal and external security and immigration, namely those affecting refugees, by Member States acting outside the competence of the European institutions, within fora such as Schengen, TREVI and the ad hoc Immigration Group, violate the aforementioned conventions and democratic principles. (Para. F, resolution on the signing of the Supplementary Schengen Agreement, Doc.B. 3–583/89)

Members of the European Parliament have expressed their dissatisfaction that 'when the Council of Ministers comes to the European Parliament for question time, as they do for a one and a half hour period during each plenary session, they refuse to answer any questions on matters discussed in the

TREVI group', and whilst some policing matters may need to be confidential the extent of the secrecy made 'the TREVI group . . . positively dangerous and undemocratic' (House of Commons 1990b: 60). In due course the 1991 Maastricht Treaty was to bring TREVI out of the shadows and into a more formal position (see below).

Data Protection: A Special Case

As most international arrangements between police forces fall short of allowing police officers to have operational powers within another country, the emphasis has come to fall on the exchange of police information between forces as being the bedrock of co-operation. Interpol has been derided as 'a post-box' and we have noted the arrival of the SIS and the TREVI initiated EIS. Any system of personal information exchange has consequences for the privacy of individual citizens, who are in turn entitled to data protection legislation to ensure a degree of information privacy. As a senior Home Office civil servant admitted to a British Parliamentary Committee, in terms of European policing and data protection 'there are major issues yet to be addressed' (House of Commons 1990b: Vol.2, p. 92).

Guiding principles on the protection of individuals in terms of data accumulation and maintenance by computers can be traced back in the European context to the Council of Europe Data Protection Convention (Council of Europe 1981) and the OECD's guidelines on transborder flows of personal information (OECD 1980). The Council of Europe has taken a sectoral approach to data protection, and has followed up the Convention with two Recommendations to its member states concerning personal information held in the police sector (Council of Europe 1984 and 1988).

Signatories to the 1981 Council of Europe Convention committed themselves to introducing national data protection legislation, if they had not already done so. The UK introduced its Data Protection Act in 1984, for example, and the Republic of Ireland its 1988 Data Protection Act. The laws were required to introduce regulatory mechanisms to oversee

the maintenance, retrieval and uses to which personal information was being put in the interests of protecting the
individual. Signatories would also use the law to introduce
Data Protection Registrars or Commissioners both to educate
people about this new form of social policy and control, and
also to 'police', with sanctions if necessary, departures from
the new regulatory laws by data users. The European
Commission encouraged its member states (who are all
members of the Council of Europe) to introduce legislation
in accord with the Convention (*Official Journal of the
European Communities* L246 (29 August 1981) p. 31).

Some European countries already had data protection
legislation and the German state of Hesse is attributed as
introducing the first data protection commissioner as early as
1970 (Flaherty 1989: 22). In France, data protection laws had
introduced the CNIL (*Commission Nationale de l'Informatique
et des Libertés*) on 6 January 1978, and its attention was soon
turned to the activities of Interpol, which was then based in
Paris. Interpol was faced with three options, according to
Anderson. It could accept regulation by the CNIL, as any
other French police authority would have to do, or lobby for
legislation that would exempt Interpol, or claim exemption
altogether because of being an international organization
(Anderson 1989: 64–5).

Interpol reached a compromise position with the French
Government. Interpol's own Headquarters Agreement of 1982
made with the French Government, as we have seen gave the
'independence, autonomy and legal personality characteristic
of inter-governmental organisations in general' (Anderson
1989: 66), but the same Agreement also created a supervisory
board known as the Internal Control Commission (ICC) to
over-see data protection matters for Interpol. The ICC was to
comprise five members of different nationalities and met for
the first time on 20 January 1986. The five members were a
French Government nominee, an Interpol nominee, a senior
judicial person to take the chair, an Interpol Executive Committee Member and an electronic data processing expert chosen
by the chair from a list proposed by Interpol. As Anderson
comments, 'the compromise seemed to lean towards Interpol
rather than the French Government's position' (1989).

More complex data protection provisions have been proposed within the Schengen Convention both for information processed and exchanged outside the SIS, in the course of international police co-operation, and for information that is processed and exchanged within the SIS. Member states are required to designate a national authority to have responsibility for its own national data base within the national data protection laws of that country, as well as an independent supervisory authority to oversee the national data base (Schengen Convention Articles 108–14).

The TSF in Strasbourg, which would only hold information the contracting parties wished to pass to it, would be over-seen by a new Joint Supervisory Authority (Article 115). Membership of the Authority would be made up from two representatives from each of the national independent supervisory authorities, ensuring that data protection principles in the Convention were met. These principles in turn were based on the Council of Europe's 1981 Convention for the Protection of Individuals with Regard to Automatic Processing of Personal Data (Council of Europe 1981) and the subsequent 1987 Recommendation from the Council on the regulation of police-held personal information (Council of Europe 1988). As with Interpol, the siting of the TSF in Strasbourg also placed it under the jurisdiction of the French data protection commissioners, the CNIL; a fact recognized by the Convention in Article 92(31).

Working to the 1981 Convention and the subsequent Recommendations, the Schengen Convention prompted some of the original signatories into putting national legislation in place. The Netherlands and Belgium had to draw up new laws. The British police and UK Government are not parties to the Schengen Convention, and one point of difference is to be found on the data protection front. Although legislation exists, Britain chose to enter reservations on two principles of the 1987 Recommendation which required people to be notified when data had been stored on them but no police action was imminent (Principle 2.2), and prohibited the collection of data solely on the basis of race, religious convictions, sexual behaviour or political opinions (Principle 2.4) (see *Hansard*, 15 October 1990: cols 721–2).

Having entered such reservations it is hard to see how the British police could ever become a party to the SIS as the Convention is currently formulated. Exactly the same issue arises with the TREVI idea of an EIS which we consider later in this chapter (see *Hansard*, 18 February 1992: col. 92).

Even where national laws are sufficient and states have ratified the 1981 Data Protection Convention, critics have still pointed to problems with the Schengen Convention itself, and its data protection safeguards for the SIS in particular. If the initial aims and objectives of any data base are not clearly defined there is a potential for unnecessary data to be stored. It has been argued that the Schengen Convention's Article 99, stating the aims of the SIS, is both vague and unduly wide (Verhey 1991; O'Keeffe 1992; Scheller 1992) and may even violate the Council of Europe's Recommendation R(87)15, where Principle 2.1 limits data collection to 'such levels as is necessary for the prevention of a real danger or the suppression of a specific criminal offence'. The Dutch Council of State has argued that this loose provision could lead to 'very fundamental infringements of personal privacy' (quoted in O'Keeffe 1992).

From this starting point of an ill-defined objective, other problems may follow. The uses to which information held in the SIS could be put may be more varied than first imagined due to poor definition (Verhey 1991), and as there is, in addition, no real reference to third parties gaining information from the SIS, it is left entirely to national laws to govern such usage (Verhey 1991).

The Director of Legal Affairs at the Council of Europe has pointed out that their Recommendation (87)15 on data protection in the police sector was issued shortly after most European states had already enacted legislation in terms of the 1981 Convention and therefore, although integrated with the Convention, did not provide sufficient detailed rules for practical purposes (the Computer Law and Security Report, January–February 1992: Conference Address). He suggested no further amendments should be attempted until the SIS was operational and evidence was available on the Channel Tunnel and its policing arrangements.

Whilst the Council of Europe is content to wait and see what happens, the national Data Protection Registrars and Commissioners of Europe are monitoring developments in international information exchange in the police sector with interest. In November 1991 Commissioners meeting in The Hague, from Belgium, Denmark, France, Germany, the UK, Ireland, Luxembourg and the Netherlands, issued a joint statement declaring a need for adequate legislative privacy protection for the Schengen Agreement and the SIS (*Statewatch* 2, 1, 1992). The UK Data Protection Registrar, Eric Howe, has re-affirmed the need for safeguards to be built into international protocols (Data Protection Registrar 1992: 3).

Not everyone accords data protection the same degree of importance. We have already seen the British police attitude to certain principles of the Council of Europe Recommendation (87)15 and the difficulties they would appear to have with the Schengen Convention. Spokespersons for the police in the UK have also referred to data protection as though it were an obstacle to effective policing. Roger Birch, Chair of the ACPO International Affairs Committee, believes 'the policing of Europe cannot wait for the total harmonisation of legislation and for the resolution of such *thorny issues* as data protection' (Birch 1992; emphasis added). Others have taken a similar perspective: 'the widespread adherence to the philosophy of 'need to know' and the requirements of governments (under pressure from civil liberties groups) for effective data protection further *restrict possibilities*' (Latter 1990: 6; emphasis added).

The British police also seem somewhat confused on the data protection question of passing information across borders between police forces, and then disclosing it to third parties for vetting purposes. Some European countries will not permit the use of criminal records and other police-held information in this way (see, e.g., Home Office 1991d: Annex Q), even though the Schengen Convention over-looks it. Senior police officers giving evidence to a Parliamentary Committee thought that in principle Interpol could do this job for the UK and that only the volume of requests that might be made would be a limiting factor (House of Commons 1990b: Vol.2, p. 109).

Maastricht and Europol

The deliberations of the TREVI group were made public in 1990 to the extent that a Programme of Action was published in the name of the EC Interior Ministers' meeting in Dublin in June of that year. The document attempted 'a synthesis of the arrangements considered between police and security services with a view to more effective prevention and repression . . . of terrorism, drug trafficking or any forms of crime including organised illegal immigration' (Programme of Action 1990).

The Programme of Action is essentially presented in two parts or chapters. Chapter 1 has the Areas of Cooperation that the Group believes requires the development of better multilateral co-operation; a third section looks at how implementation may be monitored. These areas reflect the Working Groups we have already described, and include terrorism, drug traffic, organized crime, illegal immigration and also a tentative reaching out to new areas such as 'serious disturbances of the public order' (para. 8). Allied to these areas as a focus of co-operation is the need to improve education and training of personnel to incorporate a European view, to exchange ideas on the technical and scientific side of policing, and to consider 'methods of combatting new forms of criminality' such as credit card fraud (para. 6).

Chapter 2 of the Programme of Action considers the methods of co-operation, and includes the exchanging of liaison officers and the attention to be paid to what policing is still necessary at frontier points and in common frontier zones, as well as transfrontier observation and issues of 'hot pursuit' across borders. Central to much of these efforts was the idea of a common information system which the Programme felt it needed 'to collect data and descriptions of persons and objects for purposes within the scope of this document' (para. 15.1). The Programme also revealed that as far as information on terrorism and terrorists were concerned, the TREVI group already had its own 'rapid and protected communications system' which had been agreed upon as far back as September 1986 (para. 2.4). Data protection was mentioned as such but the Programme stated that all initiatives respected national laws and the provisions of international law (para. 2.3).

The British Home Secretary was able to report on progress after the December 1990 meeting of the TREVI group in Rome. Work on the common information system was proceeding, with the creation of a European Drugs Unit (EDU) taking the lead (*Hansard*, 18 December 1990, col. 110). The House of Commons Home Affairs Committee, endorsing the need for European-wide information systems, at the same time entered reservations by pointing out the similarity to the existing Interpol communications network for Europe. In their words, they did 'not want to see the Interior Ministers of the European Community re-inventing the wheel for the sake of political innovation' (House of Commons 1990b: Vol.1, para. 108).

The Interpol versus TREVI debate on information systems was somewhat over-shadowed by an alternative debate that started up on whether European policing initiatives should go beyond information exchange to a more operational form of policing, with officers having international executive powers comparable to the FBI in the USA. Chancellor Helmut Kohl of Germany, speaking in Edinburgh in May 1991, proposed just such a style of policing, which was seen as a natural extension of the federal policing already operating in Germany (Cullen 1992: 78ff.). In the Netherlands there was only moderate enthusiasm for such policing (den Boer 1991: 25), while in Britain the Government thought it was 'aeons away' (House of Commons 1990b: Vol.1, para. 101), and the argument had been subsumed into whether or not we needed FBI style policing across the UK's 52 police forces, let alone Europe (Kirby 1990; see also Kirby 1992b).

By the time of the European Council meeting in Luxembourg June 1991 the TREVI group was able to present plans for a common information system able to help compensate for the loss of borders and also capable of taking on international organized crime. The idea of an executive European police force had been temporarily shelved, and the European Council meeting in December of the same year was able to incorporate references into the Treaty on Political Union to the establishing of a common information system, to be more

formally known as a European Police Office or Europol
(Article K.1.(9)). As already stated in the TREVI Programme
of Action, a drugs intelligence unit – the EDU – was to be the
initial move in creating the new EIS.

The Treaty on Political Union agreed at Maastricht in
December 1991 was a stepping stone in the emergence of
policing and home affairs into the political daylight. It was the
evolution of the so-called 'third pillar' of the EC – to become
the EU on 1 November 1993 – to deal with justice and home
affairs and to stand alongside the 'first pillar' (economic and
social affairs) and the 'second pillar' (foreign affairs). The
Europol idea was to be taken forward within new structures
that were to replace both TREVI and the Co-ordinators
Group. In February 1992 the EC member states signed a
Declaration on Police Cooperation as an annex to the
Maastricht Treaty.

The TREVI Group, the Ad Hoc Group on Immigration
and the MAG of Customs Officers were brought together
post-Maastricht under a Council of Interior and Justice
Ministers, which in turn delegated to a new committee of
senior officials (to replace the Co-ordinators Group) known
as the K4 Committee, taking its name from the relevant
Article of the Maastricht Treaty (Doyle 1993). The K4
Committee in turn has three senior steering groups, each
with a number of working sub-groups. (See the Appendix to
Chapter 2, and also *Statewatch*, 3, 4 (1993): 7; Benyon *et al.*
(1993): ch. 4.4.)

The last TREVI meeting effectively took place in December
1992 (*Statewatch*, 3, 1 (1993): 11) as the new structures came
into place. As far as Europol was concerned the new Ad Hoc
Working Group on Europol was formed under the auspices of
K4's second steering group with delegates from all member
states; it began meeting on a six-weekly cycle. Its first chair was
provided by the UK: the position was taken by Kevin Heal of
the Home Office until 1 July 1993 when the Belgians took over;
future chairs were to change with the EU Presidency.

A permanent Project Team to build the new Europol was
also established and took up temporary residency in Strasbourg in a Portacabin on the same site as the newly-emerging
SIS. The Project Team, headed by a senior German police

officer, Jurgen Storbeck, and with a multinational staff of around 50, started a European crime analysis project and also started looking at relevant computer software (see, e.g., 'A humble start for Europol', Police, November 1992, p. 52). Most of its work, however, was taken up with trying to draft a new Convention to legitimate the whole Europol project. The need for such a Convention, especially to cover data protection questions, relations with Interpol, drug enforcement agencies, etc., seems not to have been foreseen earlier but was now insisted on by the politicians before Europol could start business. Present activities were to be governed by a Ministerial Agreement which had been signed in Denmark and which also allowed the setting up of the EDU.

The need for a Europol Convention and the current Ministerial Agreement mirrors the early days of the 1985 Schengen Agreement and the 1990 Schengen Convention. It could be at least 1996 before agreement is reached on a Convention, and meanwhile Europol developments are seen as belonging to two phases: the *Pre-Convention phase*, which will duly become the *Post-Convention phase*. Strasbourg as a temporary site was in competition with The Hague and Rome to house Europol in the Pre-Convention phase, and Lyons and Wiesbaden were understood to be bidding to have it located with them in the Post-Convention phase; in the end the Pre-Convention phase went to The Hague. Wider political influences will be brought to bear on making the later decisions which now run parallel to the more functional 'turf issues' arising between Europol, Interpol and Schengen.

Conclusions

Three main fora have been devised in Europe to consider international policing matters. The Schengen Convention, agreed in 1990, has been seen as the model for future police relations in a frontier-free Europe. Encompassing nine of the twelve EU member states, the Schengen arrangements outline ways in which borders can be dismantled, national policing given compensatory measures and new data bank systems, such as the SIS, can be built to monitor the movement of people within the Schengen countries.

The Schengen Convention has not had an easy ride and has been beset by various obstacles to its progress. Running alongside it have been the parallel systems of Interpol and TREVI. Interpol has built upon its earlier beginnings to develop a new European focus with new technology to upgrade its service to European members. The TREVI group, formed in 1976, has provided a forum for inter-governmental meetings to discuss different aspects of cross-border policing.

In 1991 TREVI acted as the platform to launch the new post-Maastricht Europol. TREVI itself was phased out, to be replaced by the new K4 co-ordinating committee and the emergent Europol was to be based on an EDU. As operational policing matters were still the subject of heated debate, the exchange of information was seen as the way forward for European police co-operation, with only the 'thorny' problem of data protection standing in its way.

4

Practical Police Co-operation: Possible Models (2) Other Initiatives

Having concentrated on the major forms of European police co-operation embodied in Schengen, TREVI and Interpol, and their associated legal standing, accountability and data protection problems, we are not over-looking the fact that there are numerous other examples of international police activity going on across Europe and an even wider geographic span. These activities range from having quite formal legal underpinnings through to more varied informal activities and on to 'sporting, social and cultural links' to cement good relationships for future police co-operation (Devon and Cornwall Constabulary 1990).

One unique example of police co-operation is provided by the building of the Channel Tunnel to provide a 'fixed link' between France and England. The Treaty of Canterbury (1986) paved the way for this civil engineering project. The bilateral Treaty formed an English–French Inter-governmental Commission to over-see the work and a Safety Authority to look at questions of emergency, rescue and public safety. The Treaty did not mention the binational Policing and Frontier Controls working group that was formed, but did say that a Protocol would be drawn up to look at the exercise of police, immigration and customs controls (Article 4(2)).

The resulting Channel Tunnel Act 1987 enacted the Treaty and allowed the private funding consortium, Eurotunnel, to be given the concessionary agreement to arrange the building and operation of the tunnel. The Chief Constable of Kent was designated lead police authority at the English end (1987 Act, s.14(l)), working with the British Transport Police and the Metropolitan Police Special Branch who would have some frontier control responsibilities on fast 'through' trains between capital cities (as opposed to the cross-Channel only 'shuttle' trains). The Metropolitan Police had formed a Channel Tunnel Co-ordinating Group to look at their new responsibilities (Hermitage 1989), and the British Transport Police allocated two officers to working full time on the implications for them (House of Commons 1990b: Vol.2, para. 67).

In the Kent Constabulary a Channel Tunnel Planning Team first met in May 1986 and gave way to an operational Channel Tunnel Policing Unit in 1989. In terms of liaison with the French the Kent force had years of experience from the Cross Channel Intelligence Conference that had started in 1969. A full-time Cross Channel Liaison Officer had become part of the force's Central Crime Intelligence Bureau in 1982, and he had two more officers deployed to work with him from 1990. In July 1991 they were formally designated as Kent's European Liaison Unit (Gallagher 1992).

Paul Condon, then Chief Constable of Kent, could report in 1991 'excellent relationships' with the French 'developed over many years' (House of Commons 1990b: Vol.2, para. 25). In July of that year a formal 'exchange of letters' took place between the Chief Constable and his French counterpart, the Prefet of the Pas de Calais, believed to be 'the first of its kind entered into by a British police force' (House of Commons 1990b). Between them the French and the English police could divide their roles into three categories:

- the policing of the frontier
- the prevention and detection of criminality within the tunnel area
- the security of the tunnel itself

On the security question they worked jointly with Eurotunnel's own private security staff.

As soon as the engineers building the tunnel had made a physical breakthrough, and even though transportation for passengers was still some years away, an interim Order was made by the British Government to cover aspects of policing and immigration. The Channel Tunnel (Fire Services, Immigration and Prevention of Terrorism) Order 1990 came into force on 1 December 1990 to allow a limited system of police and immigration control at the UK end. In particular it enabled the police to examine and detain people entering or leaving the Tunnel in the same way as they do at ports and airports under the Prevention of Terrorism (Temporary Provisions) Act 1989.

The principle of 'juxtaposed controls' means British police will eventually operate on French soil and French police on British. Passengers will be expected to complete all frontier control formalities before embarking on the shuttle taking them through the tunnel. In effect passengers to France will be checked by the French authorities before leaving Kent, and British staff will act in a similar manner in France. Staff will be working in designated 'control zones' which will also exist on trains themselves so that frontier controls can be enacted on the fast 'through' trains, sometimes known as 'penetrating trains'.

The carrying of weapons by French police on British soil is likely to be an item high on the political and media agenda, although the Home Office has also been looking at the need for weapons by the UK police. A confidential document has been drawn up by the head of the National Technical Support Unit of the Home Office's Police Scientific Development Branch, entitled 'Police Weapons for the Channel Tunnel' (Home Office 1993c: 56).

The Protocol on policing the Channel Tunnel, having been signed in November 1991 was made public in January 1992 (Protocol France No.1, 1992). The Protocol requires the two countries to work closely together and 'to the fullest possible extent co-operate, assist one another and co-ordinate their activities in discharging their duties' (Article 3). These duties are with respect to frontier control, offences against laws relating to frontier control as well as other offences, public safety and the exchange of information in the performance of duties. Permanent liaison measures are to be established (Article 4) and police officers of both states are permitted to circulate freely in the whole of the fixed Link for official purposes (Article 26). It will also mean, of course, that French officers will have access to the SIS and their UK colleagues working right alongside them will not, as long as the UK stays outside the Schengen arrangements.

Apart from the Channel Tunnel, the long standing Cross Channel Intelligence Conference has been referred to, and its successor the European Liaison Unit has linked Kent with colleagues across the English Channel in France, Belgium and Holland. Similar arrangements will exist between other south coast constabularies and their counterparts in France, including the States of Jersey and Guernsey police and their much closer neighbours. Private port police have their own cross-Channel liaison, allowing 'information to be exchanged and action to be coordinated' (House of Commons 1990b: Vol.2, p. 72), and on the west coast police constabularies have made similar links with the Republic of Ireland and 'frequently visit the Garda Siochana' to improve co-ordination (House of Commons 1990b: Vol.2, p. 86). The UK has also had a long-standing agreement with the Republic, the Isle of Man and the Channel Islands that allows free travel between them in a designated Common Travel Area that has no frontier formalities. Denmark has had similar arrangements with its Scandinavian neighbours in the Nordic Group since 1954.

On a slightly more formal level Interpol hosts its European Regional Conference, European Drugs Conference and other international seminars. An annual European Traffic Policing Meeting for EU and Scandinavian traffic police takes place (House of Commons 1990b: Vol.2, p. 3), and British Transport Police send representatives to the European Association of Airport and Seaport Police Conference (House of Commons 1990b: Vol.2, p. 67) and to COLPOFER, an organization representing railway police and security agencies working in EC countries (House of Commons 1990b: Vol.2, p. 63); direct liaison meetings are also made with, for example, the French and Belgian Railway Police (House of Commons 1990b: Vol. 2, p. 67).

An annual conference takes place at differing venues around Europe for the Heads of Police Forces of European Capital Cities (House of Commons 1990b: Vol.2, p. 20), and the International Association of Chiefs of Police (IACP), although primarily focused on North America, organizes regular conferences in Europe (Bailey 1989). Further conferences are organized regularly in Paris by the *Institut International de Police* established in 1976 (Anderson 1989: 155) as an arm of the STCIP – France's *Service Technique de Coopération Internationale de Police* – which began in 1961 by helping African countries gain independence. Meetings are also convened in London at the annual International Police Exhibition and Conference (IPEC).

Within the European Commission itself, and based in Brussels, a form of policing has been instituted for investigating the misappropriation of the Commission's own funds. The exact extent of this fraud is unknown but is thought likely to run into millions of pounds. Following a 1987 Working Party Report entitled 'Tougher measures to combat fraud', the Commission decided to set up UCLAF. UCLAF started work in 1989 and co-ordinates all anti-fraud work throughout the EC's 23 Directorate-Generals. It has developed its own computer data base known as IRENE 3 (IRegularities, ENquiries, Evaluation) and reports to the Community Co-ordination Committee on Fraud Prevention (COCOLAF: see S. Reinke 1992; Benyon *et al.*, 1993: ch. 2.6).

To promote the international side of its work, the English and Welsh ACPO has instituted its own International Affairs Advisory Committee (Birch 1989) and ACPO (Scotland) has started its own similar international committee (House of Commons 1990b: Vol.2, p. 49). ACPO began to keep a record of its international contacts and added its weight to the European Unit started by the Metropolitan Police to analyse the implications of 1992 for the police by arranging for two provincial force officers to join the Unit (House of Commons 1990b: Vol.2, p. 24); the arrangement was criticized for not liaising well with other staff (see N. Walker 1991: 36–7) and was ended in 1993. Sir Roger Birch, the first chair of ACPO's International Affairs Advisory Committee, has also put forward the idea of a Police Council of Europe to promote police views at a European level and to act as policy advisors (see Chapter 5). The Police Federation representing police officers below the rank of Superintendent meets fellow officers

in the congress of European police unions, the *Union Internationale des Syndicats de Police* (UISP: Eastwood 1989b;
Benyon *et al.* 1993: ch. 5.12.2) and policewomen meet within
their own European Network for Policewomen (ENP; Benyon
et al. 1993: ch. 5.12).

The Home Office Police Scientific Development Branch
(PSDB), accountable to an Assistant Under-Secretary of
State at the Home Office but comprised largely of seconded
senior police officers, offers technical advice to police forces
and develops new technology to assist the policing process.
Research and development (R and D) is therefore a central
part of their work and now includes an international dimension: 'PSDB is now committed not only to an enlarged and
strengthened programme of cooperation with R and D
agencies, particularly in Europe, USA and Canada, but also
with other countries' (Home Office 1993c: 11).

The aim of this co-operation is to share R and D results to
reduce duplication of effort, costs and timescales. Co-operation is both informal and formal with the latter based on
Memoranda of Understanding (MOU) to establish 'structured
and continuing cooperation' (Home Office 1993c). Draft
MOUs exist with the German BKA and the Dutch Ministry
of Justice giving access to their R and D Sections and
National Technical Support Units, and informal co-operation is carried out with the French Ministry of the Interior and
the *Gendarmerie Nationale*. The PSDB is also a member of the
Working Group on International Technical Support (WITS)
started by the Dutch police and meeting once a year to
organize exchanges of technical information and expertise,
an equipment data base, training programmes, working
groups and an international information desk (Home Office
1993c). Most European countries are represented on the
WITS along with Israel, Canada, USA, Australia and New
Zealand (Home Office 1993c: 7).

Members of the PSDB have also been involved in a joint
initiative between the Home Office and the Department of
Trade and Industry actively to explore markets in Europe for
UK based providers of police equipment. This initiative,
known as the Public Security Sector Equipment Task Force,
has so far visited Germany, France, Italy, Spain and Portugal

to help expose UK commercial suppliers to those markets (Home Office 1993c: 7).

Within the UK, operational police activities have long since started taking in a European dimension. The Metropolitan Police has not only an advisory European Unit but an Extradition Squad within its International and Organised Crime Branch that has operational experience of working with Europe (House of Commons 1990b: Vol. 2, p. 39). The Special Branch of the Metropolitan Police is also an acknowledged centre of European expertise. In 1976 the Branch created its own European Liaison Section (ELS) which now acts as a national point of reference for liaison with Europe. Exchanges have taken place between ELS officers and their counterparts in Germany, Holland, Belgium and France (House of Commons 1990b: Vol.2, pp. 42–6). Elsewhere in the UK the RUC in Belfast is another point of reference for Europe on matters relating to terrorism in particular (R. Ford and Tendler 1992).

Members of the Met's ELS represent British interests on the Europe-wide Police Working Group on Terrorism (PWGOT) that meets every six months. The PWGOT was formed in 1979, on a Dutch initiative, following the IRA assassination of Sir Richard Dykes the British Ambassador to The Hague, and is made up of European special branches or their security services equivalent. Italy, for example, is represented by the *Direzione Centrale della Polizia di Prevenzione* (DCPP), Spain by the *Comisaria General de Informacion-Servicio de Informacion Exterior* (CGI-SIE) and the Republic of Ireland by its Crime and Security Branch-International Liaison Office of the *Garda Siochana*. Membership consists of all the EC member states together with Norway, Sweden and Finland and all have been linked since 1988 by their own dedicated communications system 'in daily use, enabling written or graphic material to be transmitted speedily and securely throughout the fifteen country network' (House of Commons 1990b: Vol.2, pp. 43–4). A separate series of meetings, known as the Club of Berne, exists for intelligence chiefs to meet to discuss state security measures going beyond a straight policing function.

The Anti-Terrorist Branch of the Metropolitan Police together with the RUC has been 'frequently called upon to assist European police, and their representatives regularly attend European anti-terrorist meetings' (House of Commons: Vol.2, p. 45). Until 1992 they were joined by 'B' Squad of the Met's Special Branch who co-ordinated British intelligence on Irish Republican terrorism. Since then, and following some acrimonious manoeuvrings, the job has been taken away from them and given to the security services (see, e.g., Norton-Taylor and Campbell 1992; Tendler 1992).

The Republic of Ireland and the UK are not the only countries in Europe beset by disputes over national borders and groups using terrorist tactics. The Spanish and French police have joined forces to combat the Basque separatists Eta (an acronym for *Euzkadi Ta Askatasuna,* or Basque Homeland and Freedom). In February 1993 'a joint French-Spanish police operation . . . uncovered what is thought to be the group's main arms and explosives factory, in the Basque region of south-western France' (Davison 1993; see also Townson 1993). Other borders have been disputed in a less violent manner and have had to be sensitively policed as a result. These include the Saarland and Alsace border between France and Germany, parts of Spain (such as Catalonia), and the island of Corsica where there has been a separatist movement known as the FLNC (the National Liberation Front of Corsica) to make it independent of France (see e.g. Nundy 1993). Other smaller terrorist groups have operated within one country such as the aptly named 'Anti-State Struggle' in Greece or the Red Army Faction in Italy, or *Action Directe* in France.

One measure taken in Ireland to try to smooth police co-operation between the RUC and the *Garda Siochana* has been the signing of the Anglo–Irish Agreement between the UK and the Republic of Ireland. Much of this bilateral Agreement concerns the creation of an Inter-Governmental Conference but Article 9 requires: 'a programme of work to be undertaken by the Chief Constable of the Royal Ulster Constabulary and the Commissioner of the Garda Siochana and, where appropriate, groups of officials in such areas as threat assessments, exchange of information, liaison structures, technical cooperation, training of personnel, and operational resources' (Anglo–Irish Agreement 1985: Article 9).

The Inter-Governmental Conference will review progress on police co-operation, and the British intend to do so by the standards of other European states in this field. The PSDB of the UK Home Office has a named Detective Superintendent as liaison officer in the *Garda*'s Technical Bureau 'D' Branch Services at its Phoenix Park Headquarters in Dublin (Home Office 1993c: 66).

At a lower level of aggression than terrorism, but seen to pose a threat none the less, is the behaviour of large numbers of football supporters. The Heysel Stadium disaster in Belgium, involving the deaths of 36 Italian football supporters at the 1985 European Cup Final, put public order policing on the European agenda. Lengthy extradition proceedings between Belgium and the UK were instituted to bring English supporters to trial, and later that year the British Government became a signatory to the European Convention on Spectator Violence and Misbehaviour (Foreign and Commonwealth Office 1985). Article 4 of the Convention called for better police co-operation and consultation.

The UK used the forum of TREVI in 1987 to set up 'a network of permanent correspondents to exchange information relevant to policing football in Europe' (House of Commons 1990a: 10). The UK also took the lead in drafting a document for TREVI in 1989 entitled 'Guidelines for Cooperation in the Policing of International Football Matches' which it hoped all members would adopt (for the full text see House of Commons 1990a: 15–18). At this time the British permanent correspondent was an officer of the British Transport Police but the role was later taken over by the head of the National Football Intelligence Unit (NFIU) created in 1989. The NFIU is a central point of reference for European police forces when foreign teams play here, and provides a service to other countries when British clubs or the national teams go abroad.

The 1990 World Cup Finals in Italy – 'Italia 90' – have been held up as a prime example of good international police co-operation in policing football spectators. Italian police were in discussions in London in November 1989 and British police and Home Office officials were in Italy in January and again in March 1990 to plan the Italian end. In May Italian police visited Liverpool and Manchester to see crowd control operations and a further 50 *carabinieri* visited other parts of the UK. Before the Finals the Home Secretary sent the names of certain convicted football hooligans to the Italian Minister of the Interior with the recommendation that they be excluded from the country for the duration of the World Cup.

Whilst the England team was in Italy, the NFIU provided officers jointly with other British police officers as a small unit available wherever the England team played, providing intelligence and liaison. In London the NFIU gave 24-hour coverage to queries received from Italy, helped monitor English air- and seaports and gave continuous intelligence updates to Italy. A similar Scottish contingent of police officers accompanied the Scottish team (House of Commons 1990a: 1–12).

By the time of the European football championship in Sweden in 1992 the Football Spectators Act 1989 had been implemented in the UK with its new concept of 'restriction orders'. In the context of international co-operation an English or Welsh fan convicted abroad for football-related offences could now be made subject to a restriction order on return home (Connett 1992). The orders last for 2 or 5 years depending on the seriousness of the offence, and require people to stay away from designated matches. Bi-lateral agreements have to be entered into with other countries in order for the so-called 'corresponding offences' to be reported back to the UK and acted upon. A bilateral agreement does not always ensure that such reporting takes place and a swift deportation without conviction means orders cannot be made. To be successful the new arrangements require good liaison and co-operation between respective police and judicial systems, but even they may not work as in the Netherlands in October 1993 for the England versus Holland World Cup qualifying game in Rotterdam (for a legal critique see Broadbent and Vincenzi 1990; an example of incorrect information being transmitted internationally on football supporters and the consequences was reported in *Statewatch*, 3, 2 (1993): 10–11).

Police measures to counter drug-trafficking have been co-ordinated in Europe by the Pompidou Group formed in 1971 and the CELAD created in December 1989.

The Pompidou Group is a Council of Europe Co-operation Group to combat drug misuse and illicit trafficking in drugs set up at the initiative of the late President Pompidou of France. The Group looks at all aspects of misuse including the specific problems of young people, the cross-flow of information between professionals as well as the role of respective criminal justice systems, and the policing of drug trafficking. Representatives from Interpol have been present with observer status at some of their sessions. In 1971 the Group comprised seven member states but now has some 21 members (House of Commons 1986: 14–19).

CELAD was a creation of the EC heads of state to widen the efforts of national drugs co-ordinators and began working in early 1990. The first UK representative was former Home Office Minister, David Mellor. CELAD attempts to co-ordinate its efforts with the Pompidou Group but has also placed a priority on lending its weight to those who would strengthen the external borders of the EC – now the EU – to stop drugs entering the Union (Benyon *et al.* 1993: para. 5.2.2).

Another European anti-drug network is the *Standige arbeidsgruppe Rauschgift* (STAR) founded in 1972 and comprising members from Germany, Belgium, Holland, France, Austria, Switzerland and Luxembourg. The US Drugs Enforcement Agency (DEA) also belongs, as does the US Customs (*Statewatch*, 3, 2 (1993): 11). The so-called Dublin Group is yet another forum attended by EC member states, the USA, Norway, Sweden, Japan and others to discuss the co-ordination of policing assistance to drug-producing and transit countries (Bunyan 1993: 175).

In preparation for closer European co-operation, the ACPO International Affairs Advisory Committee prompted all forces in Britain to appoint an ELO. The role of the ELO has been summarized as follows:

To coordinate knowledge and activity within the Constabulary regarding European matters.

To be a central point in each Constabulary through which all matters of European issues are channelled (into and out of Force). To be an adviser to the Chief Constable and his policy group on European matters.

To establish liaison with appropriate bodies (police and non/police) within the Force. (Devon and Cornwall Constabulary 1990: 82)

The priority that some forces accord to European matters may perhaps be judged by the fact that ELOs range in rank from sergeants to Chief Constables themselves (Devon and Cornwall Constabulary 1990) and the Home Affairs Committee noted a range of views 'from enthusiastic commitment to tacit support' (House of Commons 1990b: Vol.1, para. 87). The Committee offered its own support to the idea and recommended Chief Constables give some thought to the selection of suitable ELOs, and also suggested that ELOs be redesignated as Interpol Liaison Officers to improve the links between Interpol and provincial forces (House of Commons 1990b: Vol.1, para. 81). The Government was not fully taken with this idea of ILOs and suggested more thought be given to the subject (Home Office 1991c: 4–5).

The idea of the ELO should not be confused with other forms of 'liaison' which have been employed or posited as ways of improving international co-operation. British police officers have been posted abroad as liaison officers for a number of years. Often they have been located in British Embassies to reinforce their diplomatic status as being a liaison officer and not an operational officer with police powers that extend into the host country. The role is strictly one of advising, assisting and exchanging information. The TREVI group promoted liaison officers as a way of moving police co-operation forward in their 1990 Programme of Action (see below). In the past it has most frequently been employed by those policing drug trafficking, such as our own National Drugs Intelligence Unit (NDIU) or the German BKA who have some 36 liaison drug officers posted in 25 different countries (Cullen 1992: 76).

Differences of opinion have been expressed as to whether the Embassy is the right location for a British police liaison officer, and the Home Affairs Committee heard evidence from the German police that the liaison officer was best placed within the local police force. The Spanish police, on the other hand, preferred the placement to be in the Embassy. The Committee themselves came down in favour of the police department taking the liaison officer, with the Embassy giving administrative assistance (House of Commons 1990b: Vol.1, para. 125), but the Government believes individual circumstances should dictate the decision and did not want a blanket policy (Home Office 1991c: 9).

A different view again has been expressed by Interpol as to the most effective use of liaison officers. Having created their own European Liaison Bureau from the former European Secretariat, they have argued that liaison officers are best placed with their own Bureau in Lyon rather than directly into different countries. Here they can liaise with other European officers, receive Interpol's expertise as back up and provide a much more cost-efficient service than could a directly placed Liaison Officer. The Belgian police share this view (House of Commons 1990b: Vol.1, para. 124). The UK Government has hedged its bets by deciding that the two types of liaison are complementary and not interchangeable, and therefore proper co-ordination between the two is necessary (Home Office 1991c: 9).

Liaison officers coming to the UK from abroad are generally to be located in the NCIS as being the most appropriate centralized police agency (Home Office 1991c: 9). This does not preclude provincial force exchanges with direct neighbours across the Channel or the Irish Sea from taking place.

This multiplicity of police international contact and co-operation has not stopped calls for ever closer degrees of co-operation between overseas forces. The UK Home Office made an award to a senior West Yorkshire police officer who was devising a system jointly with a Dutch counterpart to log all international contacts with a view to disseminating good practice (Home Office Police Department 1993: 17). In the UK context we must also remember that the word 'police' includes the policing roles of Customs and Excise officers and Immigration officers running alongside that of the more traditional policing role. Customs Officers, for example, met in the group known as MAG 92 convened under the canopy of the Coordinators Group formed in 1988. MAG (they have now dropped the 92) had a tie in to TREVI discussions (House of Commons 1990b: Vol.1. para. 54) and expected to have a role in Europol developments (HM Customs and Excise 1992: 35). The Maastricht Treaty specifically includes customs services into its text on home and justice affairs.

The members of the MAG 92 group had set out their views on the forthcoming single European Market in the Harrogate Declaration of May 1992. The intention was to increase mutual assistance, improve liaison and information exchange, training and operational assistance. Central to the new frontier-free Europe was to be a replacement of routine 'cold' stops at borders by more targeted stops based on intelligence.

Intelligence was, in turn, expected to come from close co-operation with other agencies, especially the police, and by more covert activities using closed-circuit television, plain clothes officers, and such techniques as using so-called 'passive detective dogs' trained to sniff and sit alongside suspicious luggage. At another level intelligence was to be collated from private industry involved in international business transactions, including shipping firms and airlines. The value of these sources of intelligence had led HM Customs and Excise to sign some 7000 MOUs with industry, commerce and business between 1990 and 1993 (Russell 1993).

At an EU level Customs Officers in all member states are linked to one data base through the CIS which came on-line on 1 October 1992. The CIS built on the work of the earlier dedicated system known as SCENT, or the System Customs Enforcement Network. A specific system was established in Cologne, which was known as the Balkan Route Information System, to assist the detection and interception of drug smuggling by that particular route.

In terms of practical co-operation MOUs have been signed between the UK and France, Spain, the Netherlands, Portugal, Germany and the Channel Islands, not only to exchange information but also to engage in joint operations and training exercises (Russell 1993). The Mattheus Programme provides for the exchange of customs officers between countries for training purposes with some 58 officers going abroad from the UK in 1992 (Russell 1993; see also Vergnolle 1992). The 'Eurocustoms' project is an initiative to try to boost training in, and the efficiency of, Eastern European customs services (Russell 1993).

The policing of immigration is co-ordinated by the Ad Hoc Working Group on Immigration, and is also over-seen by the Coordinators Group; it looks at matters relating to visas, asylum applications and similar matters. This whole terrain of the policing of international migratory movements is a new one for the police and will be considered further in Chapter 5.

Conclusions

Police co-operation in Europe has been and is progressing on numerous fronts away from the main fora of Schengen, TREVI and Interpol. Specific accords and initiatives surround such enterprises as the Channel Tunnel between France and England and the Anglo–Irish Agreement concerning matters of policing the border between Northern and Southern Ireland. Elsewhere police officers are meeting in European conferences at various levels and on various specific matters. Liaison officers operating in other countries have developed enormously in recent years, and technical expertise has also been exchanged to support various policing activities.

Many of these arrangements have been 'driven' by the perceived threat posed by terrorism and drug trafficking or the threat to public order posed by football supporters travelling to European matches at club or national level. Taken together we now have a myriad different international liaisons going on between European police forces that will make contact and communication that much easier in the future.

5

Implications of Closer Co-operation for UK Policing and Criminal Justice

Closer co-operation between the police forces of Europe inevitably has a 'recoil effect' on the domestic policing arrangements of each nation involved. In this chapter we trace the nature of this 'recoil effect' on domestic policing arrangements in the UK and possible future developments. We consider, first of all, the nature of 'compensatory measures' that the British police have taken, or would like to take, as the internal borders between the EU member states have been lowered, including the creation of some new national policing structures giving the UK police a clearer voice in Europe.

We also explore, in this chapter, the still unravelling complexities of the interaction that Europeanization will have with British police training, recruitment and management. The powers and accountability of the police are also examined in the light of similar issues in Europe, and finally we look at the much-vaunted 'occupational culture' or 'cop culture' of the British police, and how it might be influenced by European considerations.

The Lowering of Borders within the EC and the Consequent Need for 'Compensatory Measures'

We described in Chapter 1 the perceived 'threat' that can be posed to British society by the lowering of frontiers with our

European neighbours. In May 1993 a conference at the National Police Staff College entitled 'Organised crime: a threat assessment', allowed senior police officers to define this international threat, which was dutifully reported by the journalists present. To counter this perceived 'security deficit', we outlined earlier the voices raised in favour of strengthening the external borders of the Community as a means of furthering its internal security. Here we consider what further other measures are thought necessary to make up for the relaxing of internal borders.

In evidence to the Home Affairs Committee the British police gave what one of the Committee's members called a 'shopping list' (House of Commons 1992: Minutes of Evidence, p. 28) of compensatory measures they thought necessary for the continuing security of the UK. These measures included extending the provisions of the Prevention of Terrorism Act (POTA), laws to get airline and shipping companies to verify the identity of all travellers, a 'Euro-warrant' to ease extradition procedures, identification cards, greater police powers on immigration matters, access to European car licensing data and more police resources to compensate for the reduced levels of immigration officers. On top of this the police wanted improved police co-operation in Europe and a harmonization of laws and judicial procedures between countries (House of Commons 1992: Minutes of Evidence, p. 96). Looking more closely, what does this list amount to?

The Prevention of Terrorism (Temporary Provisions) Act 1989 has its origins in the Prevention of Terrorism (Temporary Provisions) Act 1974. The 1974 Act was hurriedly enacted in the wake of the IRA bomb explosions in Birmingham in November 1974 as a response to what a junior Home Office Minister called 'the greatest threat [to the country] since the end of the Second World War' (*Hansard*, 28 November 1974, col. 743). The Act was redrafted and renewed in 1976 and 1984 before its most recent metamorphosis in 1989. The 1989 Act, through its section 27(b), still requires an annual renewal of its measures, and its scope has been widened to include international terrorism and not just Irish terrorism.

Criticism of the Prevention of Terrorism Acts has gathered over the years in the light of experience. The use of exclusion orders and the proscribing of certain organizations have been particularly singled out as restrictions of civil liberties (see, e.g., Hillyard 1993a). The European Court of Human Rights has twice held that the Act is in violation of the European Convention on Human Rights. In the case of *Brogan and others* versus *the UK* (1988), the European Court ruled that the Act breached Article 5(3) of the Convention by not bringing the defendants promptly before a court. The feeling was that section 14 of the Act was being used not for arrest with a view to charging but arrest with a view to intelligence gathering, or even as a restricted form of internment (see C. Walker 1992: 156–84).

In their evidence to the 1992 Home Affairs Committee inquiry into migration control at the EC's external borders, the British police were requesting an extension to the powers of the POTA, section 14. What would this imply?

Section 14(1) of the POTA empowers a police officer to arrest someone he or she has reasonable grounds for suspecting to be guilty of an offence within the meaning of the Act, or who has been preparing to commit an act of terrorism, or someone who is the subject of an exclusion order. The amendment the police were now asking for was for the Act to drop the requirement that an officer must have 'reasonable grounds' for suspicion before acting. In addition to amending s.14, the police also wanted POTA extended to transit passengers and 'along the whole of the EC Border'. POTA was seen as a deterrent to would-be terrorists by its very existence, and it was 'vitally important' that its powers should not be reduced.

The Home Affairs Committee pointed out the temporary nature of POTA to police witnesses but even so, the police argued: 'with a settlement in Northern Ireland, there would still be a need for such powers . . . there would still be an international threat and with the events in Eastern Europe and beyond and with the political atmosphere being somewhat turbulent I think . . . there is a need to retain them for the time being' (House of Commons 1992: Minutes of Evidence, p. 41)

Some academics who have looked at the statistics on the operation of POTA argue that the police are already using its stronger powers of detention for ordinary crime (Hillyard

1993a). In other words there is a process of 'normalization' of emergency legislation taking place and that process now appears to be moving into the European policing terrain. Butt Philip in his work has argued strongly that in the case of Great Britain there is no good evidence to support the need for 'internal' port controls (Butt Philip 1991b; see also Hillyard 1993b).

The police argue that the second item on their list refers to strengthening of the Aviation and Maritime Security Act 1990, which would require shipping and airline companies to vet and check the identification of all travellers. The 1990 Act was the latest in a series of enactments to try to make air and seaports as well as travel itself safer, going back to the Hijacking Act, 1971, the Protection of Aircraft Act 1973 and the Aviation Security Act 1982. The 1990 Act incorporated the International Maritime Organisation Convention for the Suppression of Unlawful Acts against the Safety of Maritime Navigation. The Act designates restricted areas at sea and air ports, and enables extended baggage checks. Its section 15(5) also allows armed police to operate on airport premises.

The police request that shipping and airline companies verify the identity of all travellers has more resonance with the requirements of the Immigration (Carrier Liability) Act 1987 which penalizes companies that allow people to travel without visas or other necessary documentation. This 'policing' by private companies is also built into the Schengen Convention (Article 26). Germany, Denmark and Belgium have similar laws to penalize carriers. In the UK, carriers can be fined up to £2000 for each person accepted without documentation. The whole process has been condemned as being in breach of the 1944 Chicago Convention on International Aviation which prohibits fines on airlines transporting passengers with inadequate documents and the spirit and intent, if not the letter, of the 1967 Geneva Convention on refugees (Spencer 1990: 35–40). The Home Affairs Committee also pointed out to the police the practicalities of verifying the identity of 2000–3000 people on a cross-Channel ferry trip of less than an hour's duration (House of Commons 1992: Minutes of Evidence, p. 28). A body known as INADPAX (International Air Transport Association Control Working

Group on Inadmissible Passengers) brings together police, immigration officials, border police and airline representatives from the EC, EFTA (European Free Trade Area) countries, Canada and the USA to iron out mutual problems (Bunyan 1993: 177).

The introduction of a 'Euro-warrant' to enable a fugitive from abroad to be brought to justice in the UK would, according to the police, avoid the necessity of involving often long and complicated extradition proceedings. This concern about extradition has a certain ring of irony about it when we consider that the 1957 European Convention on Extradition was not ratified by the UK until May 1991, after the passing of the 1989 Extradition Act. Until then it was the UK which were considered the problematic European nation with its insistence that other states present prima facie evidence before a UK court (see Chapter 3). The idea of a 'Euro-warrant' had been discussed within TREVI circles, but only to realize 'the very considerable difficulties' involved (Bunyan 1993: 31).

The idea of a mandatory identification card for all EC citizens represents the final stages in a long-drawn-out argument over the need for ID cards in which the police have been fully involved. ACPO now specifies that such a mandatory card should be the size of a normal credit card with a computer readable strip including, among other things, the individual's fingerprint. The position now taken up by the police, and supported by the Home Office (Bunyan 1993: 67), represented a decided move forward from their evidence to the 1990 Home Affairs Committee just two years earlier when 'police chiefs were lukewarm' about the idea (House of Commons 1990b: Vol.1, para. 131); however this had not stopped the Committee recommending that the idea be further looked at (House of Commons 1990b: Vol.1, paras 137–8).

At present ID cards are used on a voluntary basis in Italy, Portugal and France. Spain was reportedly developing a high-technology identity card in 1992 (House of Commons 1992: Minutes of Evidence, p. 30) whilst the UK, the Republic of Ireland, Denmark and the Netherlands had not, so far, entertained the idea.

The police request for powers to demand a passport, whether at a port or anywhere else in the UK was seen as a necessary compensatory measure given the likely reduction in the number of immigration officers in the future and the close overlap of the two jobs. For the same reason the police also demanded an increase in their manpower to assist in maintaining the former level of effectiveness. Such extra powers for the police could only be granted by amending the Immigration Act 1971. More substantial legal adjustments would need to be made to grant police their wish to have access to the Driving Vehicle Licensing Centre (DVLC) equivalents in EC countries to help them combat vehicle thefts. The British police would also have to guarantee tighter data protection regimes than offered previously, in order to access such data bases in Europe (see also Chapter 3).

The two other items on this police 'shopping list' for compensatory measures are the harmonization of EC laws to establish EC standards and the continued promotion of good policing practice and practical co-operation throughout the EC. The latter is considered throughout this volume and the former requires a separate section of its own below. Before that, however, we might examine some other projected compensatory measures that did not appear on the police list handed to the Home Affairs Committee in 1992.

Both the Scottish Police Superintendents' Association and the Scottish Police Federation have requested under the guise of 'compensatory measures' increased powers to hold suspects. In practice they want equivalence with the Police and Criminal Evidence Act 1984 in England and Wales and power to hold for 24 hours rather than the existing 6 hours they have under the Criminal Justice (Scotland) Act 1980. Six hours, it was argued, 'may be quite inadequate for any necessary international inquiries to be made' (House of Commons 1990b: Vol.1, para. 127).

A national hotel registration scheme has been mooted but not seriously considered as a compensatory measure. In use on the Continent it enables police to know who is in which hotel at any one time on any one night. Neither the police nor the Home Affairs Committee wished to show any positive enthusiasm for the idea which seems to have been considered decidedly non-British (House of Commons 1990b: Vol.1, para. 130).

The Home Office have also suggested some compensatory measures to offset the reduction in controls at interior frontiers. Paradoxically they see such relaxation as requiring greater resources for the Immigration Service (House of Commons 1992: 67). In particular they have flagged the possibility of introducing sanctions against employers who knowingly employ an illegal immigrant and point out that France introduced exactly such legislation in 1991 (House of Commons 1992: 67).

Legal Harmonization

The harmonization or equalization of criminal law in the EC has been suggested as a way of helping police co-operation and compensating for the lowering of border controls. The differing legal tolerance of certain types of pornography in Holland, Germany and Denmark, compared to the UK, for example, or the fact that 'insider trading' is not illegal in Italy when it is in other countries, complicates cross border policing. Even when laws are more or less the same the discretion with which they are policed can be seen as problematic, as in the permissive attitude towards cannabis in the Netherlands. The British police have stated their case that: 'in the absence of closer harmonisation of legislation it is questionable whether intergovernmental co-operation can effectively meet every contingency, and it should be borne in mind that there is a need to consider the harmonisation of attitudes towards enforcement in different European countries' (House of Commons 1990b: Vol.2, p. 18)

The Home Office has argued that legal harmonization is less central to effective police co-operation and that for them it was not a high priority (House of Commons 1990b: Vol.2, pp. 2 and 79), but an HM Chief Inspector of Constabulary believed that pressure from police forces in different countries would eventually lead to a great deal of harmonization (House of Commons 1990b: Vol.2, p. 81). Two years later the police were being more specific in targeting their request for 'harmonisation of certain laws' (House of Commons 1992: Minutes of Evidence, p. 96).

If we accept that a nation's jurisdiction over its criminal law and policing is a very potent symbol of nationhood, it follows that harmonization is not going to be achieved easily. Harmonization amongst police forces themselves – for example, over agreed radio frequencies, the use of DNA as evidence or information systems – may come more easily, but still not without debate. Looking at the wider picture of laws and judicial systems the outlook is not rosy. As we have already seen, the suggestion by former French President Giscard d' Estaing of an *Espace judiciaire européen* comparable to the internal market or *Espace économique européen* has been called a 'pipe dream' (House of Commons 1990b: Vol.1, p. 97). The technical, cultural and political difficulties are not under-estimated.

We have already mentioned some of the particular anomalies that have been identified between judicial systems, including 'insider trading' and pornography. Other examples include the British crime of 'conspiracy' which has no European equivalent, differing regulations on firearms, and the more restrictive banking laws of Luxembourg that hamper the tracing of laundered money. The Greek judicial system is noted as being particularly severe against hooliganism and vandalism, whilst differing ages of consent for sexual activities throughout Europe result in differing concepts of unlawful sex. Road traffic laws vary in terms of speed limits and the amount of alcohol permitted before driving. One member of the British Home Affairs Committee was moved to remark that 'some of the crimes in this country appear to be national sports in some other European countries' (House of Commons 1992: Minutes of Evidence, para. 158).

Even when laws on paper appear comparable there is the added 'problem' of unequal enforcement. The most prominent of these is the permissive attitude displayed by the police of the Netherlands to the policing of soft drugs. This attitude appears to frustrate British officers who find it hard to understand, although attempts have been made to locate its causation in cultural and historical factors in the Netherlands (de Kort and Korf 1992). The position is also not static, as many of the preferred Dutch policies of prevention and public health and concepts like 'harm reduction' and 'needle exchange' programmes are being incorporated into the UK, and in the other direction, there are reported Dutch Government crackdowns on the rising number of cafés selling hashish and marijuana in the Netherlands following UN criticism of its lenient drug policy (*The Independent*, 6 March 1993; see also 'Maastricht hit by crime invasion', *The Independent*, 18 March 1994).

Other attempts at harmonization have been made by trying to define certain criminal acts involving the physical crossing of frontiers as 'cross-frontier crime' or 'Euro-crimes'. To date these attempts have been at an informal level of co-operation, although a long-term project might be to codify a set of 'federal offences' comparable to the USA. The Project Team drafting the Europol Convention is thought to be considering ways of defining such Euro-crimes (see Chapter 3).

High profile cross-frontier crime, such as drug trafficking or terrorist actions, have already achieved a degree of consensus. International Conventions and national laws have followed. The movement of stolen art and antiques is an example of cross-frontier crime with a developing consensus, as is the laundering of money and international fraud.

The theft of cars and other vehicles is also singled out as having a clear international dimension to it. The taking of luxury cars from Western Europe to the former Communist bloc countries of Eastern Europe has been seen as a particularly severe problem (Delgado 1990). Exact figures are not available as it relies on accurate recording of the location of recovery of the vehicle and someone actively to collate information, and 'what little there is does not give a clear and reliable picture because it is incomplete' (Gregory and Collier 1992). Cars are also going to other destinations apart from Eastern Europe, with a ready market in the Middle East, the Indian sub-continent and Africa (Gregory and Collier 1992).

In general terms we have considered the way in which extradition and mutual assistance between countries has led to a degree of legal harmonization (see Chapter 3). On the movement of people, we will consider the harmonization programme of the Ad Hoc Working Group on Immigration which involves the police in new areas of work in the next chapter.

Harmonization of criminal codes and their subsequent enforcement remains beset with difficulties. 'Euro-crimes' are beginning to be identified but true harmonization will take many years. The European Commission has not until now wanted a competency in the area of interior and judicial affairs, although, as we have seen, the Maastricht Treaty opens up future possibilities in the so-called 'third pillar' for the newly-emerging Union. Already finance has been given to Spain to help reinforce its maritime border and ideas have been floated for a Directorate-General for criminal law enforcement and for an 'EU Interior Community'.

Speaking with One Voice

A major obstacle for the British police in their relations with other countries has been identified as their seeming inability to speak with a national voice. The UK model of policing presupposes a series of 52 local police forces throughout the land, all acting in an autonomous manner. Accountability is shared between the Chief Constables, the local police authorities and the Home Office in accordance with the 1964 Police Act, and the Home Office does not see itself in the same way as many of the interior ministries do in Europe, with a central directing role. In reality it is widely accepted that the UK model is very much more a centralized model than its theoretical exposition would suggest, with the locus of power having moved steadily towards the Home Office and the Chief Constables, organized through ACPO, at the expense of the local authorities (Lustgarten 1986). The result has been a structural similarity between forces and increasing standardization of equipment, procedures and training.

At an organizational level structures already exist that superimpose themselves on the local forces. Regional Crime Squads (RCSs) and the system of mutual aid between forces constitute an intermediate layer of activity. The financial arrangements for common police services are used to fund the UK Interpol NCB, and other central services including the PNC. (The PNC was supposedly deliberately named in this fashion rather than as the National Police Computer to avoid accusations of centralization.) Administrative arrangements such as the National Reporting Centre used to co-ordinate mutual aid during the 1984–5 Miners' Strike, and at other times, is always seen as a temporary measure that goes back into storage after use (see e.g. Scraton 1985).

At the end of 1991 the PNC underwent a complete upgrading, and it was pointed out that the new PNC2, building on its predecessor which had operated since 1974, had twice the processing power and almost five times the memory of the old PNC. Moreover it was felt that the new computer 'should make it easier for British police to link up with European forces' (Watts 1991). Whether or not this was so it was true that the whole information technology debate within British police circles at this time seemed, to some leading officers to be crying out for central direction (Newing 1990).

The 1989 Home Affairs Committee investigation into drug trafficking and related serious crime had received evidence from senior police officers of the need for more national co-ordination. The head of the police NDIU, Barry Price, explained to the Committee that as a non-operational unit he was not able to develop his own intelligence but was dependent on others. He suggested this could be rectified either by allowing his officers to become operational, giving him executive powers over other police officers to provide him with information, or by giving him a budget to fund local forces who could give him information (House of Commons 1989a: Vol.1, para. 152). Price thought this increased executive role for the NDIU might be achieved without recourse to new legislation, and he told the Committee: 'My arguments are being heard and accepted much more than they were twelve months ago. We will find before the year is out that there will be a move to achieve what I seek' (House of Commons 1989a: Vol.2, p. 132).

Similar sentiments were expressed by Neil Dickens, the Executive Coordinator of the RCSs, who also argued for a national intelligence unit able to improve international co-operation. A national unit would also be nationally funded and avoid undue financial burdens being placed on some forces who had more contact with Europe. The Home Affairs Committee Chairman reflected his thinking back to him:

Chairman: 'You are thinking there of the Common Police Service providing a more substantial role and financial contribution to a more organised enforcement arrangement on a multi-agency, multi-force basis.'

Mr Dickens: 'Exactly.' (House of Commons 1989a: Vol.2, p. 71)

Other voices were heard resisting such national unit ideas. The Chair of the Police Federation was not convinced that being big was being better (Eastwood 1989b), and a Chief Constable chairing ACPO's Crime Committee and perhaps with an eye to the diminution of his and his colleagues' own domains, similarly thought the concept of local policing could be damaged by such moves (House of Commons 1989a: Vol.2, p. 82). The Government was also not taken by the arguments and thought that extending the executive authority of the RCS's executive co-ordinator went beyond anything previously envisaged (Home Office 1990: para. 3.36).

In May 1989 another voice was heard in favour of national policing. Sir Peter Imbert, the Commissioner of the Metropolitan Police speaking in Oslo at the Annual Conference of the Heads of Police Forces of European Capital Cities, argued that each country needed a national voice with authority to make decisions quickly but without haste, and that consultation and local autonomy are both admirable but each can act against and delay the primary objective when discussing international matters. Imbert repeated his views later that year at the Annual Police Foundation Lecture.

By the Autumn of 1989 further developments had taken place. Skirting around the idea of a national executive police force, the then Home Secretary, Douglas Hurd, let it be known that he favoured a national criminal intelligence service to help combat serious crime. Hurd argued that a facility of this kind may also be necessary to enable us to cooperate effectively with enforcement agencies abroad

(Kirby 1989). The RCS Executive Coordinator, Neil Dickens, was asked to prepare a report in the light of 'the increasing sophistication of criminal behaviour and the likelihood that this would increase further following the relaxation of controls on movement in 1992' (*Statewatch*, 2, 2 (1992): p. 9). The British police were on the road toward getting a national voice.

Specialized national intelligence police units were not a new concept and had existed for many years. Now such units as the NDIU, the NFIU and the Arts and Antiques Squad were to be drawn into the one NCIS.

Arguments continued as to the need for the new national unit to have an executive operational capacity rather than only a static intelligence gathering function (Kirby 1990). In August 1990 ACPO gave its proposals to the Home Secretary, having held back from recommending any FBI-style operational arm to the proposed NCIS. A Steering Group was established to take the idea forward, and included in the Group were HM Customs and Excise representatives and, for the first time, representatives of local police authorities. The Home Office announced that NCIS would be: 'Solely concerned with the collection, development, analysis and conveyance to appropriate authorities, of intelligence relating to criminal activities. It will have *a particularly important role to play in coordinating information about such activities across national as well as force boundaries*' (Home Office 1991a: emphasis added).

The Home Office later outlined the objectives of the new NCIS, which included being:

> the national focal point to gather, collate, evaluate, analyse and develop relevant information and intelligence about serious crime and major criminals of a regional, national and international nature [and] . . . to establish channels of communication with domestic and overseas law enforcement agencies and to provide a national focal point for the promotion and exchange of information and intelligence. (Home Office 1992b)

NCIS brought together a number of existing national units including the NDIU, the NFIU, Regional Criminal Intelligence Offices, the National Paedophile Index, the National Office for the Suppression of Counterfeit Currency, the Commercial Fraud Index and Commercial Fraud Squad, the support and co-ordination of undercover police officers, the Public Sector Corruption Unit, and the Arts and Antiques Squad. RCSs were to be reduced in number from nine to five.

NCIS started operations on 1 April 1992 with a staff of 400. Tony Mullett, former Chief Constable of West Mercia was its first Director and Neil Dickens, the former RCS executive co-ordinator became a Deputy Director (Kirby 1992a; *Statewatch*, 2, 2 (1992): 8–9). Regional offices were opened in Wakefield, Bristol,Birmingham and Manchester, with a London office being opened south of the river to distance it symbolically from New Scotland Yard. NCIS had cost about £25 million to develop (Kirby 1992a) and was to be funded as a common police service. To start with it, was using the Metropolitan Police's INFOS computer system and the PNC (Mason 1992), but plans were in hand to develop its own designated computer system. Attempts by MPs to discover the specification of the NCIS computer and the nature of the data to be stored were blocked because of the time needed for development (see, e.g., *Hansard*, 9 June 1992, col. 76). The completion date for the new computer is now estimated to be 1995 (*Hansard*, 23 July 1993, WA No.174).

The accountability of NCIS has presented some problems, as indeed do all common police service facilities. The police local authorities, having been somewhat on the margins during the development period, had been involved in the Steering Group leading up to implementation day in 1992. Thereafter two separate committees were proposed with the local authorities only being on the Resources Committee concerned with expenditure and budgets, and not on the Standing Committee responsible for over-sight of operational intelligence matters. The Home Office saw the two committees as feeding in and out of each other, and to facilitate this the Chair of the Resources Committee would be a member of the Standing Committee, which would be composed of Home Office civil servants and senior police officers. Whether or not the Standing Committee offers any real democratic accountability for NCIS is open to debate, and not least because, although having no direct executive powers to become involved in mobile operations NCIS 'will have the authority to strongly recommend that forces take action on any intelligence supplied' (*Statewatch*, 2, 2 (1992): 10).

The creation of NCIS is the most high profile consequence in the UK of closer police co-operation with European forces. It will provide a distinct national voice for the police service and incorporate the UK Interpol NCB (Hansard, 13 March 1992: cols 739–40). Similar arrangements have come into being in Europe. The Dutch NCIS and NCB, as we have seen (Chapter 3), are now both housed in the same building and are both responsible to the one Director of the CRI. In the UK the input of intelligence and information to NCIS 'will come from UK forces, regional crime squads, Interpol, Her Majesty's Customs and Excise and other international law enforcement agencies' (*Hansard*, 20 February 1992: cols 268–9).

Although the arguments for NCIS to have an executive arm to create FBI-style national police officers were lost in 1990, the idea continues to resurface and may yet find a more fertile constituency to grow in. The question is put that raising intelligence at a national level is unproductive if we then find that local forces are too busy to use it and it ultimately has no impact. Sir Hugh Annesley, the Chief Constable of the RUC, went further in setting out his belief that locally-based policing was 'flawed', at the 1992 Annual Police Foundation lecture. Sir Hugh argued that: 'Crime is indeed local, but most major crime is . . . national and international. And whilst the delivery of general policing service is local and should be tailored to prevailing circumstances . . . the police force itself does not need to be local' (Kirby 1992c).

The idea of a national operational force is not altogether new and was put forward in a dissenting note by Arthur Goodhart to the 1962 Royal Commission on the Police and in the memoirs of a retired HM Inspector of Constabulary (St Johnston 1978). Similar sentiments have been expressed more recently by Sir John Wheeler, a former Chair of the House of Commons Home Affairs Committee (Wheeler 1993), and by a survey of senior detectives from all over the country (E.

Campbell 1993). The same survey also revealed that 84 per cent of those questioned: 'believe that organised crime will increase as a result of the single European Community Market and the Channel Tunnel' (E. Campbell 1993).

The need to have a national voice in Europe also becomes merged with the need to have efficient and effective policing, and the notion that that might be achieved by more centralization. The strengthening of the central Inspectorate of Constabulary (D. Campbell 1991) and the suggestion that it should be easier to amalgamate small forces (Home Office 1993a: para. 10.13) has reinforced the centralizing tendency. In terms of support to the police, the National Technical Support Unit (NTSU) began operation in early 1992 to provide facilities and expertise not always readily available to them in the regions. The NTSU is part of the Home Office's PSDB providing equipment, operational support, specialist skills and advice and it is clearly stated that 'the NTSU will be of increasing importance in a Europe where crime is less and less constrained by national boundaries' (Home Office 1993c: 19). The Unit also offers training to European police officers and was a founder member of the WITS (Home Office 1993c: 17–19; see also Chapter 3).

Even more specific to the needs of the UK police and their understanding of Europe was the creation by the PSDB in 1993 of the so-called EPI-Centre (European Police Information Centre). The EPI-Centre is a national resource for all UK forces offering an international police equipment and technology data base, conferencing and electronic mail facilities, access to related data bases and the 'best international advice' as well as subject-based information on specialist topics. The EPI-Centre is operational 24 hours a day and available to all UK police forces. Following full implementation in the UK it will be made available 'free to all European Police Forces and related agencies' (Home Office 1993c: 15). The EPI-Centre has cost £68 000 to set up and will cost an estimated £2000 a year to run (*Hansard*, 28 October 1993, WA No. 288).

We will look at some of these issues and the possible impact of national policing in creating a two-tier system of policing – national and local – later in this chapter.

Police Powers

The powers of police officers vary between – and often within – the EU countries. But successful co-operation will mean a full understanding of respective powers and a fair amount of research is still required in this area before a full assessment of the implications for British policing can be made.

Variations exist, for example, between the lengths of time a suspect can be held for questioning by police. A standard 24 hours is operative in Germany, the UK and Belgium with various mechanisms built in to increase that if necessary. In Italy and Portugal a suspect may be held for 48 hours, whilst in the Netherlands a review is needed after 6 hours and in the Republic of Ireland a detainee must be released or brought to court within 12 hours.

Training

The move towards more European co-operation has inevitably brought with it a demand for more training and education to help ease the process. The TREVI group included a requirement in its 1990 Programme of Action that called for regular exchange of police students and instructors at both initial and advanced levels to improve understanding of the organization and methods of respective police services and the judicial systems of member states (Programme of Action 1990: para. 7).

In the UK, police training is organized locally through Police District Training Centres which provide initial training for new recruits and which are supported by the Home Office Central Planning and Training Unit and advised by the Police Training Council. The Home Secretary has appointed a National Director of Police Training responsible for all training, provided nationally or regionally. National training is for senior officers and is provided by the Police Staff College at Bramshill. Suggestions have been tabled that in the current moves to closer European co-operation some training might take place at an international level.

The idea has been put forward that a European police academy might be created to serve officers from various countries. One of the strongest advocates for this pan-European idea has been Dr Piet van Reenen, the former Director of the Netherlands Police Academy who claims that the concept can be traced back to 1985 (van Reenen 1992). Given current differences in training and police philosophies, a simple coming together of curriculae or programmes would not be easy, and van Reenen sees his proposed European Police Institute as being only for senior officers with management responsibilities. Despite the difficulties: 'the fact that the borders within Europe are opening up is a sufficient and necessary reason to start a facility for the meeting and training of police management on a European level, no matter how different the structures and cultures of today are' (van Reenen 1992).

The positive advantages of moving training onto a European scale are that it concentrates the level of expertise, gives a clear European perspective and is more efficient if it obviates the need for each country to promote its own in-house 'European course'. The Institute could be either a central physical establishment, a secretariat that could organize courses throughout Europe, or a mixture of the two, with funding coming from member states or the EC. Van Reenen is aware that countries are cautious of setting up a European Police Institute and notes that the TREVI group temporarily turned down the idea, but is in no doubt that it will 'eventually be realised' (van Reenen 1992; see also Benyon *et al.* 1993: ch. 7.3.5).

Allied to the idea of a central European police academic institution is the British proposal for a European Police Council. Originally put forward by Roger Birch, Chief Constable of Sussex, as Chair of the ACPO International Affairs Advisory Committee, it was seen as another way to improve practical police co-operation and break down the isolation of individual nation forces (House of Commons 1990b: Vol.2, p. 20). The idea has been compared to the Customs Cooperation Council for Customs and Excise Officers from different countries to meet (House of Commons 1989a: para. 56).

The Council was to differ from the idea of a central academic institution which had the potential to become yet another large and undefined super-agency with confused accountability (Bentham 1992), and it would also be open to officers of all ranks and not just managers (House of Commons 1990b: Vol.2, p. 107). ACPO had already had discussions with Interpol who liked the idea and were happy to act as 'neutral territory to further a way forward' (Bentham 1992). The Home Affairs Committee, however, were rather lukewarm in their reception to a Police Council, and thought Interpol might be a better means of achieving the same end (House of Commons 1990b: Vol.1, para. 116). It has also been suggested that it merely reflects the UK's decentralized system of policing and the need for a national voice (N. Walker 1991: 41). This did not stop the idea being brought forward again in 1992 to the same Committee, but retitled a 'Police Programme for Europe' to avoid 'unacceptably constitutional overtones' posed by the earlier title (House of Commons 1992: Vol.2, p. 96).

At present the training of British police officers remains in the hands of their District Training Centres, and at a national level with the Police Staff College.

The National Police Staff College at Bramshill, set in its own extensive grounds in Hampshire and occupying a Grade 1 listed building, provides senior police officers with management training. The College has not been without its critics. Academics have pointed to its lack of a research base and limited publications which prevent it being a true 'University for the Police'. Others have criticized its lack of street credibility amongst lower-ranking officers in the regions (House of Commons 1989b).

Bramshill offers a Special Course for selected officers assisting them to accelerated promotion from constable, Junior, Intermediate and Senior Command Courses for officers with management responsibilities; and Carousel courses to support these courses by way of follow-ups. In recent years a European flavour has been added to the curriculum of these courses.

The Bramshill Commander meets regularly with his European equivalents at the Heads of European Police Academies

Conference initiated by a TREVI group meeting in 1977. The exchange of lecturing staff between academies is also being pursued (Home Office 1989b) and Bramshill has opened its own European Desk to keep a data base on its international contacts. Since 1979 Bramshill has also provided courses for senior French, Spanish and German officers, building on its long tradition of educating senior Commonwealth officers on its Overseas Command Course. More specific operational courses have been provided for German BKA officers on drug trafficking and terrorism (House of Commons 1989b: Vol.1, para. 37).

Senior Command Courses for British officers have now been tailored to include the study of 'international developments in crime and the need for international cooperation' (House of Commons 1989b: Vol.1, para. 59), and have included student visits to various EC countries as part of the course (House of Commons 1990: Vol.1, para.117). Note has been taken of the Home Affairs Committee's reported concern at the criticisms of Bramshill it had received from the Police Superintendents' Association and ACPO (House of Commons 1989b: Vol.1, para. 59).

The Home Affairs Committee asked ACPO representatives how they felt British training compared to training available to other forces but the delegates felt they could not really say (House of Commons 1989b: Vol.2, p. 77). Robert Bunyan, the then Commandant of Bramshill, felt that they could hold their own with European national schools but saw the question in terms of a domestic service to the British police comparing favourably to similar arrangements abroad rather than in any international training context (House of Commons 1989b: Vol.2, p. 46).

Rank and file officers not eligible for Bramshill courses are less likely to receive an international element to their local training. The Chairman of the Police Federation, Alan Eastwood, reported in 1989:

The almost complete absence of any sign that the training and information requirements of our membership are going to be satisfied in the near or long term future . . . the policing systems of Europe, and an understanding of the

differing legal systems of Member States ought to be part of
the basic initial training course at Police District Training
Centres. (Eastwood 1989a)

Throughout 1992 the Federation's own monthly journal,
Police, ran a series entitled 'Into Europe' with articles by
Interpol giving an explanatory outline of a different European
police force in different editions.

Others have noted that training at a European level 'does
not extend downwards to individual force level' (N. Walker
1991: 33). At Inspector level disappointment has been regis-
tered at the lack of initiatives ('Warnings on Europe', *Police*,
XXIV, 10 (June 1992), p. 17) and even RCS officers could say
in 1989 that their training in the structure of European police
forces was 'non-existent' (House of Commons 1989a: Vol.2, p.
68). The Home Office Central Planning and Training Unit in
Harrogate is said to be looking at ways to develop this
training, 'probably on a modular basis within the Police
District Training Centres' (House of Commons 1990b:
Vol.2, p. 24); and occasional 'one-off' events take place as,
for example, the three-day European Liaison Officers' Conference organized by the Devon and Cornwall Constabulary
in May 1990. The National Director of Police Training will no
doubt be taking the European dimension into account.

One new skill requirement for the police has been recognized in the need for language training. In 1989 senior RCS
officers identified an urgent need for language training as their
work involved increasing contact with European and other
countries (House of Commons 1989a: Vol.2, p. 68). The Home
Affairs Committee noted the general deficiency in language
skills throughout the UK and felt it was not the job of police
training to compensate for deficiencies of the education
system. The favoured approach was to see language skills
for the police as an 'operational device' that 'targeted'
learning, rather than 'indiscriminate' education of all officers. Not only should certain personnel be targeted, but the
language itself should be taught as an 'operational police
language', concentrating on legal and technical expressions
that would 'achieve a consistent and unambiguous language'
(House of Commons 1990b: Vol.1, para. 120).

Linguists could also be identified on recruitment to the police and certain forces might put more resources into training than others, such as the Kent Constabulary's need for French-speaking officers. An example of good targeting was the Kent 'Policespeak' Project, which involved them liaising with Wolfson College, Cambridge, to produce an operational police language handbook in French and English (House of Commons 1990b: Vol.2, p. 41; see also Winder 1993). The ACPO Training Committee was also in liaison with the National French Police Academy at Clermont-Feraud to use their lexicon of words and phrases covering police and judicial terms in French, German, English and Spanish and to make it available to all forces in the UK (House of Commons 1990b: Vol.2, p. 23).

ACPO was otherwise advising forces to use local colleges for their language training needs (House of Commons 1990b), just as at a more senior level the national Police Staff College at Bramshill was using the University of Reading on their six week courses run jointly with the French and German police (House of Commons 1990b: Vol.2, p. 13; see also Benyon *et al.* 1993: ch. 3.14.2).

'Managerialism'

The application of managerial theories to policing has been a gradual process from the early 1980s onwards, culminating in the 1993 Sheehy Report into police responsibilities and rewards. Considerable disquiet has been voiced by the police about this new approach to the organization of policing and the belief that policing is not an industrial production line; its whole ethos and morale could suffer if 'managerialism' is allowed to spread.

The proponents of the new thinking cite value for money, efficiency, effectiveness and economy as the rationale for making changes. They accept that policing is not a business, but argue that it can still learn a lot from the way in which business treats it customers, and that even thorny problems like accountability can be better achieved by the control of commercial disciplines. Other public services were being subjected to the same scrutiny to improve their efficiency and make them responsive to consumers rather than producers, and the whole direction of movement was being driven from the centre in the form of the Home Office.

Starting in 1989 the Government's Audit Commission published the first of a series of Papers on the Police Service. The most influential of these were Paper No. 8, 'Effective Policing – Performance Review', and No. 9, 'Management Structure and Resource Allocation', which both argued for some fundamental changes in the organiza-tion and structure of police forces. HM Inspectorate of Constabulary added weight to the arguments by pointing to already existing 'best practice' within forces. By the early 1990s the guiding principles were becoming clear. Manage-ment posts should be clearly defined, hierarchies 'flattened' to provide one tier of operational units (usually called a Basic Command Unit and usually under the command of a Super-intendent), with as close as possible a link between operational and financial management of units. Superintendents should set their policies for local needs within the Chief Constable's overall policy, and a performance review and inspectorate function was to be established above the level of Basic Command Unit to look at the quality of service.

The Government's 1993 White Paper on 'Police Reform' confirmed this movement to make the police more responsive to communities and to 'value for money' objectives, with plans to appoint more people with business and other experience to local police authorities to replace existing elected members (Home Office 1993a). The Sheehy Report on 'Police Respon-sibilities and Rewards', published the same week, took the managerialist arguments even further with talk of redundant middle managers, 'fixed term contracts' and 'performance related pay' (Sheehy 1993).

The police have been extremely critical of these moves, pointing out the unique features of policing that do not lend themselves to 'production line' management techniques (see e.g. Rose 1993). ACPO, the Police Superintendents' Associa-tion and the Federation had already jointly put out their 'Operational Policing Review' in 1990 to counter the manage-rialist approach, and all ranks demonstrated a degree of unity in their resistance. The argument from HM Inspectorate was, however, resolute:

> The challenge from the public is to open up the police service to its fellow citizens. The service needs to be thrown open to the consumer, its structures redesigned to allow the public more fully to assist in the setting of priorities. The police service needs to admit the limits of its power. In a single ugly phrase, the service needs to deprofessionalise. (Woodcock 1991)

The consequences of this strategy of managerialism is slowly being unravelled. Democratic processes of police accountability are seen as less important than direct responsiveness to performance indices, local communities and the given budget. When the strategy of 'localization' and flatter hierarchies is coupled to the wider view of greater centralization and national units like NCIS, a 'bifurcatory' process is revealed with 'the distinct possibility that we will witness the creation of a two-tiered policing system consisting of a national police organisation and a subordinate and decentralised local policing network' (McLaughlin 1992). In a European context we may well be moving into a dual system of policing comparable to other arrangements in Europe.

Numerous European policing arrangements exist on a dual force basis, and sometimes a triple force basis. These arrangements have not evolved from localized forces as in this country but were in place almost from their inception as means of counter-balancing forces in society to act as a check on each other. The French *Police Nationale* weighs against the *Gendarmerie Nationale*, whilst in Portugal the *Policia Judiciára* is counter-balanced by the *Policia de Siguranca Publica* and the *Guarda Nacional Republica*. In Luxembourg officers must move from one force, the *Corps de Police* or the *Gendarmerie*, to the other each time they are promoted in rank.

A corollary to different forces within one country, with different status attached to each force, may be the rise of dual entry systems to the police in the UK. Such ideas have always been resisted here, with police officers who become Chief

Constables having to start at the bottom and work their way up in common with every other entrant. The concept of an 'officer class', with direct entry to senior positions has been anathema to the British police service; even accelerated promotion with the aid of the National Staff Police College at Bramshill has been looked at askance, with upwardly mobile officers being referred to in derogatory terms as 'butterflies' who never stay in one place for very long. Ireland, Denmark, Germany and Greece have similar single entry systems.

If a dual system of national and local policing comes into being in the UK in an incremental way it will undoubtedly bring status rivalries with it, and once entrance schemes have been devised from one force to the other the pressure may well increase to develop direct entry schemes at senior levels in both forms of policing. In the UK it has been the very existence of a single-point of entry for all recruits that is said to have in part reduced some of the excesses of a large officer and other ranks divide and even to have encouraged 'a somewhat greater ambivalence amongst senior officers as regards the various tenets of the managerialist approach' (N. Walker 1991: 13).

Trade Unions

The British Police Federation representing all officers below the rank of Superintendent meets with its European equivalents in the UISP, which is based at Hilden near Dusseldorf in Germany (Benyon *et al.* 1993: ch. 5.12.2). The British Federation is a Government created association for police officers that came into being after the 1919 police strikes and is overtly not a trade union. As such it cannot, for example, join bodies like the Trades Union Congress and must be independent of, and totally unassociated with, any body or person outside the police service (Police Act 1964, s.44(2)). Even allowing the Federation to join the UISP required legislative provision in the shape of the 1972 Police Act, which amended the 1964 Police Act, section 44.

Having made contact, the British Police Federation seems to have suffered something of a culture shock on meeting

European colleagues. For a start many European officers openly joined trade unions, many of whom were competing for their membership. Political stances were openly declared and police officers have 'total freedom of political action' (Eastwood 1989a). On operational police matters it seemed that domestic worries about terrorism, drug trafficking and the potential lowering of border controls produced hardly any anxiety at all amongst European officers, a fact that the Chairman of the Federation could only attribute to the British having an 'island perspective' (Eastwood 1989a).

In practice there is now much evidence that the Police Federation is quite openly involved in political activity in this country, despite its formal constitutional position (see, e.g., Reiner 1983 and 1992: 91–6). When that position was formally reviewed by the Edmund-Davies Committee of Inquiry of the late 1970s the Federation's position was contrasted with that of its European equivalents. The unique role of the 'Office of Constable' and its accompanying status was pointed to as the rationale for continuing to limit the political freedom of the Federation, when compared to the European police who were either of the military or 'grouped with public service workers and civil servants with whom they have pay links' (Home Office 1979: para. 210).

In France Anderson estimates there are over 20 police unions of which perhaps the largest and most important is the *Syndicat Général de la Police* (SGP) representing the lowest ranks of the uniformed National Police. Others include the extreme right-wing union, the *Fédération Profes-sionelle Indépendante de la Police* (FPIP); the FPIP is quite small in numbers and not representative of a generally reformist attitude amongst French police unions, although none of them have the right to strike. The military nature of the *Gendarmerie* forbids them from forming or joining unions although, following a semi- public expression of discontent with their conditions of employment, the Government pro-vided in 1989 a means of voicing collective grievances for the *Gendarmerie* (Anderson 1991: 17–19).

The police of the Netherlands are also well unionized 'and do not usually hesitate to call for actions, demonstrations and strikes in view of various demands' (den Boer 1991: 19), while in Germany 'a huge police protest on the streets of Freiburg' took place in the Baden-Wurttemberg *Land* in December 1991 against low pay, poor resources and large amounts of overtime (Cullen 1992: 22).

In stark contrast, however, the Greek police service has experienced great difficulty in even getting a union or federation recognized by its government. In 1989 the Federation had had to invoke the Greek courts in order to register itself as a trade union, and allegations have been made that police officers trying to organize a federation 'are being posted to faraway places, or assigned special duties, so as to prevent them from attending meetings, and in some cases they have been fined large amounts, as much as one month's pay, for small breaches of discipline' ('A Greek Travesty', *Police*, December 1991, p. 28).

Whether or not the British Police Federation is engaged in any mutual learning process through their contact with the UISP remains to be seen. Twenty-one thousand officers gathered in London in July 1993 at a protest rally against changes to conditions of employment proposed by the Sheehy Report, reportedly the largest ever demonstration by police officers in Britain.

Occupational Cultures

A number of studies in the UK have sought to illustrate the nature of the occupational culture of policing and its influence on day-to-day police activities carried out by rank and file police officers. Occupational cultures are not peculiar to policing but provide for any working group a set of values and expectations that cushion workers from the trials and tribulations of the job and create a shared view of 'commonsense' reality. In the case of policing it is a way of coping with unsocial hours and often dangerous and anxiety provoking situations (see, e.g., Holdaway 1983; Waddington 1984; Fielding 1988).

At its worst occupational culture leads to a closing of ranks, introspection and preserving of poor work values and low expectations which become firmed into methods of working impervious to new ideas and change. The police have been criticized for developing just such a restrictive culture that recognizes only insiders (the police) and outsiders (everyone else), and is suspicious and defensive. It has variously been described as a 'cop culture' or 'canteen culture'. Within such a culture informal contacts become more important than formal contacts, and short-cuts are rationalized as being worthy means to an end which save you having to 'go by the book'.

Occupational cultures in policing can cause division along both horizontal and vertical lines. Horizontal divisions create a gap between rank and file officers who see themselves as having to do the 'real' frontline work out in the streets, and management officers who organize and administer the police service. When such a division opens up and two cultures of policing occur at different levels (see, e.g., Ianni and Ianni, 1983), it is possible for policies coming down from the top not to be completely subverted by the lower culture but certainly to be refracted to make them acceptable to more junior ranks.

Occupational cultures of policing can also lead to unhelpful vertical rivalries growing up between police forces or police officers and, for example, specialized policing units. Rivalry may exist between one force and another based on perceived levels of work. Provincial forces may distance themselves from the Metropolitan Police, and vice versa. At best it may be symbolic and harmless rivalry, but at worst it leads to a breakdown in communication, inability to share information and a restriction on the effectiveness of police activities. Local detectives may, for example, not share information with RCS officers, or information and intelligence developed by NCIS might have no practical impact due to local police having other priorities, and resenting outside 'interference'. Police officers engaged in international activities may be seen as elitist and attendance at international conferences regarded as little more than junketing. Walker has suggested that 'in this respect the problems associated with the operational use, neglect and criticism of the UK NCB of Interpol may be instructive' (N. Walker 1991: 43).

It remains to be seen how such occupational cultures operate within an international European environment, whether as oiling the wheels of co-operation or as a restrictive element that creates rivalries and yet another policing 'turf issue' (e.g., N. Walker 1991: 42–4). It also remains to be seen how other occupational police cultures differ from or are similar to the home grown variety. In general terms we might note that the German police seems to lend itself to 'legalism' in its day-to-day work, the UK police has greater discretion, while the police forces of some European countries are more inclined to a form of 'militarism'. In France occupational cultures within the police are much debated but little researched, and as elsewhere are seen to lie behind that 'peculiar mixture of cynicism and sense of public duty' that infuses the day-to-day life of the police officer (Anderson 1991: 17).

A number of reports are beginning to show how police in the UK are priding themselves on the growth of their informal contacts within European police forces. Formal contacts come from the initial meeting or conference, and from there it is the personal contact that becomes all-important. The position has been succinctly put by a police officer representing the UK on the Europe-wide PWGOT:

We know these people, they are our personal friends, they come here to the Yard when they happen to be in London. We make contact with them when we go abroad, regardless of what we are looking for. It has become a very solid group of working colleagues. We trust each other implicitly and pass information to each other without question. (Bresler 1992: 162)

What could even be happening is the emergence of an international occupational culture – a 'Euro-cop culture' – that police officers of different countries are beginning to feel comfortable with. Many of the fora we describe in Chapter 3 lend themselves to the making of informal contacts where work objectives are agreed. As one Dutch police officer has suggested, it is the bar and the lounge that was cementing European police co-operation where 'many excellent agreements on cooperation were made, and often they were even more effective than the ones made through the official channels of The Hague' (quoted in Benyon *et al.* 1993: ch. 5.12.4).

On this basis ultimately procedures can be circumvented altogether and even personal information passed 'without question', and presumably without reference to data protection legislation as well. Despite, for example, the long held policy of the Republic of Ireland not to disclose police held criminal records for purposes of pre-employment vetting of people wanting to work with children (Home Office 1993b: para. 48), a senior UK police officer has described how:

> Many forces, my own included, make *direct access inquiries* with Eire . . . The reason is one of *expediency*. A common language simplifies the inquiry. The response time from the Garda Siochana is good and one can immediately see the advantages in terms of *less time delay and lessening of bureaucracy by dealing direct.* (Devon and Cornwall Constabulary 1990: 224–5, emphasis added)

Here is a given national policy neatly sidestepped by direct contact across a national border between police officers.

Conclusions

Police co-operation in Europe is having a clear 'recoil' effect on national police forces throughout Europe. Using the British police as a case study we can see the effect operating at different levels.

With their localized policing model the British have difficulty in putting forward a national police voice. In recent years attempts to overcome this deficit have resulted in national initiatives such as the NCIS, which may become a forerunner for other national services or even the idea of a national police force comparable to other parts of Europe.

Elsewhere compensatory measures are being called for by the British police in anticipation of frontiers being removed. Measures might include a strengthening of the POTA, easier extradition procedures or other methods of achieving greater 'harmonization' between the criminal codes of different countries. Within the UK Identification Cards might compensate for a freer movement of people in Europe as a whole.

The British police are being pushed into looking at other aspects of Europeanization; understanding different policing arrangements and the nature of international crime; and looking at language training needs and the possible development of a European University of Policing.

6

Europe: A New Police Terrain (1) Justifications

The development of a notion of 'permanent security deficit' has been crucial in helping to determine and, as we argue, restructure police work in the new Europe. Within the context of the steps towards European union, no matter has been more the subject of intense discussion and debate than that of border controls: it has had an 'activating presence' (a term borrowed from Bauman 1978). The removal of border controls and their relationship to the 'threats' of illegal immigration and cross-border crime have structured this internal security field (Bourdieu 1989). Much of this is termed 'new' and is itself the product of the creation of institutions to 'deal with' these perceived 'new threats'. At the heart of this restructuring are processes of 'linking and glossing', whereby separate activities of drug trafficking, terrorism, money-laundering, illegal immmigration, extreme right movements and football hooliganism are assembled into a causal 'field of intervention'.

In this chapter we examine aspects of this 'field of inter-vention' and in particular immigration and organized and cross-border crime. However, Europe as a new policing terrain is also constructed through interplay with another factor, and in Chapter 7 we examine the central part played in developing co-operative counter-measures in this new 'Europe' by the production of information systems across jurisdictional boundaries. We suggest that these systems, extending across inter-governmental and towards suprana-tional levels, present an important and perhaps transforma-tive 'informatization' of policing and play their own part in the construction of police work in the new Europe (see Raab, 1994).

The Threat of Immigration

At the centre of European debates on immigration one can identify two central contradictions that concern the *role* of the nation-state in the regulation of immigration into the EC (Miles 1992). The first is between the continuing reproduction of the ideology and institutional reality of the nation-state and its inability to accommodate certain changes consequent upon the process and consequences of immigration. The second is between the dominant discourse of the member state concerning immigration *control* and the declining ability of the state to effect control. The restructuring of the processes of exclusion that lies at the confluence of national interests and Europeanization is central to understanding the formation of this 'regime', and of police terrain within it. Before examining how these processes have been developed, let us consider some background.

Baldwin-Edwards and Schain (in press) in their review of trends in immigration point to the fact that *legal* immigration into Western Europe has been low if steady since the oil crisis of the 1970s, when most countries restricted immigration from non-EC countries. During the decade of the 1980s and into the early 1990s, the percentage of foreign legal residents in Western Europe increased (see Table 6.1), with the largest proportionate increases in the Netherlands and Austria (SOPEMI Continuous Reporting System on Migration 1994). In absolute terms, the foreign population increased most in Austria and actually declined in Germany.

The legally present foreign population of Italy increased threefold during the 1980s, but remained under 800 000. Perhaps more important, for the first time in modern history Italy, along with other Southern European countries, has become in the past decade a country of net immigration rather than of emigration. Despite these changes and with the exception of Austria, the overall distribution of foreigners across Europe has remained largely unchanged, with the vast

Table 6.1 *Percentage of Foreign Population in Selected OECD Countries (1982–91)*

	1982	1984	1986	1988	1990	1991
Austria	4.0	3.6	3.6	3.9	5.3	6.6
Belgium	9.0	9.1	8.6	8.8	9.1	9.2
France	6.8				6.4	
Germany	7.6	7.1	7.4	7.3	8.2	7.3
Italy	0.6	0.7	0.8	1.1	1.4	1.5
Netherlands	3.8	3.9	3.9	4.2	4.6	4.8
UK		2.8	3.2	3.2	3.3	3.1

Source: SOPEMI (1994), p. 187.

majority located in Germany and Belgium, followed by Austria, France, the UK and Switzerland.

Starting in the late 1980s, new flows of migrants have occurred (see Salt 1992). These include increases in both family reunions and guestworkers; flows from Eastern Europe, mainly affecting Germany and Austria; largely illegal immigration, originating from Africa, into southern European countries; and a marked increase in the number of asylum-seekers.

Asylum-seekers

The number of asylum-seekers increased dramatically in the late 1980s and early 1990s (see Table 6.2). The largest increase in absolute numbers was in the newly unified Germany, although proportionately short-term influxes are substantial in Italy and continue in Belgium and the UK. Even before unification, more asylum-seekers were entering Germany than the rest of the EC. With the collapse of Communist regimes in the Soviet Union and Eastern Europe, and with the expansion of the war in former Yugoslavia, the number of asylum-seekers grew rapidly in every country in Western Europe. This was particularly true in Germany, but only in Germany,

Table 6.2 *Asylum-Seekers into Selected OECD Countries (thousands, 1982–92)*

	1982	1984	1986	1988	1990	1991	1992
Austria	6.3	7.2	8.6	15.8	22.8	27.3	16.2
Belgium	3.1	3.7	7.6	4.5	13.0	15.2	17.6
France	22.5	21.6	26.2	34.3	54.7	47.4	28.9
Germany	37.2	35.3	99.7	103.1	193.1	256.1	438.0
Italy		4.6	6.5	1.4	3.6	24.5	2.6
Netherlands	1.2	2.6	5.9	7.5	21.2	21.6	17.1
UK	4.2	3.9	4.8	5.7	38.2	67.0	

Source: SOPEMI (1994), p. 188.

Belgium and Sweden did the number continue to increase during 1992. In France, the number of asylum-seekers declined after 1989, in Spain after 1990, and in Italy, the Netherlands and Austria after 1991 (SOPEMI 1994).

The decrease in the number of asylum-seekers is generally a result of legal and administrative changes that have made it more difficult for asylum-seekers actually to enter countries in Western Europe and also to gain refugee status. These changes include, at the national level, such devices as carrier or airline sanctions; strict visa requirements; penalization of undocumented asylum-seekers; the invention of so-called 'international zones' in airports, circumventing both constitutional requirements and international legal obligations; the notion of 'safe countries' of first asylum, generally defined as those countries signatory to the 1951 Geneva Convention and the 1967 Protocol; the concept of 'safe' countries of origin, denying access to asylum procedures; and accelerated procedures, which deny a full hearing for the applicant.

At the transnational level, both the Schengen Convention and the Dublin Convention incorporate many of these devices, as well as addressing the issue of multiple refugee applications. Indeed, it is clear that the evolution of these institutions is intrinsically bound up with the desire of national governments not only to keep away asylum-seekers but also to evade judicial control. The policies determining structures affecting border controls, immigration and asylum are considered in more detail later in the chapter.

Illegal Immigration

Illegal immigration has been widespread throughout Western Europe in the post-war period, yet is only recently that unanimous condemnation of the phenomenon has been voiced, in the context of immigratory pressures (Baldwin-Edwards and Schain, in press). Illegal migrants gain admission by a variety of routes, and also for different reasons, making it difficult to characterize and to estimate. It has been suggested that more than 75 per cent of refused asylum-seekers remain illegally (Böhning 1991); other commentators point to 'over-stayers' as a significant proportion of illegal residents (Salt 1992: 62); clearly, weak immigration controls, combined with a large informal economy and geographical proximity to North Africa, make southern Europe a prime location for illegal immigration (see Baldwin-Edwards 1991). Baldwin-Edwards and Schain conclude, 'Perhaps one generalization is valid, though: that restrictions on legal immigration have had the inevitable consequences of promoting illlegal migration' (Baldwin-Edwards and Schain in press: 5).

Estimates of the extent of illegal immigrants in Western Europe are difficult to obtain or verify. The ILO estimated for 1991 that there were 2.6 million illegal residents representing some 15 per cent of the total foreign population (see Table 6.3). The countries most affected seem to be Germany with 650 000 and Italy with 600 000.

In general, mass publics have been less than receptive to changing patterns of immigration. According to the latest *Eurobarometer* survey on attitudes towards immigration, a majority of respondents (some 52 per cent) across the EU feel that there are too many non-Union immigrants (*Eurobarometer*, June 1993). This shows little change from both 1991 and 1992 surveys; however, individual countries exhibit more complicated trends. In countries in which immigration has been high since 1945 (the UK, Germany, France, Belgium), this trend has been evident for the last twenty years. Opposi-

Table 6.3   *Estimate of Illegally Present Non-Nationals in 1991*

	Illegal Migrants (persons who did not enter as asylum-seekers)	Illegal Refugees (refused asylum-seekers whose presence is not tolerated)
France	200 000	
Germany	350 000	300 000
Italy	600 000	
Spain	300 000	
Switzerland	100 000	
Other	400 000	350 000
TOTAL	1 950 000	650 000

Source: Böhning (1991), p. 450.

tion to the presence of Third World immigrants has been spreading more recently even to countries in which immigration is low but increasing, such as Greece, Italy and the former East Germany.

On the other hand, none of the particular differences of immigrants seems to disturb more than a relatively small minority of mass publics in EU countries. More than 80 per cent of Europeans find these characteristics 'not disturbing', with no change over the past three years. Asylum-seekers are accepted throughout the Union, but with restrictions. Only a quarter of those surveyed are prepared to accept them without restrictions.

What is most evident from these cross-survey data is that there is little consistent relationship cross-nationally between proportions of immigrant stocks and patterns of attitudes towards immigrants. The feeling that there are too many immigrants is strong even in many countries with small immigrant populations. Expressed tolerance for differences of nationality, race and religion is strongest in some countries with few immigrants (Ireland, Spain and Portugal), but is also strong in Italy where immigration has been growing, and in UK and Germany, where the proportion of immigrant stock is relatively high. The intolerant minority is strongest in France and Greece (around 30 per cent).

Despite the legal fact of citizenship of the EU, the level of acceptance of other Union nationalities without restriction was only 35 per cent, and the pattern corresponded to that of acceptance of asylum-seekers: there is a rough correspondence between stronger acceptance among countries which have been traditional exporters of labour and weaker support among countries which are traditional importers of labour.

However, if we are looking for the sources of mass attitudes, an examination of the political process, rather than of demographic structure, may be more fruitful. As Zolberg (1981) has argued, popular perception of the origins of resident foreigners is constructed by the political dialogue in Europe itself.

Despite the dire predictions in the press in 1989–90, the 'invasion' of Western Europe has not taken place, in part because of much tighter restrictions on border controls and their enforcement, in part because the predictions themselves were highly inflammatory. Thus, the 'crisis' of immigration is less a crisis of cross-border flows than it is a political crisis of elite and mass reaction to foreign-born people, only a few of whom have arrived in the last five years.

Baldwin-Edwards and Schain (in press) argue that although immigration is frequently seen as a problem with which policy-makers and mass publics are unhappily confronted, changing immigration patterns can also be understood as a process, or rather as a network of processes. The first process is that of the pull/push of migration, the process that impels migrants to leave their native countries and migrate to Europe. While much of the 'push' is related to larger trends in Europe and globally, the 'pull', argue Baldwin-Edwards and Schain is to a large extent under the control of policy-makers.

The recent debate involves the construction of policies that would limit the pull by creating obstacles to migration, whatever the cause. These obstacles include tighter border controls, increased visa requirements, employer sanctions, greater use of deportations, redefining the criteria for asylum, accelerated procedures, and co-ordination of national policies. There also exists a sub-debate, conducted largely within international organizations such as the ILO, the

European Parliament and the European Commission. This stresses the inevitability of migratory pressure from the less developed world, not least in the context of massive population growth in North Africa and serious economic disparities in the world economy. Demographic factors are worth noting. Baldwin-Edwards (1992) states that while European fertility rates have generally been falling since the mid-1960s and are shifting the age structure towards a very high old age dependency ratio (see OECD 1989) the picture is very different in the Mahgreb and Turkey. There, population growth is extremely high and the expected age structure between 1990 and 2025 changes to one with a very high proportion of working/mobile age. Table 6.4 illustrates these two trends.

The particular focus of limiting the 'pull' advocates development aid in various forms as a means of reducing the 'push' factors: its principal disadvantage lies in its cost and the need for the industrialized world explicitly to address the structural nature of poverty and exploitation within global capital.

The second process is that of incorporation or integration, a process which has had implications for a whole range of policy areas, but one that has had an impact on the structure and relations among political institutions. In this process, immigrants are not only the objects of policy, but have become political actors who have had an impact on the process itself.

Table 6.4 *Projected Population Growth and Age Structure, 1989–2025*

	Population (millions)			Age Structure (%) (0–14)		(15–64)	
	1989	2000	2025	1989	2025	1989	2025
Algeria	24	33	52	44	26	52	69
Morocco	25	32	48	41	26	55	68
Tunisia	8	10	14	38	24	56	68
Turkey	55	68	92	35	23	61	68

Source: World Bank (1991), table 26.

Increasingly, the politics of immigration involves conflicts between different visions and models of integration: conflicts that challenge long-accepted models of national identity and the nature of national integration (see Baldwin-Edwards and Schain in press).

Developing the Regime

A cornerstone of the steps towards European union has been the elimination of internal barriers to freedom of movement. The 1957 Treaty of Rome's provisions on freedom of movement within Europe has been extended by the Treaty on European Union (1992). While states have thus far refused to cede sovereignty over immigration law to the EC, nonetheless they have recognized that the ending of internal border controls makes effective exercise of *de jure* national competence over immigration nearly impossible: once an individual has successfully entered the common territory, he or she is unlikely to be inspected again. Governments have as a result, in classic regime-type process, sought agreement on common criteria to regulate the entry of foreigners into the Community. Governments have decided to treat migrants from the less developed world as an undifferentiated evil: refugees, economic migrants, terrorists and drug traffickers are officially categorized as presenting a unified threat, and will all confront a common policy of deterrence. As Hathaway (1993) points out, much of this is a reflection of the fact 'foreigners' have come to be seen as threats to regional stability and security: 'To a great extent the distinction between refugees, illegal immigrants, drug traffickers and terrorists has become blurred in the public mind and they are all seen to be problems that can only be resolved by stricter border controls' (Loescher, 1989: 624).

The origin of this association of concerns derives (in part, but see below) from the work of the inter-governmental group TREVI which was charged with the examination of asylum issues in the context of broader discussions of violence, international crime and terrorism and drug trafficking, and of course these associations are still present: 'Maastricht . . .

retains the dangerous practice of associating asylum and immigration issues with criminality: the articles dealing with asylum policy also refer to "combatting terrorism, unlawful drug trafficking and other serious forms of international crime"' (*North/South Issues*, 18 (1992): 3).

TREVI is the group constituted in the mid-1970s to allow the immigration and justice ministers of EC states to co-ordinate policy on security matters. In 1986, TREVI established the more specialized Ad Hoc Group of Immigration to enable immigration ministers and officials to address concerns associated with the plan to end internal border controls. A sub-committee of the Ad Hoc Group has produced three major accords: the 1990 Dublin Convention on responsibility to examine asylum requests; a 'parallel convention', approved in principle in June 1992 by EC immigration ministers, and intended to allow non-EC states to accede to the regime; and a draft Convention on the Crossing of External Borders which deals with such matters as mandatory external border controls, unified visa requirements and the sanctioning of carriers which transport passengers without proper documents.

King (1993) identifies three broad trends with respect to border controls, immigration and asylum: first, increasing policy decision-making in this area by inter-governmental and other bodies and networks not accountable to EU institutions; second, towards the strengthening of border controls and harmonization of policies for exclusion; and third, increasing convergence of structures and policies. As Cohen notes, there is a resulting process of incorporation and exclusion, 'a process of herding and sorting which is taking place as sheep are separating from goats, outsiders from insiders, the excluded from the included' (Cohen 1992: 336).

King (1993) sets the scene:

There are a multiplicity of interlinked and overlapping Western European structures engaged in this process under the umbrella of immigration, asylum and freedom of movement. Structures specifically relevant for the areas of concern here range from bilateral or multilateral border agreements . . . to intergovernmental (but non-EC accountable) policy-making bodies like the TREVI Group of

Ministers of the Interior. Of special importance, however, within the EC context are the Schengen Accord, the Ad Hoc Working Group on Immigration, and the Co-ordinating Committee, all established with the aim of 'harmonisation' of control . . . the new Union Treaty has provided (under Article B) that the question of EC powers in these respects will not be reviewed until 1996. (pp. 184–5)

So how have the Coordinating Group, the Ad Hoc Group and Schengen made their contribution? Let us first consider the Coordinating Group.

At Rhodes the EC Council of Ministers set up, in 1988, a 'Group of Coordinators'. Composed of very senior officials of the 12 EC states, its first task was to draw up a document whose proposals for measures to be implemented, known as the Palma Document, were adopted at the Madrid Summit in June 1989. Measures the group described as 'essential' included:

- a common negative list of countries whose nationals require an entry visa
- a common list of inadmissible persons and procedures for dealing with them
- a procedure for preventing asylum-seekers from applying for asylum in more than one member state
- acceptance of identical international commitments on refugees
- definition of common measures for checks on external borders, and system of surveillance, with improved co-operation and exchange of information between police and customs
- combating illegal immigration networks
- establishing an information exchange system on wanted and inadmissible persons

This programme of policies of harmonization and exclusion has, as we shall see, many features in common with Schengen. The suggested actions on the programme are either in the process of being or have already been instituted. It is becoming increasingly clear that the Rhodes Coordinators Group performed a key role in linking concerns across the new policing terrain: it essentially co-ordinated the activities of the Ad Hoc Group on Immigration, the TREVI sub-groups, the customs MAG, CELAD and others (Cruz 1993: 16).

The work involved in furthering the Palma Document measures mentioned earlier fell to the so-called Ad Hoc Group on Immigration. The Ad Hoc Group, comprising interior ministers of the EC states, produced in 1990 the draft convention to prevent asylum-seekers making more than one application in the EC: the Dublin Convention. In the same year it produced a draft convention on harmonization of controls at external borders. This draft was considered at Maastricht in December 1991, although not signed due to continuing problems between Britain and Spain over Gibraltar. The draft External Borders Convention closely follows the provisions of Schengen in terms of external borders and the harmonization of visa controls. There is a clear process of convergence in this area (King 1993).

In 1991, the Ad Hoc Group set out proposals for fingerprinting asylum-seekers, and set up a 'rapid consultation centre' on immigration problems (see Webber 1993). EC immigration ministers approved, in June 1992, the Group's draft of the parallel Dublin convention eventually intended to be signed by EFTA and other non-EU states. They called for joint reports, from information collected by EU states' embassies, on countries of origin of asylum seekers. At the November 1992 London meeting, ministers asked the Group to expedite work on EURODAC, the automated fingerprint matching system to be used to check all asylum seekers to ensure that they have not claimed asylum before or elsewhere in Europe. In addition, both CIREA, the centre for information, discussion and exchange on asylum and the more recent CIREFI, the centre for information, discussion and exchange on the crossing of borders and immigration, have been established under the Ad Hoc Group auspices.

Turning now briefly to Schengen, Hondius describes the 1990 Convention, which has been mentioned in previous chapters, as a 'typical law enforcement instrument. It quotes the price for liberalising borders, namely, stringent rules on the controls at external borders' (Hondius 1991: 302). Schengen provides for a general intensification of policing controls at the external borders of the nine 'Schengen states' and is particularly directed towards 'aliens' attempting to enter Schengen territory. The Convention's Articles, among other things, define 'external borders' as common 'land and sea borders and their airports and sea ports, provided they are not [otherwise defined] as internal borders', and 'Aliens' as 'any person other than a national of a member state of the European Communities'. Particular control emphasis is placed upon aliens of 'Third states', harmonization of visa policies and special rules governing asylum.

The New Europe's Expanding Cordon Sanitaire

This trend towards convergence of exclusionary policies for some European states has led to marginalization of others. To this extent, one can depict what is happening in terms of border and immigration controls in Europe as a 'fortress', with expanding perimeter walls (King 1993). Of course, within it, there are differing levels of control: the Schengenland of the nine EU states forms an 'inner core', moving outwards through the full EU states towards the EFTA and Eastern Europe front.

Perimeter expansion is occurring for several reasons: many EFTA countries have applied for EU membership; several countries (such as Austria and Switzerland) are engaged in pre-Schengen type harmonization policies (see, e.g., *Platform Fortress Europe*, April 1992); the previously mentioned 'parallel' Dublin convention is being prepared for signature, with the aim of extending the 'country of first asylum' principle to EFTA and central and eastern Europe. However, the drive is so great that many 'inner core' states are not waiting for signature of the 'parallel' convention and are engaged in a series of bilateral agreements. It can be suggested that these agreements create 'buffer-zone' areas on the periphery which now bear the hallmark of the new Europe's immigration policing.

For example, Schengen states signed an agreement with Poland in 1991 which obliged Poland to take back refugees transiting through its territory who arrived in a Schengen state. Austria has signed mutual readmission agreements with Hungary, Poland, Romania, Slovenia and the Czech Republic, and has since 1990 deployed over 2000 military police personnel on its borders. Belgium has signed agreements with Poland and Slovenia, and in June 1993 was negotiating with Rumania, the Czech Republic and Slovakia. Denmark has agreements with Latvia and Lithuania, and is negotiating with Estonia. On Europe's southern borders, Spain has agreements with Poland and with Morocco; under the latter, 2000 Moroccan border personnel guard the coastline to prevent the departure of fishing boats full of asylum-seekers. And the list could continue.

These readmission agreements represent the formal and public tip of the expansion. In October 1991 ministers from 33 European countries met in Berlin to discuss ways of co-ordinating immigration control and, in particular, combating illegal immigration across Europe. The agreed items included provision for:

(i) Mutual support in developing the border-securing infrastructure, in particular as regards the equipment and training of frontier protection forces, including the fields of communications and information processing
(ii) Intensification of frontier surveillance between border points deploying mobile forces of a strength appropriate to the situation at known or suspected weak points and, to this end, act in close concertation, which may include arrangements on the deployment of frontier protection forces at critical points, on the basis of joint analyses and up-to-date situation reports. (*Migration News Sheet* 1991: 3)

This Berlin group, so called after its first meeting, met again in Budapest in 1993, and discussed enlarging the Schengen-Poland agreement to cover more Eastern European states such as Hungary, the Czech Republic, Slovakia and Rumania (*Statewatch*, 3, 6, 1993: 16).

Yet another grouping, the Vienna Group, originally set up in 1978 to combat terrorism by the interior ministers of Austria, France, Germany, Italy and Switzerland, called a conference in 1991 to discuss migration movements from Eastern to Western Europe, to which it invited EC and Central and Eastern European ministers. From that conference emerged the Vienna Group (Immigration), which in turn produced the 'Working Party on a Solidarity Structure' with a brief to examine collective European co-operation with respect to the movements of people.

The Vienna Group working party first met in March 1993. A report for its second meeting in June 1993, said by the author to represent the general thrust of what was agreed at the first, makes it clear that the solidarity referred to is interpeted as prevention of 'disorderly movements' across Europe. Refugees travelling without visas are declared 'irregular'. The report reveals that this co-operation has so far included Austria sending police patrol cars to Hungary and training immigration police in the Czech Republic; and Germany, France, Norway, Switzerland and even Ireland training immigration officials in Central and Eastern Europe. The report also indicates clearly that buffer-states procedures are being tightened up in response to the internal security deficit ideology in Western Europe, according to the maxim, 'pressure will always be exerted on the weakest link of the chain'.

While at the policy level the trend is towards convergence and harmonization of controls in Europe, the practical effects are usually less well highlighted. The new policing terrain can be seen most sharply focused at the German buffer-state borders. At the border towns of Slubice and Frankfurt-am-Oder, German and Polish police work closely together and from the same office block. Around 2500 permanent officers are based at the eastern border. In addition, there are numerous Schengen exchange liaison officers, and military personnel in police uniforms operating heat-seeking equipment to detect potential asylum-seekers.

It is becoming increasingly clear that through Schengen and the other inter-governmental EU structures, immigration and asylum-seeker control policies form the dominant agenda. As this agenda reworks relationships between police, military, border personnel and customs officers, it is also clear that at national level the links between immigration and the other 'threat' are also having an impact on reshaping control structures. Charles Pasqua, France's interior minister, presented his view of his country's internal security situation in April 1993 to the EC Council of Ministers. According to Pasqua, France has been confronted with increasing insecurity. 'Its main components', he said, 'are drug trafficking, illegal immigration and urban violence – which are increasingly linked to each other' (*Platform Fortress Europe?* May 1993: 3). It is to the role of crime in the new Europe that we now turn.

Open Borders and Crime Connections?

Heidensohn writing in 1991 still felt able to opine: 'Crime has not yet achieved the same high profile as a European topic as have for example, wine lakes and butter mountains or the European Monetary System' (Heidensohn 1991: 7). The situation has changed. For many policy-makers, as well as police, crime in Europe is one of the highest matters on political and professional agendas, with the central issue being whether a more open 'Europe' will result in more crime.

In the space available, it is useful to consider three dimensions to this issue: first, general implications and suggestions from criminological research; second, an evaluation of what European crime 'data' including official statistics and commissioned surveys contribute to our understanding; third – and from our point of analysis the most important – the presentation of the 'threat' of cross-border and organized crime.

At the general criminological level, the crime rate in any given country and in a given unit of time (i.e., per annum) depends on the number of offenders as well as on their 'productivity' (i.e. the number of criminal acts they commit per unit of time). Theories explaining criminal motivations may be more helpful in understanding the high or low number of offenders who are active in a given space and time, whereas the opportunity structure (i.e., situational variables) might be more helpful in explaining the 'productivity'. How will these factors be affected by national boundaries or by open borders?

On the one hand, it seems likely that facilitated mobility might increase the mobility of offenders as well. But as Killias (1993) points out, open borders are also likely to induce osmotic pressures which, in turn, could reduce the economic attractiveness of certain 'rich' areas. Of course, if Europe's Union and open borders favour production, exchange and availability of consumer goods, we might expect a general increase of crime as a result of changed opportunity structures (see Felson 1993). The change, however, would probably be general and not concentrated in certain areas: that is, it would probably leave unaffected what one might call cross-border crime.

The criminological work of Field (1990) provides a framework within which one can examine whether factors concerning economic performance relate to recorded crime rates. He concluded that the change in the level of personal consumption has an inverse relationship to the change in the rate of property crime. First, if there is a *rapid* increase in personal expenditure then the increase in property crime is less rapid or tends to fall. However, this is a short-term effect as the overall rate of property crime is unaffected by the surge of growth in consumption. Second, change in the rate of personal crime (for example, crimes of violence) increase as consumption rises. To explain this Field lists three main economic effects on crime: the *opportunity effect* (as the number of available goods increases so does the opportunity for theft and vandalism); the *motivation effect* (a rise in consumption indicates a capacity for lawful acquisition and thus a decrease in property crimes); finally, the *routine effect* (changes in lifestyle are dictated, to a certain degree, by economic factors which provide increased opportunity for certain types of crime). Demographic factors are also noted as an important influence upon crime trends; much criminological research has indicated that young people are more likely to be involved in crime, and consequently the age profile of the population is an important indicator of the potential amount of crime: 'It follows that if we can predict future economic and demographic circumstances, we can forecast future levels of crime' (Field 1990: 54–5).

In the same study Field also examined the relationship between crime change and consumption change in other countries, notably France, Germany and Sweden. The study demonstrated that in these countries there was a relationship, but some of the data presented more complex relational patterns.

While such general insights are illuminating and thought-provoking, recent historical trends in recorded crime in Europe can also be usefully examined. Crime statistics are deceptively simple but cannot be easily interpreted because of, among other things, variations in definitions of criminal categories, reporting and recording rates (for a full specification of the problems in interpretation of criminal statistics see Bottomley and Pease 1986; for cross-national research see van Dijk, Mayhew and Killias 1990). However, it can be said that most European countries have experienced a sharp rise in recorded crime since 1945. Van Dijk's (1993) analysis suggests that while there was some indication of stable or falling overall rates during the 1980s, by the start of the 1990s the official figures show an upward trend.

Linked to the official data, some limited survey work on international comparisons has been published (see van Dijk, Mayhew and Killias, 1990; van Dijk and Mayhew, 1993). There have now been two sweeps of the International Crime Survey. Six EU countries participated (Belgium, France, Germany, the Netherlands, the UK and Spain) in the 1989 Survey, with interesting differences emerging across offence types. For example, Spain had the highest prevalence victimization rate for 'Robbery' (3 per cent), compared with an average European rate of 1 per cent, and France had a rate of 0.4 per cent. In relation to sexual offences, Germany (West Germany, pre-unification) came highest (2.8 per cent) followed by the Netherlands (2.6 per cent), compared with an average of 1.9 per cent. A repeat of the survey in 1992, encompassing more countries, produced broadly similar findings. Benyon *et al.* (1993) point to what they see as two important findings which relate to pan-European police co-operation:

First, the two ex-Communist countries in the survey (Poland and Czechoslovakia) had much higher levels of crime than indicated by police-recorded crime figures. This may be a function of victims' unwillingness to report offences to the police, or to a general rise in crime in east European countries . . . Secondly, a tentative interpretation was offered that property crime rates were partly determined by crime-specific opportunity structures, so that vehicle crime related to the supply of available targets and burglary rates reflected the number of semi-detached and detached houses. (Benyon *et al.*, 1993: 21)

Benyon *et al.* conclude from this that taking these two points together one may suppose that if the EU expands to former Communist states, and as affluence increases, the downside of such economic prosperity may well be increased crime rates. This clearly has resonance with our earlier comments on Simon Field's analysis.

It is our view that both the available official data and the survey data clearly present an interesting but incomplete measure of the crime 'problem'. Much more detailed comparative empirical research is required to allow us a reasoned picture of crime in Europe (see Hebenton and Spencer, 1994).

Re-presenting the 'Threat': Cross-border and Organized Crime

For anyone approaching the literature on police co-operation in Europe, it is clear that a dominant discourse centres on the 'challenge posed' to law enforcement by forecasts in growth of crime. It is not too far fetched to draw (as den Boer 1992 does) tentative analogies between the defence terms of the Cold War situation and the policing terms of the post-Cold War era. Three aspects are important here: first, 'discussion' of moves and counter-moves in the Cold War was always re-invigorated by new rhetoric of emerging 'problems'; second, 'discussion' was essentially 'stimulus-response' based; third, there was little scope (or perceived need) for analysis since there was a consensus that scenarios could not be different.

Our view is that, in addition to the earlier examination of crime in Europe, the construction of a police operational notion of permanent security deficit rests on the very shaky premise of an ever-growing threat within the context of a border-free Europe. On this policing terrain, dominant accounts are concentrated around *cross-border crime* (e.g. auto-theft, where stolen objects are physically transported across frontiers) and the growth in *organized crime* (e.g., drug trafficking and money-laundering) more generally. It is our argument, however, that there is, at present, an empirical poverty in our understanding of both cross-border and organized crime. In addition, the complexities of 'criminal markets' are such that dominant accounts which engender a notion of security deficit organized around powerful and long-standing myths about 'foreigners' and 'aliens' can at best be only partial in their description of the situation. More importantly, the continuing adoption and mobilization of such a conventionalist account results in the restriction of real debates about control of crime.

In developing an economically united Europe, there is in this process, the potential for growth in organized crime since, it is argued, entrepreneurial criminals will seek out weaknesses in the economic, political, social and legal controls in order to capitalize on the process to their own illicit gain. In essence, organi*zing* criminals act as mobile risk takers responding to changes in market opportunities (for the development of this kind of analysis, see van Duyne 1993).

More generally in this vein, the United Nations in a recent economic assessment observed that: 'there are consequences of the trends toward greater ease of communication through-out the world, which relentlessly force a new openness in economic affairs on all countries of the world, with or without formal arrangements. To control the movements of people, funds, or illegal drugs is virtually impossible (United Nations 1991).

This, of course, coincides with the four freedoms of the EU: people, goods, services and capital. Easier travel, business growth, reduced border delays, international professional recognition, financial services, broader consumerism, free competition, and standardized and enhanced telcommunica-tions will not only enrich the economic vitality of the Union, but will, it is argued, facilitate cross-border crime and organized crime.

Discussion of this threat is contextualized more broadly, particularly by US analysts (see Carter 1992; Lee 1992). Carter, writing about the period until 1991, for example, argues that at the *policy level* little attention had actually been directed towards organized crime as it related to the EC, in contra-distinction to terrorist groups. The nature of international crime is evolving according to these analysts; it is in a transformation. There is a 'functional interdependence that increasingly links the traditionally separate areas of criminality. Common crime (violence and theft), political crime, organized and economic crime are all increasingly drawn into the [transitional] process. Even some forms of petty crime (e.g. drug-related) appear to be, wittingly or not, more dependent on and linked to organized crime' (Savona 1990). Moreover, organized crime and white-collar crime 'must be considered on a continuum which includes illegal, and does not exclude legal, activities' (Savona 1990). For these analysts:

> transnational activities of organized crime include, inter alia, illicit drug trafficking; traffic in people for the purposes of sexual enslavement or economic exploitation and, in recent years, illegal adoption of children; large scale counterfeiting; illicit currency manipulation, illegal transfer of capital and of unlawfully acquired assets, fraudulent bankruptcy and large scale maritime insurance fraud; smuggling, and certain forms of piracy. The near future may add substantial additions to this list, as new fashions emerge and as technological advances continue. (United Nations 1990)

Concern for non-traditional forms of crime was also recently expressed in a report by a special United Nations Congress. The report noted:

> An alarming increase in transnational criminal activities has taken place in recent decades. This new international dimension of crime has emerged, to a considerable extent, as the reflection and outcome of modern advances in electronic and transportation technologies, which have

brought about the development of instant communication over great distances, as well as the massive displacement of goods and persons. Thus, licit international trade and commerce and world-wide travel have been paralleled by the rapid growth of an international criminality that utilizes the same means of transport and communication. (United Nations 1990)

Carter (1992) argues that this is consistent with the logic presented earlier concerning changes in the politico-economic character of the EU.

However, grounding of such an account must begin, we would argue, by recognizing that there is very little hard data available about the numbers of cross-border crimes in Europe, or about their economic cost to states or the EU as a whole. As Levi (1993) points out, there are currently no specific research studies which demonstrate the proportion of crimes across the board which possess a cross-border dimension, even as regards recorded, still less unrecorded, crime. Taking the example of car theft, Gregory (1992) notes a series of problems, and more specifically the inadequacy of available data. Car theft is only partly identified in annual Home Office crime statistics which show thefts of motor vehicles. It includes the theft of motor cars, motor cycles and heavy goods vehicles. However, it does not include the theft of contractors plant in the same category, although it is estimated that annually the construction industry loses plant worth £4 million. Neither does it include the theft of vehicle parts which is included in the category of theft from motor vehicles. Both of these are important when considering the subject of cross-border crime. Whilst statistics of the total UK crime in this area are available, the data for cross-border crime are much less easy to calculate. The PNC2 records all vehicles stolen in England and Wales. However, there are currently no computer codes to identify locations abroad. Gregory is of the view that new applications of PNC2 will still not go far enough to allow easy identification of the size of cross-border car theft. In relation to car theft, therefore, there is no easily obtainable evidence. There are, however, small samples data available from three sources: the Metropolitan Police Autocrime Unit at the port of Dover; Interpol; and survey commissioned data. Gregory concludes: 'Plenty of anecdotal evidence exists to show that the international traffic in stolen vehicles, plant and vehicle parts is a thriving business. However, there is currently very little statistical evidence available to measure the size of the problem. What little there is does not give a clear and reliable picture because it is incomplete' (Gregory 1992).

Levi (1993) confirms this picture. He points out that during 1991, the Metropolitan Police Stolen Vehicles Squad made 275 arrests and recovered 790 vehicles worth £10 million. Of the vehicles recovered, 114 were overseas and the number of arrests involving these cross-border car thefts was around 50. This ratio 'of one in seven vehicles recovered being a cross-border theft cannot reasonably be extrapolated to whatever proportion of the 582 000 cars taken without authority in England and Wales are never recovered, and the proportion found in the EC is unknown' (Levi 1993: 70). However, Levi points to a survey by the Association of British Insurers and their European equivalents conducted in 1990 which revealed that in the eight European countries surveyed, out of 130 million vehicles reported stolen in the study period, 100 000 (to the value of £1000 million) had disappeared illegally out of the country. But in answer to the question, 'Has the cross-border vehicles crime problem been getting worse?', Levi suggests that information overall is not sufficiently reliable to make deductions.

Other areas of cross-border crime illustrate similar problems: for example, art and antiques theft. Home Office statistics are inadequate and police are currently incapable of producing statistics to demonstrate the size of cross-border theft. Current statistics show that no more than 5–10 per cent of all stolen art and antiques are recovered. The other 90 per cent moves around the world with apparent ease. Often those items that have been recovered have travelled across international borders before they are finally recovered. It is argued by many that the best estimates of stolen art and antiques come from the commercial world. Here, in 1990 it was estimated that a total of 60 000 works of art, each worth over £5000, were stolen throughout the EU. This is thought to represent some 10 per cent of world-wide art theft. It has been suggested that the reporting rate for art theft can be as low as 15 per cent (Gregory 1992).

Again, Levi commenting on this draws similar conclusions, and highlights in the context of England and Wales:

> serious problems of statistical collation and of communication between divisional officers attending burglaries and the specialist squads. The art theft dockets provided by the police are four pages long . . . and though easy to fill out, are infrequently used by local officers. Relatively little is known about the art thieves themselves, and there is some controversy about the networks of dealers that give false provenance to what are in fact stolen art and antiques. (Levi 1993: 71)

Of course there are individual forms of crime which allow for cross-border dimensions to be assessed in some form and clearly drug trafficking is such an exception. Drug trafficking is an extremely interesting example since it can be seen as the case par excellence of the dominant account of the 'threat'. In its Preamble, the European Parliament's Committee of Enquiry into drug trafficking presented the 'threat' in the following way: 'The power of the criminal organizations which control the drugs traffic is growing at an alarming rate. It is having increasingly serious effects on society and on the political institutions of the Member States. It is undermining the foundations of the legitimate economy and threatening the stability of the States of the Community' (European Parliament 1992: 4). Clearly, the considerable threat posed requires consideration; however, much of what passes for such consideration often lacks any substantial empirical basis. Benyon *et al.* talk of the ill-informed basis of much of the discussion and say that such 'rhetoric can be seen in statements on the same theme (drug trafficking) by the Chair of the Police Federation of England and Wales' (Benyon *et al.*, 1993: 25). Similarly, more recent statements by NCIS in its 'Threat Assessment' (see NCIS 1993) also appear to lack detailed empirical underpinning.

In relation to estimating the scale or level of drugs trafficking in Europe, the only way of doing this is to survey the data on seizures and probable origins. Both Interpol and the United Nations Drug Control Programme in Vienna prepare detailed reports and analysis on such seizures. Seizures, of course, provide an indication of illicit drug movements but, by their very nature, they cannot be interpreted to give an absolute quantifiable level of drug trafficking. One might surmise that either volumes of traffic had increased, or that enforcement agencies had had more success with their interception. In order to calculate the likely amounts of, for example, heroin now used in Europe, other indicators are necessary. They may include estimates of opium/heroin production and estimates of numbers of users.

On this matter, Benyon *et al.* note:

> The two UK customs officers' unions, the National Union of Civil and Public Servants (NUCPS) and the Civil and Public Services Association (CPSA) have stated, quite simply, that 'There is no sure way of knowing what quantities of drugs are imported into this country' . . . similarly the House of Commons Home Affairs Committee noted that 'Quantifying the extent of an illicit activity such as drugs trafficking is notoriously difficult.' (Benyon *et al.*, 1993: 27)

Of course, some indication is available from seizure data. Benyon *et al.* (1993) cite UK Customs data in the period 1987–90: heroin seizures rose steadily from 190 kilos in 1987 to almost 600 kilos in 1990. Similarly, with cocaine there was an increase from 362 to 561 kilos in 1990. Interpol data for seizures in Europe for the same period suggests increases for heroin from 3,700 kilos to over 6000 kilos in 1990, and cocaine from around 2500 kilos in 1987 to over 13 000 kilos in 1990 (European Parliament 1992). These figures point in the same direction, although they may reflect either increased and more effective customs work or a real rise in trafficking, or indeed both.

In spite of the foregoing, it is clear that what one may call the dominant account of an integrated Europe, without internal border controls enhancing crime and drug trafficking, has over recent years held and helped to construct the response to 'understanding' crime in Europe. In the UK, the worries of politicians and senior police officials are now well documented. Some examples will suffice.

Douglas Hurd, then UK Home Secretary in his statement to the House of Commons Select Committee on European Legislation accused EC Commissioners 'of seriously underestimating the value of internal frontiers in the fight against terrorists, drug smugglers and other criminals in their determination to bring forward plans to abolish frontier controls in 1992' (*The Guardian*, 20 February 1989). Also in 1989, the House of Lords European Select Committee Report on 1992 and border controls summarized the concerns in the following way: 'There is a genuine fear that abolition of border control of people will lead to an enormous increase in drug smuggling, organized crime, terrorist attacks and to the uncontrolled movement of immigrants' (House of Lords 1989: 6).

Representatives of the UK police services in their evidence to the 1990 House of Commons Home Affairs Committee inquiry into Police Co-operation in Europe, stated: 'It is reasonable to assume that the relaxation of frontier controls will enable criminals and fugitives to move more freely throughout Europe than has previously been the case and displacement of crime may acquire an international dimension' (House of Commons 1990b: 18).

Similarly, *The Independent* (4 April 1991) under the headline 'Open frontiers could boost crime', notes:

The abolition of frontier controls in the European Community . . . could encourage international crime, senior police officers were warned. Peter Lloyd, the Home Office minister, said police needed to respond to the changes, some of which were already creating law enforcement problems. Mr Lloyd told the European Regional Conference of Interpol in London: 'The developments . . . are very welcome. But we must recognize that they also have the potential to encourage the growth of international crime, much of it targeted on Europe.'

Again, Chief Constable Roger Birch develops the theme in a Home Office article:

> it is my belief, shared by many European colleagues, that there are many good class criminals who will be encouraged to expand their activities across internal boundaries in the belief that 1st January 1992 will produce a sudden relaxation in police and customs activity. I accept that the perception may be more significant than the reality, but nevertheless, there is a danger that the criminal will feel less restricted and will act accordingly. (Birch 1992: 4)

One can distinguish in all of this what den Boer (1992) calls a 'reiterative pattern', with senior civil servants, government ministers and senior police officers drawing on what can only be seen as a stereotypical analysis of the consequences of removal of border controls. She continues: 'When the arguments are selected and presented . . . without a detailed substantiation of the premises underlying the assumptions, they tend to be fairly consistent. However, a closer inspection of the actual statistics and analyses would lead to the establishment of a number of frictions or contradictions' (den Boer 1992: 19). They become, in other words, rhetorical statements without a substantiating context. For Dutch and German examples of these 'reiterative patterns' see Grosheide (1993) and Wilkitzki (1991).

Of course, the insistence of the UK government, Customs officials and police that the power to intercept transshipments of goods and movements of persons at borders is a really significant factor in controlling the international drugs trade is problematic. Between 1979 and 1989, it is estimated that annual expenditure (in real terms) on drug enforcement activity by HM Customs and the police rose by 38 per cent and 74 per cent respectively (Sutton and Maynard 1994). The cost to the taxpayer of drug enforcement activity reached more than £335 million in the financial year 1992/3, 66 per cent of total government expenditure on drug policy (Standing Conference on Drug Abuse, or SCODA 1992). Despite such increases in expenditure, little is known about how such enforcement activity affects drug markets, and as a result, the degree of effectiveness of such enforcement activity by Customs and police is as yet undecided.

In one of the very few econometric studies to date, Sutton and Maynard (1994) examined the impact of Customs and police on the illicit heroin market for the period 1979 to 1990. Their study considered a range of output measures, such as the number and weight of seizures, interception rates, the number of people dealt with by the police, Customs and the courts for offences and the risks imposed by law enforcement agencies on drug smugglers, dealers and users. As mentioned above, while there have been large increases in expenditure in real terms, Sutton and Maynard conclude on the basis of their analysis that trends in law enforcement output have not followed the same pattern.

The estimated Customs heroin interception rate (the proportion of the total amount of heroin shipped to the UK which is seized by Customs) rose for most of the 1980s, but fell between 1985 and 1988 at the time of the largest increases in expenditure. Thus, for example, while the estimated quantity of heroin shipped to the UK was around 5372.7 kilos (see Sutton and Maynard 1992 for details of assumptions made in the calculations), Customs seized 211.4 kilos, or under 4 per cent. Measures of the outcome of enforcement activity by the police show a consistent trend over the 1980s. Improvements in impact were recorded over the period 1979–85, but the heroin interception rate and the risks their activity imposed on heroin dealers and users have fallen consistently since 1985. Thus, for example, in relation to interception rates, while the estimated quantity of heroin reaching the distribution level of the market in 1988 was 5719.3 kilos, the police seized some 24.3 kilos, or a rate of 0.42 per cent; by 1990 the interception rate had dropped to 0.35 per cent. Of course, as the authors point out, some of these changes may be indicators of switches in enforcement focus between different drug markets. It seems that changes in the success of Customs intervention in the heroin market were more marked than they were in other markets, such as those for cocaine and cannabis. As the weight of heroin seized by the police declined over the period 1987 to 1990, increased amounts of cocaine, cannabis and amphetamines were intercepted. Nevertheless, the disruption of domestic drug markets through the arrest and conviction of smugglers, dealers and users by the police certainly declined in the period from 1985 to 1990.

Sutton and Maynard also combine the cost and output information to provide an illuminating cost-effectiveness index of enforcement activity. Figures 6.1 and 6.2 indicate how the cost-effectiveness of enforcement activity for Customs and police changed over the 1980s relative to 1979. The cost-effectiveness indices are given by the ratio of expenditure to a measure of output. Since no estimates are available of the level of drug enforcement expenditure devoted to the heroin market, it is not possible to calculate the cost per unit of output. Trends in cost-effectiveness are indicated by changes in cost-effectiveness indices from the base year 1979.

Since cost effectiveness indices are calculated as the level of expenditure divided by the level of output, increases represent deteriorations in cost-effectiveness and decreases represent improvements in cost-effectiveness.

Between 1985 and 1988 there was a large deterioration in the cost-effectiveness of Customs activity, indicated by the rising cost-effectiveness indices for both the interception rate and the risks faced by smugglers, but in 1989 this trend was

Figure 6.1   *Trends in Cost-effectiveness of Customs Drug Enforcement Activity, 1979–89 (1979 = 100)*

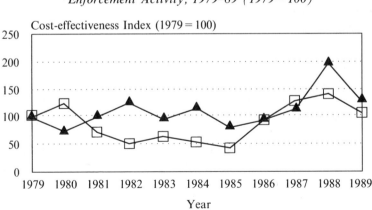

Source: Sutton and Maynard (1994), p. 41.

Figure 6.2 *Trends in Cost-effectiveness of Police Drug*
Enforcement Activity, 1979–90 (1979 = 100)

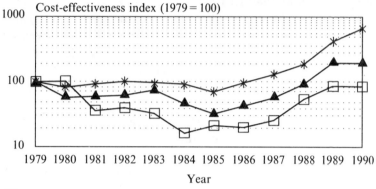

☐ Interception Rate   ▲ Risks faced by dealers   ✳ Risks faced by user:

Source: Sutton and Maynard (1994), p. 43.

reversed. For the police, trends in indices are similar, with the
first half of the decade being a time of cost-effectiveness
improvements followed by a decline from 1985.

Due to the limitations of available data, Sutton and
Maynard point out that the study's results should be seen as
indicative rather than authoritative and, as a consequence of
the dire paucity of data, they conclude that 'public accountability for the £335 million expended on drug enforcement
activity is quite limited' (Sutton and Maynard 1994: 2).

A further challenge to the insistence of the efficacy of the
British approach to control has also been made in Europe,
particularly by the (then) West German minister of the
interior, Wolfgang Schauble, in 1989 (cited in Kattau 1990:
6). Two German studies and one Swiss study are worth noting
in relation to this. Kattau's (1990) survey of crossings over the
border of the Federal Republic in the period 1977–88 suggests
that 'only' about 100 000 of the 70 million annual crossings
resulted in police action, and that 'only' 14 per cent of these
100 000 resulted in arrest. About 33 per cent of these arrests
(4700 cases) involved drug- related offences. Kattau concludes: 'The number of arrests and the quantities confiscated
. . . indicates that major-scale drug or arms trafficking is not

detected at border controls' (Kattau 1990: 5). Similarly, Kuhne (1993) analysed border statistics in Germany between 1980 and 1989 and suggests an arrest rate of less than 3 per cent per 100 000 crossings. Finally, Killias (1993), commenting on Switzerland, states:

> over the last few years, there were, approximately 400,000 offences registered by the police at federal level. According to the same sources, roughly 20 percent of the offenders known to the police have no legal residence in Switzerland. If we assume that these persons should theoretically have been prevented from crossing the border, the border control officers would have needed to stop maybe 100,000 potential offenders at the border. This figure is to be contrasted with the 75 million legal and unproblematic passages of the border . . . not surprisingly, drug offences cleared at the Swiss border control posts represent about four percent of all cases of drug trafficking. (Killias 1993: 8)

The issue of border controls and drug trafficking has been an important part of the dominant account. However, it is clear that there is little evidence to support the case. Professional drug entrepreneurs have never been so impressed by border controls as to be frightened out of business. Given a certain market demand, stricter border controls have usually only served to increase consumer prices which meant a higher net profit per unit for the criminal. This was the outcome of the USA's 'war on drugs' after the intensified efforts of the 1980s (see Martin and Romano 1992). Of course, this applies to Europe too. For traffickers, the most dangerous points of entry into the European market have always been the sea- and airports (the outer borders). The internal borders have always been slack and carried a huge volume of traffic, estimated in 1990 to be 320 million travellers through the major European airports alone (Interpol General Secretariat, February 1993).

We would argue, alongside Dorn *et al.* (1992) and van Duyne (1993), that it is more important to see the drug market as an open market, irregular and flexible, and to examine the prospects of the different drug market segments. The developments in these markets do not appear to be primarily determined by the unification of the EU but by market demand and profit (van Duyne 1993). It is comparable with any other open irregular market, as a former Commissioner of New York remarked: 'Organization in the drug business is largely spontaneous, with anybody free to enter it at any level if he has the money, the supplier and the ability to escape arrest or robbery' (Block and Chambliss 1981: 57). Any future is difficult to predict, but the present EU market terrain may lead to two parallel developments.

First, most market extensions, such as the synthetic drug ('Ecstasy', MDMA) market, are characterized by a rapid influx of small and medium sized enterprises trying their luck by meeting the market demand (van Duyne 1993). The potential of such a market to attract is not local or national in its effects. The data of the national drug bureaux in Germany, the Netherlands and Interpol indicate an increase in multinational participation. Given the general attraction of the rich countries of the Union for immigrants and political or economic refugees this should not be surprising. A second, parallel development is the emergence of a wholesale drug trade, particularly specialized in importation and transit, as is the case with, for example, the Dutch wholesale marijuana traffickers. Though wholesale trafficking organizations are certainly not considered as 'open' co-operatives, they are in constant need of cross-border assistance and co-operation. There is always a fluid and flexible network of connections. Over a longer time span these networks may develop into well established trading communities, as indicated in van Duyne (1993). One can argue that such criminal trading communities develop along economic trading lines which may be considered economic crime regions (connected regions of crime trade which are characterized by a stable personnel and economic cohesion).

Of course the changing landscape of Central Europe and the Commonwealth of Independent States is also reconfiguring markets. Central Eastern Europe is, according to Carter (1992), significant in having under-gone economic evolution and opportunity within a reactive economic environment. This reactive environment is, it is claimed, fertile for the growth of organized crime. More generally, it is predicted that as countries move from a centrally planned to a market economy there will be increasing crime rates (Castle-Kanerova 1992).

In Central or Eastern European countries the development of such organized crime in the first instance is more likely to be linked with the economic demands for hard currency. For many of these countries currency acquisition is a fundamental requirement for economic growth and development; hard currency provides the means with which to purchase raw materials, industrial technology and know-how. For citizens, hard currency provides access to a range of consumer goods which are otherwise unavailable. The attractions for organized crime to deal in hard currency are its profitability and potential to access the state organization through bribery and corruption, for hard currency is a powerful determinant of status and power acquisition. The acquisition of power and status may, in the long run, provide the opportunity for organized crime to legitimate certain of its activities, thus providing a better screen to the continuation of its illegal activities.

Hard currency also provides the opportunity to acquire arms and weapons which have been freely available in the shadow economy. The availability of weapons, from hand-guns upwards, has developed due to the lack of controls to administer the restructuring of army and state security apparatus. For example, many Russian soldiers awaiting their return to an uncertain future in the Commonwealth of Independent States have exploited the lax arrangements and sold arms. The restructuring of state security services has provided some former security officers with the opportunity to sell arms on the shadow markets (*The Guardian*, 20 July 1992). The purchasing of weapons in the shadow economy serves two different markets: the criminal market which requires weapons in the execution of crime, and the self-protection market which is concerned with individual protection against crime.

In relation to the former USSR, Lee (1992) presents several factors that are acting on the illicit drugs market. First, he considers the policies to increase rouble convertibility. If

international drug traffickers can sell drugs to Soviet customers in exchange for dollars, francs or marks, the traffickers
will have much greater incentive to penetrate the market.
Second, the privatization of economic activity is allowing,
for example, profit-sharing co-operatives the opportunity to
act as legal cover for laundering of drug money. Third, rapid
expansion in trade and economic ties is allowing greater
penetration of Western organized crime 'know-how'.

In Central and Eastern Europe, the drugs most commonly
used are heroin and hashish (Joutsen 1993). The primary
source is the Central Asian republics, although low-grade
heroin is also made from home-grown poppies in other
areas. Some indication of the size of the market is given by
official statistics, according to which the (former) USSR had
some 120 000 addicts in 1989 or 42 per 100 000 head of
population; the true number is undoubtedly higher. Poland
is estimated to have between 20 000 and 40 000 addicts
(Moskalewicz and Swiatliewicz, 1992). Currently, home-
grown heroin is the preferred drug in Poland and in some of
the Baltic republics (see Maertens, Sailas and Joutsen, 1992).
Following Dorn *et al.* (1992) it could be said that the market
in these countries is still in an early stage of development.

This chapter has set out an account of the two main
justificatory fields for enhanced police co-operation in the
new Europe: immigration and crime. In the following related
chapter the important and, as we see it, transformative role of
information exchange in the construction of the new terrain of
European police work forms the final dimension for examination. Several broad conclusions which inter-relate the themes
of this and the following chapter are drawn at the end of
Chapter 7.

7

Europe: A New Police Terrain (2) Informatization: Police, Technology and Data Protection

Information throughout the Western world has come to be seen as a resource, and the tool which has facilitated this is the computer. Computerized communication, information storage and exchange have come to be seen as being at the heart of counter-measures against the 'security deficit' in the new Europe. Although usually presented in the context of a resource-led measure to increase efficiency and deal with increased crime levels, it is clear that police computerization and the collection, storage and use of personal information has its own, separate trajectory. Our view is that understanding the shape of this 'informatization' of police work can aid in predicting the emergent key practice of policing the new Europe.

The importance of rapidly communicated, secure accessible information to the goals of European policing is, it can be agreed likely to structure further harmonization and integration of such systems, and perhaps their supranational centralization; a tendency that is already apparent within individual member states of the EU, with the creation, in the UK, of the NCIS as an interesting case-study. Other examples in the British context include the recent updating of the PNC (PNC2) and the rationalizing of police records (see Hebenton and Thomas 1993). Several authors have examined the historical development of the inexorable rise in proactive information-centred policing in the UK (see, e.g., Bunyan 1976; D. Campbell and Connor 1986), and they illustrate how, in the process, the new technology reconstructs both the aims of policing and the 'target' groups of policework. Cannings (1990: 165–97) reviews the development of the information and intelligence function in British policing in the context of '1992', and shows how the formation of specialist units such as, for example, the NDIU or the FIU were predicated on an ideal of the centrality of information and more specifically, 'intelligence' to the police.

Of course, as Robertson (1992) points out, to the police 'intelligence' often means nothing more than information produced by a covert source, such sources being either the use of covert technical equipment in the form of visual or aural surveillance, or covert human sources in the form of informers or under-cover officers. Furthermore, he notes the important fact that the police use of intelligence is usually tactical, the aim being to use information to assist a particular investigation. In our opinion, while this tactical use remains, informatization is able to allow the development of long-term strategic information as a Europeanized resource.

In the past, domestic policing has most often been seen as being concerned with the arrest and prosecution of offenders and with providing a service which can respond to immediate demands from the public. If each crime is treated in a compartmentalized way then information becomes relevant only if it aids the investigation of a specific incident. Again, in the past, the operational or tactical focus of the effort to collect information has been reinforced by the under-capacity to analyse (see Chatterton and Rogers 1988 for a good illustration, and more generally Tremblay and Rochon 1991). 'Knowledge of crime' studies have examined whether individual officers were more knowledgeable about aggregate crime patterns than ordinary citizens (e.g., Feild and Bienen 1980). The answer was no. A meaningful interpretation of this can be provided by simply examining what police in general mean by 'being knowledgeable about crime matters'. It is quite clear, for instance, that in the past they did not consider 'crime trends' as providing 'real knowledge'. Real knowledge meant: (a) knowing about individual offenders and their 'significant others' and being able to sort through 'gossip'; (b) being able to obtain information directly either through interrogation and informants or indirectly through exchange with other officers; (c) being skilled in using this information so as to accuse or neutralize targets.

Informatization is altering the previous tactical and under-analysed context of information. The demand for sophisticated information and communication links is under-going far-reaching changes brought about by the pace of technological progress, and the way in which users can see their interests reconfigured around information-based policework. Robertson (1992) fails to recognize this when, in commenting on police 'intelligence', he suggests that:

> The identification of patterns may be limited to those which are part of an investigation in progress rather than to a more general and long-term aim such as reducing the ability of terrorists to carry out attacks or reducing the capacity of drug traffickers to move money and supplies. The fact that police officers are law officers not only restricts their methods to those which are lawful but also focuses attention on the process of arrest and prosecution rather than upon goals such as altering the environment within which criminals operate. (Robertson 1992: 2)

However, Saltmarsh (1993) illustrates the new tactical context when, from the UK's NCIS perspective, he notes:

> I am becoming increasingly attracted to what has been described as 'preventive operations' and not waiting for the full crime to occur. Backed by a fully operational and aggressive intelligence agency the goal of a covert preventive operation is either to prevent the crime occurring at all, or to prevent harm if it does. By using *every* lawful means at our disposal we often clandestinely seek to limit, inhibit or block the capacity to carry out criminal enterprise operations successfully. The emphasis is on suspect weakening and/or target hardening. Disruption and subversion with arrest this time around not being the necessary goal. (Saltmarsh 1993: 7, emphasis author's own)

Even sharper focus can be seen in the words of the Northern Ireland contibutor to the NCIS 'Organized Crime' Conference (held at the Police Staff College, Bramshill, in May 1993). He states, in the context of dealing with organized crime financing terrorism, that:

> The complexities of business, commerce and finance in the nineties mean that traditional investigation and prosecution procedures are unlikely, on their own, to be the most effective means of curtailing . . . major criminals or dismantling organized crime structures . . . Dissemination and professional exploitation of structured and high-grade intelligence gathering, collation, evaluation and analysis is critical. (NCIS 1993: 55).

European Communications and Information Networks

At national level, police agencies are enhancing facilities. In the UK, for example, the Police National Network now allows a greatly enhanced communicative facility between forces and provides potential for greater interface with NCIS. Police agencies from within the EU can communicate bilaterally through electronic means such as FAX and TELEX. The TREVI Secure Fax Network is illustrative of this development.

Computerized data bases have proliferated, and the European police terrain now is criss-crossed by exchange of information networks. Given their significance, it is worth describing three in some detail, namely Interpol's networks, Schengen and the EIS.

Interpol's networks

Interpol's information exchange can be seen as serving some 174 countries (as of 1993), with over one million messages transmitted through the network in 1992. Currently, about 80 per cent of the telecommunications flow is sent by or to the 44 countries in Interpol's European section and nearly 50 per cent of Interpol's work relates to Europe (see Benyon *et al.*

1993: 222). The central function of Interpol's Communication Network is to pass on information and requests for action in the form of international notices, of which there are five types (as noted in Chapter 3). The notices contain identification data as well as information on other suspected offences, photographs and fingerprints. In addition, crime modus operandi sheets are also transmitted.

The Interpol Criminal Information System data base was created to improve methods of storing and retrieving information on crimes and criminals emanating from the NCBs that form the Interpol network. The data base currently comprises files containing details of names, drug seizures, cases, counterfeit currency and property (see also Chapter 3). Some 60 per cent of messages relates to drugs. Property includes art works that have been stolen, lost or recovered. The counterfeit currency database is the largest in the world.

To enhance the Criminal Information System, an Electronic Archive System became operational in October 1989. In the past, requests for information involved manual retrieval of files. All Interpol criminal record files are now preserved electronically, on optical disks. Within 15 seconds, staff can now access the file, including fingerprints on screen, compared with 7 days under the manual system. Documents are indexed by the operators on microcomputers and the index is then held on a computer linked to a 'juke-box' capable of holding 80 optical disks online and also linked to the Criminal Information System. Together the Criminal Information System and the optical disks provide a formidable means of storing and accessing large amounts of data.

Interpol's Message Response Branch, established in 1989, enables criminal information to be recorded and processed and for requests from NCBs to be responded to using the Automatic Message Switching System (AMSS). It currently handles over one million messages per annum. With an Automated Search Facility that came online in 1992, NCBs can now search, with some exceptions, the central Criminal Information System data base.

On Interpol's informatized status, Benyon *et al.* conclude that these systems 'provide Interpol with one of the most sophisticated automated search and image transmission systems in the world. It enables rapid, reliable and secure exchange of information. NCBs will have access to an enormous store of data . . . the idea that Interpol is just a 'letter-box' is clearly out of date.' (Benyon *et al.* 1993: 226). In addition, Cameron-Waller (1993) emphasizes a newly developed analytical capacity, the Analytical Criminal Intelligence Unit (ACIU). He states in unequivocal terms the fact that Interpol intends to increase its activities in the area of crime intelligence as opposed to simply acting as a clearing house for information, and points to the fact that 'the development and dissemination of crime intelligence demonstrate[s] the determination of Interpol to stay in the forefront of improving international police co-operation' (Cameron-Waller 1993: 16).

The Schengen Information System

As described in earlier chapters, Schengen is, alongside Interpol, TREVI and Europol, one of the four major structures relevant to the EU and police co-operation. We now move on to examine its 'information system', together with its data protection provisions. The broader issues of privacy, protecting personal data and accountability of the system will be dealt with in our final chapter.

Described by Schutte as the 'most spectacular novelty' (Schutte 1991: 559), in the Schengen Convention and by O'Keeffe as 'one of the most innovative features' (O'Keeffe 1992: 204), the SIS is a joint computerized information system to be set up and maintained to enable national authorities to access reports on people and objects for the purpose of border checks and police inquiries. SIS is not a system linking existing police information data bases or computer systems, but a separate international register. Structurally, therefore, SIS consists of a central data bank and materially identical national data files, connected to the central information system. Article 93 of the Convention sets out the purpose of the SIS as being to maintain public order and security and for use in connection with the movement of persons. As O'Keeffe (1992) insightfully points out, the Convention's provision is that it mixes detailed rules as to the functioning of the SIS with prescriptive rules on immigration and asylum. This nexus demonstrates the key position of the SIS within the Schengen framework. Once SIS has been installed, at all places where external border controls are to take place there should be terminals connected with SIS.

The Convention details the six categories of data file to be entered on SIS, as set out below.

1. Data relating to persons who are wanted for arrest for extradition purposes. Such entries into the system are to be accepted as requests for provisional arrest as intended in applicable extradition Treaties, although the *Convention* requires the state making an entry to submit the necessary additional information supporting the request for provisional arrest to the other countries through traditional channels (Article 95).

2. Data relating to aliens, reported for purposes of refusing their entry into the territory of the Parties to the *Convention*. If such an alien is found within that territory he or she has in principle to be removed (Article 96).

3. Data relating to persons whose whereabouts are to be reported. This may concern missing persons who are to be served with judicial writs (Article 97).

4. Data relating to witnesses/ suspects summoned to appear before a court in criminal proceedings (Article 98).

5. Data relating to persons who are to be kept under discreet (covert) surveillance or specifically checked, in order to get information about their movements or behaviour (Article 99).

6. Data relating to objects sought, for the purpose of seizure (Article 100).

An SIS information report by the police on an individual is to include only:

- name
- identifying physical feature
- date and place of birth
- sex
- nationality
- whether violent

- whether armed
- reason for the report
- action to be taken

In general, access to SIS is reserved for authorities responsible for: (a) border checks; and (b) other police and customs
checks carried out within the member state, and the co-
ordination of such checks. In terms of structural responsibilities, national SIS is to be over-seen by a national central
authority to be established by the member state concerned.
The central SIS, located in Strasbourg and for which France
has responsibility, will over-see and monitor input, and will be
the only part of the system with information held from all
Schengen countries. This central component of SIS (referred
to in the Convention as the TSF) will be supervised by a Joint
Supervisory Authority comprised of representatives of the
national supervisory bodies. It has two tasks: to check that
the Convention provisions with respect to central SIS are
properly implemented; and to examine and mediate on
problems arising from the application of SIS.

While the above structure may appear clear-cut, the
proposed operation is far from simple to interpret. It is to
these matters that we now turn.

The sole rationale for the Schengen process is to strengthen
collaboration between member states. The mutual exchange of
personal data forms an integral part of this process and as
such the Convention, in addition to specifically establishing a
joint information system (SIS) also provides for possibilities of
mutual exchange. In what follows, we distinguish between
arrangements that the Convention sets out for the operation
of SIS and exchange of personal data outside SIS.

Operation of SIS according to the Convention. The SIS
originally dealt with by the Police and Security Working
Group (Working Group 1) is now handled by a separate
Steering Committee, which reports directly to the *Central
Negotiating Group*. National SIS in each country are net-
worked to the central SIS (C-SIS) in Strasbourg. The Strasbourg C-SIS began work in 1990, with an initial target date of

1 March 1993. According to Cruz (1993), C-SIS has reached operational status amongst the five original signatories, but technical problems remain, for instance in harmonization of regulations on surnames. *Statewatch* (2, 5, 1992) reports that two regions of the Netherlands, Rotterdam and Arnhem, used the test version of SIS in October 1992.

Articles 102–18 set out provisions for the protection of personal data and security of data on SIS. One of the initial and most important points to note in this regard is that the Convention provides that in so far as it does not lay down *specific* provisions, then the legislation of the member state shall apply to the data included in the national SIS. In an attempt to deal with disparity of national legislation, the Convention states that prior to it coming into force, member states must achieve a level of personal data protection at least equal to that resulting from the principles of the 1981 Council of Europe *Convention for the Protection of Individuals with regard to Automatic Processing of Personal Data*, and the Committee of Ministers of the Council of Europe Recommendation (87) 15 *Regulating the Use of Personal Data in the Police Sector*. While these principles set the 'default' values, a number of detailed provisions are set out in the Convention, and we now proceed to describe and comment on these.

First, the use of personal data. Here, the concept of purpose limitation applies. As a general rule of data protection it means that information may be used only for the purpose for which it was gathered. The Convention states that data recorded in SIS may be used only for the purposes laid down for each type of report. This is clearly an important principle, however, it is not clear whether this notion of 'purpose' refers to purpose as indicated in an individual's data record under 'reason for report' (e.g., criminal prosecution) or to the more general six categories of data file. Scheller (1992: 167) concludes from her analysis of of the relevant provision (Article 102) that it refers to the latter. If this is the case then its effectiveness as a safeguard is severely limited. States can derogate from the 'purpose limitation' principle where it can be justified 'by the need to prevent an imminent serious threat to public order and safety, for serious reasons of State security or for the purposes of preventing a serious offence' (Article

102). On this, O'Keeffe comments that 'derogation . . . could render guarantees about the use of data nugatory' (O'Keeffe 1992: 207).

The Convention also sets out who may have direct access to data on SIS. While authorities responsible for border checks and other police and customs checks are included, this is only a very general indication which has to be supplemented by national lists to be drawn up by member states. In addition, Verhey points out that authorities responsible for the implementation of aliens regulations have direct access in accordance with Article 96 (Verhey 1991: 124).

Second, we have the issue of data subject access to SIS. In principle, subjects are accorded the right of access (Article 109). Importantly, the Convention clearly indicates that such access can only be exercised in accordance with the law of the member state in which the right is invoked. Thus any person is at liberty to determine to which state he or she will address his or her access request. The principle of right of access is, however, constrained, and not only by the national law. The Convention provides that prior to agreement on access, the *reporting* state should be given the opportunity to contest the matter. Quite how this process of legal challenge to right of access would work is left unstated, as is any analysis of the problem of how a difference of view between *requested* and *reporting* states would be resolved. In addition, access can be refused if it undermines the execution of the legal task relating to the SIS report, or in order to protect the rights and freedoms of others, or in relation to the task of discreet (covert) surveillance.

It is possible for any person to have factually inaccurate data relating to him corrected or have legally inaccurate data deleted. Verhey (1991: 125) sees as highly significant the provision which allows a person to bring an action to correct, delete or provide data or obtain compensation before the courts or the competent national legal authority. Final decisions taken are binding. Thus, for example if a German court finds an SIS report recorded at the behest of the French authorities to be unlawfully stored, they would have to delete the report from SIS. However, there is no direct legal remedy for the data subject offered by the Convention at either the national or supranational level.

Third, we come to the supply of personal data from SIS. While the Convention provides that national SIS reports may not be copied to other national data files, it is left unclear whether this excludes supply of personal data to third parties where the data being stored is not specifically in a personal data file. Furthermore, because it is left unstated, can it be presumed that national domestic law would govern such supply of data originating from SIS ?

Finally, we reach the issue of reporting on SIS. As we have set out previously, there are six general categories of data file on SIS. However, the category dealing with reporting for the purpose of discreet (covert) surveillance is worthy of more detailed examination (Article 99). According to O'Keeffe it allows reporting on SIS for aims which 'are both vague and arguably too wide' (O'Keeffe 1992: 207). In particular, concern has been expressed because it provides that a report may be made where an 'overall evaluation' of the person concerned gives reason to suppose that he or she will commit serious offences in future. Indeed, in April 1991 the Council of State of the Netherlands in its opinion on the Convention took the view that such a provision may well be in conflict with Principle 2.1 of the Recommendation (87) 15, which states that the collection of personal data for police purposes 'should be limited to such levels as is necessary for the prevention of a *real danger or the suppression of a specific criminal offence*' (emphasis added). The Dutch Council of State felt that such a provision on reporting on SIS could lead to very fundamental infringements of personal privacy. A further matter of reporting on SIS is the vagueness of the provision relating to aliens (Article 96). Here aliens can be reported for the purpose of being refused entry on the basis of a threat to public order or national security and safety which the presence of an alien in national territory may pose.

Information exchange outside SIS.   As mentioned earlier, the Convention generally aims at enhancing collaboration on mutual exchange of personal data. In particular, it specifically refers to exchange on:

- processing of asylum requests (Article 38)
- police co-operation on preventing and investigating crimes (Article 39 and Article 46)
- mutual assistance in criminal matters (Article 48 *et seq.*)
- control of the acquisition and possession of firearms (Article 91)

As O'Keeffe (1992: 207) indicates, Title VI of the Convention was added at a late stage in negotiations and covers the protection of data other than on SIS. The provisions are very intricate, but it is not at all clear why they are so complex and why they allow for the range of exemptions specified.

The primary distinction made is a tripartite one which recognizes three forms of information exhange:

- automated processing of personal data (Article 126)
- personal data recorded in a non-automated personal data file (Article 127)
- personal data recorded in another manner (Article 127)

Differing levels of *general* protection are specified for each of the three forms of information exchange and this is supplemented by other specific provisions. In terms of general levels of protection, the first two forms are subject to a level of protection equal to the principles of the 1981 Council of Europe Data Protection Convention. The third form is subject additionally to the principles of the Recommendation R (87) 15 regulating the use of personal data in the police sector.

Specific provisions (Article 126) in relation to automatic processing of personal data relate to: compliance with the principle of purpose limitation, accuracy and legality of supply, confirmation of liability in cases where inaccurate data is transmitted and the obligation to record each transmission and receipt of personal data. However, as Verhey (1991: 117) notes, these measures do not apply in all circumstances.

For example, neither the general level of protection nor the specific provisions apply to the transmission of data on handling asylum applications. In addition, other *partial* exemptions include exchange of data on extradition, mutual assistance in criminal matters and the application of the *non bis in idem* principle.

In relation to non-automated data files, the measures mentioned above are in principle also applicable, and with the same exemptions. However, with this data the data protection provisions do not apply at all to extradition, mutual assistance in criminal matters and the application of the *non bis in idem* principle.

The third form of data exchange involves application of the safeguards as for automated data. In addition, there are supplementary provisions. They relate to: the obligation to keep records of transmission and receipt, the use of personal data and access to data. As with the non-automated form of exchange, these provisions do not apply to extradition, mutual assistance in criminal matters and the application of the *non bis in idem* principle.

In respect of data exchange in relation to general police co-operation there are again specific provisions. These provide that: data may only be used for purposes set out by the member state supplying the data, data may only be disclosed to police and other authorities, and that a supplying member state may request a receiving member state to indicate what use was made of the data and the subsequent results.

In relation to information exchange outside SIS, two other provisions regulate purpose limitation. Article 126 (3a) states that personal data may only be used for the purposes for which transmission of such information is provided for in the Convention, thus allowing for very wide interpretation.

Article 129 referring to police information exchange outside SIS without request (Article 46) only allows the use of data for the purposes specified by the transmitting country. In any particular case, however, information for other individual cases is not prohibited. As Scheller (1992) suggests, however, this may lead to problems if national legislation and implementation practice differ greatly in, for example, covert surveillance (Article 99). Under Article 99, the requesting state does not even apply the law of the state which carries out the measure but instead exclusively applies its own. Therefore, one state may supply information on behalf of Article 99 and this information might then be used, let us say, in a minor case in which covert surveillance could not have been carried out in the supplying state. Scheller describes this as 'circumvention of national law by international co-operation' (Scheller 1992: 168).

A separate code is introduced via Article 38 for the exchange of data concerning asylum seekers, which in certain areas may offer less protection than the general rules to be found in Title VI. Cruz (1993) points out that the Schengen group has given assurances that the SIS will never serve as a network of exchange of information on asylum seekers. But Cruz astutely indicates that nothing has been said on rejected asylum seekers served with expulsion orders to leave the Schengen 'territory'. Failure to comply with such orders renders one a clandestine immigrant. Article 96 provides for the inclusion in SIS of personal data on any 'alien (who) has been the subject of a deportation, removal or expulsion measure which has not been rescinded or suspended, including or accompanied by a prohibition on entry or, where appropriate, based on non-compliance with national regulations on the entry or residence of aliens'.

While it is clear that SIS itself will handle 'information' as opposed to criminal intelligence, the proposed EU-wide information systems appear set to handle and co-ordinate a wider range of material. It is to these that we now turn.

European Information System and Customs Information System

As mentioned in an earlier chapter, the 1990 TREVI 'Programme of Action' resolved that EU member states consider the development of a computerized information system. It is intended that the EIS will cover criminal information and intelligence, immigration and asylum and other matters (Bunyan 1993: 27).

As far as can be determined from extant sources, the draft Convention covering the proposed EIS is due for signature under the German Presidency of the EU in late 1994. However, although the operating detail of EIS is unclear at the moment, it appears nevertheless that the scope of both SIS and EIS is virtually the same. Senior British sources have indeed suggested that part of the reason for slow progress on EIS was the lack of willingness on the part of SIS officials to make available their 'Technical Manuals'. This would appear to indicate a very substantial probable overlap. Benyon *et al.* are of the opinion that 'A stand-alone EIS would have the political cachet of incorporating all European Union member states, but it would mean an enormous duplication of effort alongside the SIS' (Benyon *et al.* 1993: 236). We consider the contradictions and conflict of this in the final chapter.

Before turning to the CIS it is, in this context, worth noting that the EIS is not the only TREVI-inspired information network. Europol (now established in The Hague) is to act as the link between the European criminal intelligence agencies such as the British NCIS and the Dutch CRI. The EDU also acts to facilitate the exchange of information about drug trafficking and associated money laundering.

The other EU wide system, the CIS, became operational in October 1992. With the UK Headquarters at Heathrow Airport, the system – funded by the European Commission – links EU Customs officials through 300 terminals in Europe. The purpose is to exchange information and intelligence. CIS is based on the existing encrypted message system called SCENT, but it is an enhancement. Messaging becomes more user-friendly by use of a series of pre-set screen formats. Standard messages, such as 'Stop-and-search' are numerically coded, so avoiding language barriers. The CIS passes information in five main categories: persons; method of transport; commodities and trends. A dedicated CIS database handles intelligence material.

Of course, the EU-wide systems are not alone. Individual countries are also developing and helping shape the 'informatized' security terrain. In Switzerland, DOSIS, the new electronic anti-drugs data base, has an exceptionally wide information-capture. According to one senior Swiss police official, 'when, for example, an address book with hundreds of addresses and phone numbers is found on a dealer, we want them all in our drug investigation system, otherwise it would make no sense' (*Platform Fortress Europe?* March 1993: 7). Similarly, in Austria, information on foreigners (except tourists) is filed on a data base. A 1992 law (seen as part of Austria's pre-Schengen harmonization policy) permits the police a general registration function on those foreigners intending to stay in the country beyond a tourist stay. According to the Interior Minister, Loschnak, an estimated 500 000 people are affected by the new law (*Platform Fortress Europe?* April 1992: 4).

Before drawing this section to a close, it is important to consider, in the context of the centrality of 'information' to the new policing of Europe, the emerging role and functions of the internal security services. The perceived European 'internal security deficit' has removed old rationales about internal security planning and in its place the new ideology that the removal of border controls presents common EU 'problems' has created a situation where, in Peter Klerks' words, 'European security services are shifting from a perspective dominated by counter-espionage and counter-subversion to a new "threats" agenda' (Klerks 1993: 66). In the UK context, the exchanging of primacy for dealing with anti-terrorism from police Special Branch to MI5 in May 1992 is significant. But of course, other European countries have been developing co-operative and training links between the police and the security services for some time. In the Netherlands, for example, a 1991 Working Group, headed by Apeldoorn chief of police, J. W. Bakker, recommended the importance of integrated training programmes for the police and the security service, the BVD (*Binnenlandse Veiligheidsdienst*). Structured co-operation was advocated to ensure effective and influential use of intelligence (*Statewatch*, 1, 4, 1991).

It is now clearly emerging that both Britain's MI5 and MI6 together with Germany's BND (*Bundesnachrichtendienst*) are developing key roles in relation to drug trafficking, arms dealing and related matters (*Financial Times*, 22 November 1993). These security service links now involve Eastern European states. The Czech security service (BIS) together with the Hungarian and Polish services have received substantial training assistance from MI5. Interesingly, of course, much of the new co-operative linkage with formal police agencies is taking place in the context of a new and reworked pan European 'threat' of organized crime: here, Brunton (1993), a UK Metropolitan Police detective, presents the case for viewing organized crime as 'multicommodity' with each activity supporting the other in what is known as the 'wrap-around' principle. Attention can move from drug trafficking to weapons, military equipment and even national economies. In justifying the increased role of the security services, Brunton presents an example:

> After the political changes in eastern Europe, criminal organizations from the former Soviet bloc moved in to use Germany as a base for their enterprises. Many of these groups are run by, or have recruited, senior 'spooks' from former state security agencies such as the East German STASI and the KGB. Their training, knowledge of operational systems and language skills are superb. They specialise in arms trafficking; fraud and white-collar crime. (Brunton 1993: 17)

He concludes by advocating the importance of the security service rôle:

> The fact is that some of these same spies are re-grouping in terrifying criminal organizations. Police officers already involved in such investigations will privately and candidly say that the Security Service gather vital intelligence. And, they will add, they have the capability and will to liaise and assist agencies internationally against groups which do indeed threaten state security . . . in short, the police need closer links with the security agencies. (Brunton 1993: 17)

Conclusions

From Chapters 6 and 7 there are three broad conclusions which we wish to draw, together with some themes which we wish to highlight and which will be further considered in the final chapter.

The first broad conclusion is the apparent importance of the prospective abolition of inner border controls between EU states as a generator of the perceived security deficit. The justifications of an increase in international criminal networks and the impact of migratory flows have acted as constructors for a new form of police work, or at least of forms of co-operation. As we have tried to demonstrate this has been effective at a number of levels in intensifying police co-operation. Dorn, for example, notes that such an approach 'definitely has popular appeal. It fits in with the resurgence of nationalistic feelings in Europe and eastern Europe, and with suspicion of all things "foreign" ' (Dorn 1992: 7) At a deeper level, EU institutional development has had the underlying influence as part of the political dynamic. From the TREVI Ad Hoc Group and the Rhodes Coordinating Group, the Treaty of European Union permits continuity of influence. Under the Treaty, the first meeting of the Council of Interior and Justice Ministers has taken place (November 1993). This new Council has taken over the work of TREVI and the Ad Hoc Group and is serviced by the new K4 Committee which replaces the Coordinators Group. In terms of the EU structure, COPREPER now sees through agendas and negotiates consensus. A cursory examination of K4's three steering groups makes clear the inter-relationships: immigration and asylum; security, law enforcement, police and customs; judicial co-operation. In addition, K4 is now over-seeing the development of the two EU-wide computerized information systems, EIS and CIS.

A second broad conclusion which we would wish to draw relates to informatization. We see this as acting as a facilitating condition, which has encouraged the growth and shape of the internal security field. Particularly at the present conjuncture in European policing, where forms of operational support short of joint organizational capacity are being developed, information technology has a pivotal pioneering role to play (den Boer and Walker 1993). Informatization will continue to play this role in the medium term for several reasons. First, the new information systems are underwritten with considerable political authority and a general commitment to pan-European policing is an important part of the EU Treaty 'third pillar'. Second, this commitment is recognized by private information technology industries. For example, UNISYS, the computer and communications company, recognizes pan-European law enforcement concerns as a challenge facing it. At the UNISYS-organized annual European police seminar in 1991, the Chairman illustrated its reasoning and strategy:

> As the volume of data exchanged between Law Enforcement agencies increases, both within national boundaries and on an international scale, the demands on Information Technology for the improvement of networks, retrieval systems and for many operational support requirements are becoming more pronounced. The reason why UNISYS is continuing to run an annual seminar on this scale, with many principal European police officers and country officials, is because of the contribution their presence can make to the cooperation process. As Seminar chairman, and having overall responsibility for UNISYS' Police business, I bring together two themes to support this point. Firstly, UNISYS has a large base of Law Enforcement . . . accounts worldwide, thus giving us the experience and standing to be market leaders: secondly, cooperation means interoperability. Once again, UNISYS is a leader in respect of the abilities to connect computer systems successfully. (UNISYS, 1991: 3)

Furthermore, the power of modern processors allows unprecedented analytic capacities for intelligence 'production' (something seen as vital to the new European police work).

A final broad conclusion to be drawn at this point, is that while the idea of a European internal security field has become gradually embedded in the institutions and 'discourse' of the new Europe, it is also arguable that for many political actors the sequestration of some aspects of policing and interior matters to the supranational domain represents what has been called a 'transfer of illegitimacy'. In other words, in the sensitive area of internal security policing, there may be a positive encouragement to cede responsibility to a new centre. This also, of course, has its counterpoint in debates around accountability, allowing perhaps a greater autonomy at a supranational level (McLaughlin 1992). Provisions around personal data protection may be a case in point.

In the final chapter that follows we try to develop some of the themes underlying these conclusions. Special emphasis is given to questions of legitimacy and accountability, together with an attempt to relate current trends in policing to the future development of the EU.

8

Policing Europe:
Understanding the Future

In this final chapter we undertake the task of (a) returning to some previously identified themes and trying to represent and analyse them against a wider canvas, and (b) identifying some deeper structural issues that may affect police work and how we come to understand policing in Europe towards the millennium. We begin by returning, in the first section, to the ideological notion of a European security deficit. Chapters 6 and 7 illustrated how the presentation of 'threat(s)' had helped in the construction of this ideological standpoint, and within this, the role of information and 'intelligence' was identified as a key practice. We try to contextualize this still further. In the second section we examine a theme only partially developed elsewhere in the book, namely legitimacy and accountability in the policing of the new Europe. The relationship between these concepts and the *evaluation* of current policing arrangements is analysed, and we also try to contextualize these against what appear as deeper trends in the structural dimensions of policing and police work. These trends, already well documented in England and Wales and elsewhere, may be significant in understanding the future shape of policing in Europe. In the final section, proposals around an agenda for research are considered and some tentative conclusions drawn.

Police, States and Fear

Security always implies the preservation of an established order against whatever seems to threaten, disturb or endan-

189

ger it from within or from without (Spitzer 1987). Policing is an activity that seeks to maintain, in Hobbesian terms, the fundamental order upon which other orders are built: for example, the order of financial markets. In the context of Europe and the EU we have tried to illustrate the particular perceived significance of threats to such 'order'. As we discussed in Chapter 5, one of the key public rationales for intensified police co-operation has been the prospect of abolition of border controls between member states of the Union, which it is argued will undermine the traditional filter function of frontiers, and remove a major impediment to cross-border criminality. Another identifiable factor has been the emphasis on the dangers of uncontrollable growth in illegal immigration.

In our analysis throughout the book we have pointed to the fact that it is unclear to what extent claims about these matters can in any simple sense be substantiated. Instead, the constant linking of these themes in discussion by politicians and senior police officers has created a mutually reinforcive 'security deficit'. Such a security deficit presents a continuum from terrorism through international crime to immigration. As we argued in earlier chapters, this has become embedded at the institutional level. The trend away from specialist fora and groups towards more all-encompassing arrangements is illustrative; regardless of the initial 'purpose' many co-operative agencies (like TREVI) have enveloped other policy domains. The current K4 arrangements fit this pattern (see the Appendix to Chapter 2).

As we indicated in Chapter 2, while developments in the policing of Europe should perhaps not be seen as exemplifying a simple linear trend, particular themes and concerns have been identified by critics of the process. McLaughlin (1992) takes this head-on:

> It is obvious, given the concern about drug smugglers, immigrants, terrorists, and the securing of internal order, that the objective of Euro-'community' policing will not be service with a smile. It is going to be at the hard end of the policing spectrum. Given these developments, it is little wonder that civil liberties pressure groups have expressed

concern about the implications for the 15 million non-EC nationals who form the migrant work force in the EC and those citizens of member countries who are defined in official documentation as 'non-white' . . . These marginal groupings, who are already disadvantaged and discriminated against are being defined as an unwanted presence in the new increasingly insular and xenophobic social order and will be vulnerable to the attentions of this new policing system. (McLaughlin 1992: 483)

For others, writing even earlier, the implications of the working-out of the new policing 'internal security field' are equally clear; Spencer notes that '1992 highlights the risks involved for two reasons. Firstly, there may be a growth in internal surveillance with the proposed withering away of intra-Community frontiers. Secondly, 1992 will accelerate the existing trend towards cross-border exchanges of information' (Spencer 1990: 78). He concludes that: 'The fields of policing and criminal justice could turn out to be another instance of harmonization being a one-way process, with benefits for Big Brother but potential losses for the individual.' (Spencer 1990: 97). Bunyan (1991a; 1993) continues this 'Fortress Europe' approach, by illustrating how developments are shaping the transformation to what he terms the 'authoritarian European state'. He opines:

States also acquire legitimacy by protecting society and citizens from commonly perceived 'enemies'. The ending of the Cold War, with its 'threat' of nuclear war and communist subversion, removed the rationale for much internal security planning. In its place is the ideology that the removal of frontiers presents common 'problems' to the EC. This shift left many agencies casting around for new roles, and they have found them in the perceived external 'threats' from terrorism, drugs and immigration. Internal opposition is portrayed as against the interests of all with the internal security services and police defining new 'threats' to be ideologically marginalized and targeted for surveillance. Taken together with the policies on immigration and asylum . . . the European state institutionalises the 'cordon sanitaire' at its external borders and sets up draconian mechanisms for internal control which will affect the whole community. (Bunyan 1993: 33)

These processes of inclusion and exclusion are, according to Bunyan and others, integral to the working of the new policing security field. However, such processes also, in our view, have a wider resonance.

Closure and exclusion also operate at the 'explanatory' level – in relation to definitional matters (Chomsky 1988). A good illustration of this is the argument presented in *The Terrorism Industry: The Experts and Institutions that Shape our View of Terror* (Herman and O'Sullivan 1989). In the judgement of Herman and O'Sullivan, this industry is international, with close ties between government intelligence, foreign policy agencies, private sponsors, private security and individual experts. Meeting and publishing regularly, these sources have established themselves as the accredited agents speaking out on the topic of terrorism – this allows ideological mobilization of interests. In the same way, it can be argued that the European policing security field influences how crime is explained and what steps are accepted for its control. Let us take an example.

In Chapter 6, we looked briefly at the 'threat' of drug trafficking. There, we argued that the available research evidence suggested that control strategies within the European policing field had misread the relationship between border controls and the nature of the 'market(s)'. From within the internal security field one is presented with a causal account which equates money laundering to the growth in the traffic of drugs that occurred in the 1980s. Such an account has all the elements of closure and exclusion, and works through and around very straightforward and powerful stereotypes. The escalating international traffic in drugs is seen as a product of the extraordinarily clever dissemination of highly addictive and very profitable substances by essentially very evil foreign criminals, whose control over markets is assured by ruthless violence. Money laundering, from this angle, is the process whereby such drug barons transfer 'hot money' earned in the drug economy into offshore banking facilities, there to be recycled into more legitimate business. This account has under-pinned the highly unsuccessful approach to drug control in other areas of the world (Martin and Romano 1992: 51–79).

In part, the problems in this official account of money laundering arise because of the insistent emphasis on the idea of 'hot money' and drug trafficking as a pivotal explanatory couplet, underwritten by the demonology of evil criminals introducing a menace of drugs into an otherwise uncontradictory Europe. This closed account, offered from within the security field, has a number of significant lacunae. One crucial absence, for example, is any kind of sociological explanation of the social or economic conditions within Europe which actually allow and encourage the consumption of drugs. The deindustrialization of Western economies and the restructuring of the international political economy provide a much more appropriate vehicle for understanding (Lash and Urry 1987). Such an understanding would also, we believe, have to encompass processes linked with concomitant key features of European culture including its accelerated work ethic, the loss of a clear sense of individual meaning and identity, and the declining sense of a connecting teleology or purpose to social life itself (Giddens 1991).

Clearly this is not the place to recount such argument in any detail. However, the point must be made that at the level of international political economy, the demise of mass production has had uneven effects, both within the developed world and especially within the so-called under-developed world. Although many Third World countries have pursued export development strategies and domestic regrowth, such development strategies are not equally available to all countries. Countries like Peru amd Colombia, on the one hand, and Pakistan, Burma, Thailand and Laos on the other, do not have large wealthy domestic markets, and they have not been able to develop the kind of productive infrastructure which would enable them to compete with other Asian or Latin American economies, either in export-led or domestically-oriented mass production. The consequence is the continued pauperization of the mass of their populations and the search for any kind of production – including, for example, the systematic production of coca – with which to sustain a livelihood. The fact that there is a growing market in Europe for the products of such an international business (e.g., cocaine), is also of vital importance. Our concern here is to suggest that the explanation of the continuing production of drugs such as cocaine in the Third World is crucially bound up with uneven development opportunities. *Such a condition is substantially unaffected by the move towards free trade and the abolition of frontier controls in Europe, or by the policing security field itself.*

Similarly, in respect of money laundering, the complexity arises from the need for businesses to be actively engaged in the international money markets, the broader economic context, the internationalization of finance markets and the competitive struggle for a secure store of value, within which any significant transfer of capital and value must now take place. There is a logic here which applies to legitimate as well as illegitimate capital. Investment strategies become not that much different from those of other 'legitimate' investors: thus Petracca (1993) in the context of Italy, outlines these as now involving:

- acquisition of the control of specific economic activities in particular areas of the country
- intervention in those economic sectors affected by recession
- intervention in those economic sectors with better prospects of development
- investment of illicit money in foreign economic activities.

The role of successfully laundered 'narco-dollars' in under-pinning legitimate purposes, including capital investments, poor relief and the financing of political parties is one that leaves simple 'internal security' solutions problematic.

Critics of developing police co-operative arrangements in the new Europe have importantly drawn attention to the implications of the processes of inclusion and exclusion for citizenship (Bunyan 1993). As we argued in Chapter 7, a facilitating factor in reshaping both the aims of policing and the 'target' groups for police work has been the process of 'informatization'. This concept can usefully be drawn more widely as 'knowledge', and in so doing some insights from recent social theory can be brought to bear, albeit speculatively, on the constituent and emergent properties of the European internal security field.

In this regard, it has recently been argued by some social theorists that social institutions increasingly construct risks as threats, underpinned by an assumption of distrust in human relations (Giddens 1991). Such institutions increasingly respond to their own constructions through probability calculations and through knowledge systems for efficient risk management of those threats. Previously dominant values become displaced in this risk society (see Beck 1992), with crime control values decreasing in importance and administrative surveillance assuming greater importance. Here, the state itself is de-centred and less important than the administration of the production distribution and usage of whatever knowledge is deemed necessary to conduct efficient surveillance. The system level becomes paramount, with knowledge production about 'suspect' populations becoming the key practice. The hard end of crime control gives way to ensuring access, storage and retrieval of knowledge. The police are knowledge workers, spending increasing amounts of time producing and communicating knowledge which serves both their needs and other institutional needs that require police knowledge for their own systems of risk management and security provision. Such surveillance is consequentialist, or forward looking. The concern is to ensure availability of detailed knowledge about people in the hope that it will come in useful in future system dealings with them or, more likely, in the dealings which other linked institutions might have with them. This is a particularly pertinent point, given the nature of the European response to 'threats' to social order which is increasingly operating as a continuum.

Ericson (1993) has recently presented an analysis of the British criminal justice system in these terms, and such an approach may prove useful in trying to make sense of emerging aspects of the internal security field at European level. This is especially so if it also proves possible to draw into such an account (a) that all forms of information technology in the police have an indeterminate effect at structural level (Manning 1992), and (b) that information use can also be a source of symbolic capital (Bourdieu 1989) within the internal security field itself.

Beyond Legitimacy and Accountability?

In Chapter 3 we briefly examined matters of accountability in relation to Interpol, Schengen and the EC co-operative structures on policing. We did so in a way which took for granted the important, but as yet unconsidered, issue of the evaluation of these new policing arrangements. Of course, any such evaluation traditionally comes up against the issue of the 'criterion' of evaluation. In police studies, this is usually presented as the distinction between accountability and effectiveness. This relationship between accountability or legitimacy and effectiveness is essentially a normative one; it would seem appropriate to argue that while there are clear and varying circumstances in policing at the domestic level in Europe, any such policing arrangements have to be satisfactory in terms of *both* accountability and effectiveness (den Boer and Walker 1993).

Clearly, in respect of effectiveness and accountability there is a complex interaction between structural dimensions of policing at both the national level and the European level. In what follows, we try to illustrate how some of this can be captured conceptually. In addition, we feel it is also useful to try to locate the discussion against what appear as deep-rooted trends of social change and, although we use the example of the situation in Britain, the importance of the underlying processes lies in what they reveal about the nature of the 'police function' in a future Europe.

Taking the effectiveness of current European policing arrangements as our starting point, we would argue that one is immediately faced with a basic uncertainty; what are our criteria for judgement? Difficulties arise from a number of sources: first, as we saw in Chapter 5, the exact nature, scope and extent of the 'crime problem' is unknown (or at least subject to controversy), so how do we begin to judge success? Second, as we saw in Chapters 2 and 3, the European policing field is criss-crossed with a plurality of initiatives and fora and there is little empirical data to permit assessment of relative performance. Third, it can perhaps be argued in the last analysis that until there is an appropriate supranational (i.e., EC/EU) police function, then any evaluation of effectiveness will be confounded by an interaction effect of cross-national with national (domestic) factors (den Boer and Walker 1993).

While for the foregoing reasons any head-on evaluation of effectiveness is almost impossible, it is useful to speculate on how effective alternative configurations of the European policing arrangements may be. As we saw from Chapter 2, while the Treaty on European Union has now assumed a kind of hegemony, there are still other contenders. For analytic purposes, one can perhaps distinguish between three 'ideal-type' configurations. At one end an integrated configuration, which allows for legal competency across crime areas and at the institutional level, links operational and policy matters. The closest we have to this, but yet still far short of it, are the EU Council of Ministers (K4) arrangements. In terms of effectiveness, it could be argued that the integrated configuration may greatly facilitate practical policing 'action' around arrest, hot pursuit, and information gathering. However, it may entail the disadvantages of (a) exacerbating the traditional tension in policing between strategic management policy formulation and 'on the ground' operational matters, and (b) permitting the creation of a centralized core either over-responsive to transient political forces or under-responsive to influence from below (or indeed externally).

At the other end, a pluralist (or mixed) configuration is based on boundaries at the organizational level between police specialisms, together with no clear hierarchical or strategic influence at the territorial level. Such an arrangement could have the advantages of allowing greater flexibility of response to crime at the territorial level and permit clear policy/operational mandates.

In the middle, we have a mixed configuration. The newly born Europol bears all the hallmarks of such a 'mixed' arrangement, with its co-ordinating role as a facilitator of co-operation between discrete national police forces, and as a centre for operational information exchange.

However brief, what such an analysis illustrates is the inherent uncertainty surrounding the effectiveness of such configurations. Nevertheless, it is argued by police and policy analysts that organizational arrangements do, in the end, have implications for effectiveness. The unanswered question is what are these implications? Or to rephrase, does organizational configuration make a difference? Almost everyone thinks so.

On the one hand, police and public may feel that, for instance in England and Wales, structural decentralization is 'essential' while on the other hand response to crisis – whether growth in crime or other threats – is often met with by a reach-for-organizational-reform. Organizational change is often analysed by commentators as being 'significant', but are changes in police organization really instrumental? As Bayley (1992) points out, what is really needed is a serious examination of the assumptions about the importance of organizational variables. In order to do this, one must stipulate (guess ?) areas of likely impact and then study the differences that change in organization make. The very limited available research about the effects of police organization on goals and objectives suggests a 'don't know', with the entire subject 'shrouded in unexamined assumptions often unintelligently applied' (Bayley 1992: 509).

Moving on to the other evaluative dimension, namely accountability and legitimacy, one has to concur with McLaughlin that 'What is significant in the debates that have taken place about the future shape of Euro-"Community" policing is the lack of discussion of accountability' (McLaughlin 1992: 483). In considering the parameters of accountability and legitimacy, den Boer and Walker (1993) provide an illuminating and thoughtful analysis based on an original schema by Baldwin (1987). Baldwin has suggested that institutional legitimacy claims are assessed by five main means. The first concerns the extent to which the institution and its practices are authorized by a legislative mandate. The second concerns arrangements for holding the institution to account democratically. The third concerns matters of 'due process', rules and procedures whereby individuals have rights of redress. The fourth refers to the degree of expertise seen to reside in the institution and related to performance. Finally, there is reference to overall institutional effectiveness in reaching objectives.

The legislative mandate in the European policing field has been largely lacking. Interpol, as we saw in Chapter 3, is notorious for its lack of statutory underpinning. TREVI, when it existed, operated outwith the EC Treaty framework, while the two Schengen treaties are agreements in international law between nine EC countries and are potentially in conflict with Community law. In addition, Schengen envisages no judicial authority to interpret and implement the treaties and, although an Executive Committee is to perform this role, it is not a court and operates completely outside the constraints of domestic or supranational law (for a detailed examination of Schengen's relationship to other legal arrangements, see Baldwin-Edwards and Hebenton 1994). The Treaty of European Union divides competence for judicial and security matters between a Community method and an inter-governmental method. Even this division is not watertight, and a system (known as the 'passerelle' under Article K9) has been prescribed to allow a subject to be transferred from the inter-governmental to the EC framework. Europol, recognized in the Declaration to the Treaty on European Union, must look to inter-governmental means for a more detailed legislative mandate.

In keeping with this weak (and confused) legislative base, democratic accountability controls over the relevant policing institutions are equally lacking. Neither Interpol nor the Schengen arrangements require account to a separate agency across their functions. On the EU and K4 arrangements one can only conclude at the moment that they are opaque in practice. It is unclear what 'influence' the European Parliament will be able to exert.

On due process, again as den Boer and Walker indicate, various safeguards are under-developed. If one takes information exchange and data protection as a case in point, then there is no reason to be sanguine about the privacy protection afforded, given the political and policing imperatives that drive the process of co-operation. In the case of Schengen, Baldwin-Edwards and Hebenton conclude that 'the standards of Schengen will amount in practice to little more than a complex, almost impenetrable, legitimation of state and inter-state invasion of personal privacy' (Baldwin-Edwards and Hebenton 1994: 156). On Europol, if it

> were to acquire operational powers, including those of search, questioning and arrest, the need for rights of due process would become even more pressing. In such circum-stances, it is arguable that, as with many domestic systems, what would be required as well as a detailed set of procedural rights would be a special complaints process and tribunal through which such rights could be effectively vindicated. (den Boer and Walker 1993: 22)

Clearly, claims to legitimacy and accountability are weak on all the above three fronts. However, when one turns to the remaining two bases, namely knowledge/expertise and orga-nizational effectiveness then one can see that a stronger case can be 'presented'. After all, as we argued earlier in this section and in Chapter 6, quite how one can objectively answer these appeals to expertise and effectiveness is un-clear; the value of these two bases for police legitimacy lies, one can suggest, in their very 'irrefutability'. Given the nature of the arguments, appeals to such claims achieve a kind of ideological closure.

In concluding this (albeit brief) evaluation of effectiveness and legitimacy, our argument would be that at this conjunc-ture in the policing of Europe, it is important to recognize the basic problem of (lack of) knowledge and understanding. Combined with this, one can further argue that there is a pressing need to ensure that all interested parties can con-tribute to the shaping of the agenda on policing Europe at domestic and supranational level.

As mentioned earlier, questions of legitimacy and account-ability must also be seen against the background of rapid social change, and here one is faced with trying to account for the transformative impact of such change on police and the 'policing' function. The transformative implications of policing in post-modern societies can be usefully illustrated with the example of British policing.

Debate about reform of British policing is again high on the political agenda. To set the scene fully and to understand the entire 'narrative' leading to this point in the early 1990s would require revisiting the policy debates of the 1980s and perhaps even earlier and would certainly need far more space than we can possibly allocate (see Reiner 1992b for the now classic statement on these debates). Instead, we prefer to try to distinguish, for our own purposes in this chapter, both 'surface' and 'deeper' matters of significance around legitimacy and accountability.

It can plausibly be argued that, in Britain, police legitimacy (certainly since the Second World War) had been based on a unique cocktail of cultural and social forces which are unlikely to recur and which were not duplicated elsewhere. Although a generalization, it can be stated that elsewhere, police wielded power rather than authority in the Weberian sense. The power of the British police was transmuted into authority primarily because they came to stand for a largely mythical national culture of order, harmony and restraint. Their power was legitimated by tradition. Elsewhere in Europe, any legitimation the police achieved was on a rational-legal or charismatic basis. However, while these bases seem less secure than that of 'tradition', it is certainly the case that the British police have fallen from grace.

In elucidating the 'fall' or undermining of British police legitimacy, Reiner (1992b) identifies eight specific aspects of change in police organization and policy that played a significant role: changes around recruitment; training and discipline; allegations of corruption; police malpractice and abuse of powers in law enforcement; change towards militarization; acquisition and use of riot equipment and firearms; perceived political partisanship; the incomplete change to a service role.

However, there is a 'deeper logic' underlying these 'surface' factors (Reiner 1992a) which relates to social change at the economic and cultural level. Two such changes are identifiable:

(a)   the structurally generated formation of a completely
      marginalized section of society (a major source of the
      huge growth in crime, disorder and tension around
      policing);
(b)   a cultural trend which involves the decline of traditional
      patterns of deference and the unquestioning acceptance
      of authority, a process aptly named desubordination.
      The police as symbols of social authority evidently suffer
      from this culture of desubordination.

In theorizing these changes, commentators such as Reiner
draw increasingly on social theoretical frameworks around
post-modernity. Such engagement is, in our view, entirely
appropriate and immensely helpful in locating policing
against the backcloth of rapid change in general, and in its
heuristic role of indicating where the determinants of future
patterns of European policing lie. The post-modern world is,
according to such theorists, bound to processes of pluralism,
disaggregation and fragmentation (Lash and Urry 1987;
Giddens, 1991). In such a society, the social structure is
subject to fragmentation and the systems for maintaining
order become increasingly pluralistic. In that situation, policing is subject to what Reiner calls an organizational
'bifurcation': on the one hand, a small number of centralized
agencies at national and supranational levels; on the other
hand, a large number of decentralized or fragmented agencies
at the local level. This bifurcation also consists of a complex of
public, private and hybrid 'policing agencies'.

In essence, it is argued that the role of the police institution
is being transformed within the array of policing processes;
such a transformation is inevitable given that the rise of the
nation-state police had been predicated upon the project of
organizing society around a central, cohesive notion of order.
Such arguments imply, therefore, an increasing need to
develop a conception of policing and, more generally, order-
ing that is consistent with a view of the social world as
'irreducibly and irrevocably pluralistic, split into a multitude
of sovereign units and sites of authority, with no horizontal or
vertical order, either in actuality or in potency' (Bauman 1988:
425). These emerging conceptions may conjure up an image of

a Europe in which corporate 'private security' exists alongside nation-state governments in an 'integral plurality' (Fitzpatrick 1984) of shifting relations and claims with respect to sovereignty that change over both time and terrains. Such an understanding permits a recognition of private corporations (or interests) which compete in a global market as sites of governance from which assurances of security and order are sought and relied on. This is occurring at the same time as the emergence of global markets is challenging the boundaries of nation-states and indeed the very notion of nation-state as a basis for political organization.

In trying to rethink the structural dimensions of such 'policing', this may increasingly need to be seen across two parallel continua of (a) sectoral forms (from the public/state to the private) and (b) spatial levels (from local to supranational: see Johnston 1992: 195–6). The commodification of policing may be likely, with a market in which different policing systems trade their products. In this order of things, intersections between (international) spatial levels and (private) sectoral forms may be the likely determinants of future patterns of European policing.

Policing Europe and Research Agendas

As academics engaged in writing on police in Europe, it would be remiss if we were to complete a book on the subject without the obligatory plea for 'more research'. This is the conventional end to any academic work, and it would certainly be unthinkable to argue for less research. In arguing for greater research emphasis, it is clear that the European 'worksite' of police co-operation offers a veritable feast of research delights. For the political scientist, there is a rich field around sovereignty, citizenship rights and the emergence of new types and conceptions of security. For legal analysts there are important questions about the harmonization and integration of law at national, European and international levels. For theoreticians of police studies there are important issues about the extent to which police institutions can be viewed as simply epiphenomena to be 'read off' from the wider social and political framework at state level, and how new configurations at supranational level encourage and set limits to developments in the policing field.

However, there are also apparently more basic research needs in this area. One valuable research focus could be around the nature of the diversity of European policing. Organizational structures vary immensely, across state/regional and national/state. A comparative study highlighting commonalities and differences and their *significance* would be invaluable. On police powers, again a comparative study of legislative under-pinning and exercise of discretion would be useful (similarly with recruitment and training and so-called occupational cultures).

At the intermediate level, there is a need for a clear account of existing police formal and informal networks, together with an evaluation of their effectiveness. On police information exchange, there is a need to examine how the trajectories of police co-operation and of data protection relate because, as we have illustrated elsewhere in the book, they often overlap within the same policy space.

At the level of national and EC arrangements, there is an important study in elucidating what underpins national policing responses to co-operation. For example, the British police response (here regarded as 'unitary') has been described as pragmatic and ecumenical (N. Walker 1993: 131). There has been strong interest in effective co-operation in certain key areas of crime and terrorism, and likewise in certain technical areas around radio communications and fingerprint recognition. The reasons for this particular approach are no doubt many and varied, but do require investigation.

It would be relatively easy, then, to construct a 'dream shopping list' of future research needs. Nevertheless, at this stage in the understanding of the Europeanization of policing, it is probably more useful to consider the direction of future research than its specific content. One direction would be to displace past practice in police studies: that is, traditionally, police research has been dominated by a 'producers-side' focus, the emphasis being placed on the police (as producers of the service) rather than on *how policing is constituted.* Europeanization of policing permits a change of focus. Through its co-existence with other institutional control responses, policing constitutes an intricate pattern of relations between sources of authority, a set of goals, the selected means and available resources for achieving them, and the environment in which such activity takes place. It has been our analytical contention in this book that the particular interactions of interest, power and authority which distinguish the structures and functions of police work should be viewed as constructed around expectations for policing within a given cultural, political and situational context. Direction signs around this agenda for research would be both innovative and revealing.

Throughout the book, our approach has drawn on a notion of the economy of practice, with assumptions of fundamental links between actions and interests in specific contexts or 'fields' within which people act. A field is always a site of struggles in which people seek to maintain or alter the distribution of forms of resources specific to it. Those who participate in these struggles will have differing aims – some will seek to preserve the status quo, others to change it – and differing chances of winning or losing, depending on where they are located in the structured space of positions. However, there is always a fundamental complicity on the part of those who struggle about the value and stakes of the game. This is our conceptualization of the European policing 'field'.

Such a conceptualization carries with it a heuristic research principle, in the sense that it calls upon the researcher to elucidate the specific interests at stake in the practices and conflicts which take place, for the content of interests cannot be determined abstractly. What those interests are – that is, what they amount to in particular instance – can be determined only through empirical inquiry.

Just what the emerging new Europe will look like remains uncertain. We are a lot clearer about what we are leaving behind than about what we are moving towards. Policing, because it lies at the heart of any order, however, provides a dark glass through which we may be able to catch glimpses of the shape of the world we are tumbling towards. What this peep through the prism of policing reveals is that the emerging European order is one in which 'security' matters will be paramount.

Selected Further Reading

For those who, like us, have become intensely interested in the evolution of the policing of Europe, there are several good and reasonably up-to-date sources of background information. We list them in no preferred order.

Police Co-operation in Europe: An Investigation, Benyon, J., Turnbull, L., Willis, A., Woodward, R. and A. Beck (Leicester: University of Leicester Centre for the Study of Public Order, 1993).

Statewatching the New Europe, Bunyan, T. (ed.) (London: Statewatch, 1993).

Policing Across National Boundaries, Anderson, M. and den Boer, M. (eds) (London: Pinter 1994).

Policing the World. Interpol and the Politics of International Police Co-operation, Anderson, M. (Oxford: Clarendon Press, 1989).

Organizations and Sources of Information

NCIS (National Criminal Intelligence Service): PO Box 8000, London, SE11 5EN, UK (tel. 071-238-8364).

INTERPOL International Criminal Police Organization: BP 6041, 69411 Lyon Cedex 06, France (tel. + 72 44 70 00; FAX +72 44 71 63).

EUROPOL: Raamweg 47, 2596 HN, The Hague, The Netherlands.

European Parliament Office in UK: 2 Queen Anne's Gate, London SW1H 9AA (tel. 071-222-0411; useful library but check on opening hours).

Institut des Hautes Etudes de la Sécurité Intérieure (IHESI): 19 Rue Peclet 75015 Paris, France (tel. (1) 45 30 50 70; produces an interesting French language journal, *Cahiers de la Sécurité Intérieure*).

Centre for the Study of Public Order, University of Leicester: CSPO, University of Leicester, 6 Salisbury Road, Leicester LE1 7QR, UK (tel. 0533 522458; FAX 0533 523944).

Statewatch: PO Box 1516, London, N16 OEW, UK (tel. 081-802-1882; FAX 081-880-1727; produces an independent and critical bi-monthly bulletin of very useful information on policing developments and related matters).

Platform Fortress Europe?: Blomstervag 7, S-791 33 Falun, Sweden (tel./FAX + 46/23 26 777; an international network of groups and individuals concerned with European harmonization in the fields of policing and internal security which among other things produces a very useful newsletter; the UK is contact R. J. Jenkins, 125 Stonhouse Street, London, SW4 6BH).

OMEGA Foundation: 6 Mount Street, Manchester, M2 5NS UK (tel./FAX 061-834-8223; undertakes research on security/arms exports and related matters).

Bibliography

Abel, P., Hebenton, B., Thomas, T. and Wright, S. (1991) 'The techno-politics of exclusion: an assessment of the constitutional and political implications of the new tools for policing Europe after 1992', Paper presented at the European Group for the Study of Deviance and Social Control, 19th Annual Conference, Potsdam, September 1991.

Ackroyd, S., Harper, R., Hughes, J. A., Shapiro, D. and Soothill, K. (1992) *New Technology and Practical Police Work* (Buckingham: Open University Press).

Alexander, G. M. (1981) 'The demobilisation crisis of November 1944', in Iatrides (1981).

Amnesty International (1993) 'Racism: torture and ill treatment in Western Europe', *Focus*, February pp. 3–6.

✳ Anderson, M. (1989) *Policing the World, Interpol and the politics of International Police Co-operation* (Oxford: Clarendon Press).

Anderson, M. (1991) *The French Police and European Cooperation* (University of Edinburgh: Dept. of Politics).

Anderson, M. and den Boer, M. (eds.) (1992) *European Police Cooperation: Proceedings of a Seminar* (University of Edinburgh: Dept. of Politics).

Anderson, M. and den Boer, M. (eds) (1994) *Policing Across National Boundaries* (London: Pinter).

✦ Anglo-Irish Agreement (1985) *Agreement between the Government of the United Kingdom of Great Britain and Northern Ireland and the Government of the Republic of Ireland November 1985*, Cmnd 9657 (London: HMSO).

Bailey, S. (1989) 'Meeting the international challenge', *Police Review*, 21 April.

Baldwin, R. (1987) 'Why police accountability', *British Journal of Criminology*, 32, pp. 97–105.

Baker, G. (1988) 'When boundaries disappear', *Policing*, 4, 4 (Winter), pp. 281–92.

Baldwin-Edwards, M. (1991) 'Immigration after 1992', *Policy and Politics*, 19, 3, pp. 199–211.

Baldwin-Edwards, M. (1992) 'The context of 1992', *Runnymede Trust Bulletin on Europe*, February.

Baldwin-Edwards, M. and Hebenton, B. (1994) 'Will SIS be Europe's "Big Brother"?', in Anderson and den Boer (eds) (1994).

Baldwin-Edwards, M. and Schain, M. (in press) 'The politics of immigration', Introduction in Baldwin-Edwards and Schain (eds), Special Edition of *West European Politics*.

Bauman, Z. (1978) *Hermeneutics and Social Science: Approaches to Understanding* (London: Hutchinson).

Bauman, Z. (1988) Sociology and postmodernity. *Sociological Review*, 36, pp. 790–813.

Bauman, Z. (1992) *Intimations of Postmodernity* (London: Routledge).

Bayley, D. (1985) *Patterns of Policing* (New Brunswick: Rutgers University Press).

Bayley, D. (1992) 'Comparative organization of the police', in Tonry and Morris (1992).

Beck, U. (1992) *Risk Society: Towards a New Modernity* (London: Sage).

Bentham, K. (1992) 'A European Police Council', in Anderson and den Boer (1992).

Benyon, J., Turnbull, L., Willis, A., Woodward, R. and Beck, A. (1993) *Police Co-operation in Europe: An Investigation* (University of Leicester: Centre for the Study of Public Order).

Berlière, J. (1991) 'The Professionalisation of the Police under the Third Republic in France 1875–1914', in Emsley and Weinburger (eds) (1991).

Bessel, R. (1991) 'Policing, professionalisation and politics in Weimar Germany', in Emsley and Weinberger (1991).

Bevins, A. (1992) 'Row grows over lifting of checks at borders', *The Independent*, 26 May.

Bigo, D. (1992) 'The European internal security field', Paper to European Consortium for Political Research, Joint Sessions, Limerick.

Birch, R. (1989) 'Preparing for 1992', *Police Review* 17 February.

Birch, R. (1992) 'Why Europe needs Interpol', *Police Review*, 17 January.

Bittner, E. (1971) *The Functions of the Police in Modern Society* (Washington, DC: US Government Printing Office).

Block, A. and Chambliss, W. (1981) *Organizing Crime* (New York: Elsevier).

Böhning, W. R. (1991) 'Integration and immigration pressures in Western Europe', *International Labour Review*, 130, 4.

Bottomley, A. K. and Pease, K. (1986) *Crime and Punishment: Interpreting the Data* (Milton Keynes: Open University Press).

Bourdieu, P. (1989) *La Noblesse D'Etat* (Paris: Minuit).

Bowden, T. (1978) *Beyond the Limits of the Law* (Harmondsworth: Penguin).

Bowlby, C. (1986) 'Blutma: 1929: police, parties and proletarians in a Berlin confrontation', *The Historical Journal*, XXIX, 1, pp. 137–58.

Bresler, F. (1992) *Interpol* (London: Sinclair Stevenson).

Bridge, A. (1992) 'A nation of secret policemen', *The Independent*, 10 February.

Broadbent, G. and Vincenzi, C. (1990) 'World Cup 1990: law and order v. civil liberties and EEC Rights?', *Solicitors Journal*, 134, 25, pp. 698–702.

Brodeur, J. P. (1983) 'High policing and low policing: remarks about the policing of political activities', *Social Problems*, 30, 5 (June), pp. 507–20.

Brogden, M. (1982) *The Police: Autonomy and Consent* (London and New York: Academic Press).

Browder, G. C. (1990) *Foundations of the Nazi Police State* (The University of Kentucky).

Brunton, G. (1993) 'Global pillage', *Police Review*, 5 February.

Bulmer, S. (1993) 'Community Governance and Regulatory Regimes', Paper to the European Community Studies Conference, Washington DC.

Bunyan, T. (1976) *The Political Police in Britain* (London: Quartet Books).

Bunyan, T. (1991a) 'A Europe to be steeped in racism', *The Guardian*, 28 January.

Bunyan, T. (1991b) 'Towards an Authoritarian European State', *Race and Class*, 32, 3, pp. 19–27.

Bunyan, T. (ed.) (1993) *Statewatching the New Europe* (London: Statewatch).

Butt Philip, A. (1991b) 'European border controls: who needs them?', *Public Policy and Administration*, 6, 2 (Summer), pp. 35–54.

Butt Philip, A. (1991a) 'Dismantling Border Controls', *Chatham House Papers*, May.

Cain, M. (1979) 'Trends in the sociology of police work', *International Journal of the Sociology of Law*, 7, pp. 143–67.

Cameron-Waller, S. (1993) 'The future role of Interpol in Europe', in NCIS (1993).

Campbell, D. (1980) 'Society under surveillance', in Hain (1980).

Campbell, D. (1991) 'Police G7 that's promising action', *The Guardian*, 7 August.

Campbell, D. and Connor, S. (1986) *On the Record* (London: Michael Joseph).

Campbell, E. (1993) 'Detectives back FBI-style agency', *The Guardian*, 17 July.

Cannings, D. (1990) *Policing in Europe Towards 1992* (Devon and Cornwall Constabulary).

Carter, D. (1992) 'A forecast of growth in organized crime in Europe: New challenges for law enforcement', *Police Studies*, 15, 2 (Summer), pp. 62–75.

Castle-Kanerova, M. (1992) 'Czechoslovakia' in Deacon (1992).

Chaigne, Y. (1989) 'The new dimensions of crime, and how these can be tackled', Seminar paper presented to the IPEC, London, September 1989.

Chapman, B. (1970) *The Police State* (London: Macmillan).

Chatterton, M. and Rogers, M. (1989) 'Focused policing', in Morgan and Smith (1989)

Chomsky, N. (1988) *The Culture of Terrorism* (Boston, MA: South End Press).

Clavelous, D. (1990) 'Drug barons cast long shadow', *The European*, 15 June.

Cohen, R. (1992) 'Migrants in Europe: processes of exclusion and inclusion', *New Community*, 18, 2, pp. 332–6.

Connett, D. (1992) 'Convicted fans may face ban on travelling', *The Independent*, 19 June.

Council of Europe (1960) Exchange of letters between Mr Lodovico Benvenuti and Mr M. Sicot (Feb. 1960), Document TN 142/ KO.WM.

Council of Europe (1981) *Convention for the Protection of Individuals with Regard to Automatic Processing of Personal Data* (Strasbourg).

Council of Europe (1984) *The Criminal Record and Rehabilitation of Convicted Persons* (Recommendation R(84) 10) (Strasbourg).

Council of Europe (1988) *Regulating the use of Personal Data in the Police Sector* (Recommendation R(87)15) (Strasbourg).

Critchley, T. A. (1967) *A History of Police in England and Wales* (London: Constable).

Critchley, T. A. (1978) *A History of Police in England and Wales*, 2nd edn (London: Constable).

Cruz, A. (1993) *Schengen, Ad Hoc Immigration Group and other European Intergovernmental bodies*. Churches Committee for Migrants in Europe Briefing Paper 12 (Brussels).

Cullen, P. J. (1992) *The German Police and European Cooperation* (University of Edinburgh: Dept. of Politics).

Das, D. K. (1991) 'Comparative police studies: an assessment', *Police Studies*, 14, pp. 23–35.

Data Protection Registrar (1992) *Eighth Report of the Data Protection Registrar* (London: HMSO).

Davis, J. A. (1988) *Conflict and Control: Law and Order in Nineteenth Century Italy* (London: Macmillan Education).

Davison, P. (1993) 'Police uncover Basque arms factory', *The Independent*, 16 February.

Deacon, B. (ed.) (1992) *Social Policy, Social Justice and Citizenship in Eastern Europe* (Aldershot: Avebury).

de Kort, M. and Korf, D. J. (1992) 'The development of the drug trade and drug control in the Netherlands: a historical perspective', *Crime, Law and Social Change*, 17, pp. 123–44.

Delgado, M. (1990) 'Stolen car trails lead to Poland', *The European*, 28–30 December 1990.

den Boer, M. (1991) *The Police in the Netherlands and European Cooperation* (University of Edinburgh: Dept. of Politics).

den Boer, M. (1992) 'The Quest for European Policing: Rhetoric and Justification in a Disorderly Debate', Paper to the European Consortium for Political Research, Joint Sessions, Limerick.

den Boer, M. and Walker, K. (1993) 'European policing after 1992', *Journal of Common Market Studies*, 31, 1, pp. 3–28.

Desborough Committee (1920) *Report of the Committee on the Police Service*, England, Wales and Scotland. Cmd 574 (London: HMSO).

Devon and Cornwall Constabulary (1990) *Constabulary European Audit for 1992.*

Domenico, R. P. (1991) *Italian Fascists on Trial 1943–1948* (Chapel Hill, NC: University of North Carolina Press).

Dorn, N. (1992) Drug Enforcement within Europe: police cooperation in the age of free movement for EC nationals, Howard League for Penal Reform (mimeo, unpublished).

Dorn, N., Murji, K. and South, N. (1992) *Traffickers* (London: Routledge).

Doyle, L. (1992) 'U.S. police chiefs attack Interpol over Habash case', *The Independent*, 4 March.

Doyle, L. (1993) 'Secret plans for brave new world of E.U. security', *The Independent*, 12 November.

Eastwood, A. (1989a) 'Preparing the police officer for 1992', Seminar paper presented to IPEC, London, September 1989.

Eastwood, A. (1989b) 'On to '92', *Police*, September/October.

Emsley, C. (1991) *The English Police* (Brighton: Harvester Wheatsheaf).

✦ Emsley, C. and Weinberger, B. (1991) *Policing Western Europe* (Westport, CT: Greenwood Press).

Endean, C. (1990) 'Migrant invasion fears fuelled by border deal', *The European*, 30 November–2 December.

Ericson, R. (1993) 'The Royal Commission on Criminal Justice System Surveillance', Paper to Criminal Justice in Crisis Conference, Legal Research Institute, Warwick University, 18 September 1993.

Eurobarometer (1993) *Eurobarometer*, 39 (June) (Brussels: Commission of the European Communities).

European Parliament (1992) *Report drawn up by the Committee of Enquiry into the Spread of Organised Crime Linked to Drugs Trafficking in the Member States of the European Community* (Luxembourg: European Parliament).

Feild, H. and Bienen, L. (1980) *Jurors and Rape* (Lexington, MA: Heath).

Felson, M. (1993) *Crime and Everyday Life* (Pinewood Forge Press).

Fernandes, M. (1992) 'Abolition of Border Controls', *Solicitors Journal*, 13 November, pp. 1142–6.

Field, S. (1990) *Trends in Crime and their Interpretation*, Home Office Research Study No. 119 (London: HMSO).

Fielding, N. (1988) 'Socialisation of recruits into the police role', in Southgate (1988).

Fijnaut, C. (1987) 'The Internationalisation of criminal investigation in Western Europe', in Fijnaut and Hermans (1987).

Fijnaut, C. (1989) 'Looking at policing: a view from the continent', in Hood, R. (ed.), *Crime and Criminal Policy in Europe: Proceedings of a European Colloquium* (Centre for Criminological Research, University of Oxford).

Fijnaut, C. (1990) 'Europeanisation of the Police: what does it mean?', Paper presented at the Congress of the International Sociological Association, Madrid, 9–13 July.

Fijnaut, C. (1991) 'Police Co-operation within Western Europe', in F. Heidensohn and M. Farrell (eds), *Crime in Europe* (London: Routledge).

Fijnaut, C. and Hermans, R. H. (eds) (1987) *Police Cooperation in Europe* (Lochem: Van den Brink).

Fitzpatrick, P. (1984) 'Law and Societies', *Osgoode Hall Law Journal*, 22, pp. 115–38.

Flaherty, D. (1989) *Protecting Privacy in Surveillance Societies* (Chapel Hill, NC: University of North Carolina Press).

Fooner, M. (1989) *Interpol: Issues in World Crime* (New York: Plenum House).

Ford, G. (1992) *Fascist Europe* (London: Pluto Press).

Ford, R. and Tendler, S. (1992) 'RUC is the strongest thread in web spun to destroy the IRA', *The Times*, 23 April.

Foreign and Commonwealth Office (1985) *The European Convention on Spectator Violence and Misbehaviour at Sporting Events and in Particular at Football Matches*, Cmnd 9649 (London: HMSO).

Foreign and Commonwealth Affairs Office (1992) *European Convention on Mutual Assistance in Criminal Matters with Additional Protocol*, Cmnd 1928 (HMSO: London).

Fraser, G. P. A. (1981) 'The applications of police computing', in Pope and Weiner (1981).

Frean, A. (1991) 'Top law officer rejects plan for EC-wide force', *The European*, 12–14 July.

Galeotti, M. (1993) 'Perestroika, perestrelka, pereborka: policing Russia in a time of change', *Europe-Asia Studies*, 45, 5, pp. 769–86

Gallagher, F. (1992) 'Kent County Constabulary – Its European perspective', in Anderson and den Boer (1992).

Gallant, T. W. (1988) 'Greek bandits: lone wolves or a Family Affair?', *Journal of Modern Greek Studies*, 6, 2 (October), pp. 269–90.

Giddens, A. (1985) *The Nation State and Violence* (Cambridge: Polity Press).

Giddens, A. (1991) *Modernity and Self-Identity* (Cambridge: Polity Press).

Gleizal, J., Gatti-Domenach, J. and Journes, C. (1993) *La Police* (Paris: Presses Universitaires de France).

Goldsmith, C. (1991) 'European Security (Tackling Terrorism)', *Intersec*, 1, 2 (June), pp. 40–2.

Greer, S. (n.d.) 'De-centralised policing in Spain: the case of the autonomous Basque police' (unpublished).

Gregory, F. (1990) 'Border control systems and border controllers: a case study of the British police response to proposals for a Europe sans frontiers', *Paper presented to Public Administration Committee Conference*, University of York, August 1990.

Gregory, F. (1992) 'Unprecedented linkages in crime control', Paper presented to the European Consortium for Political Research, Joint Sessions, Limerick.

Gregory, F. and Collier, A. (1992) 'Cross frontier crime and international crime – Problems, achievements and prospects with reference to European police cooperation', in Anderson and den Boer (1992).

Grosheide, J. (1993) 'Cooperation in the field of criminal law, police and other law enforcement agencies', in Schermerr, H. *et al.* (1993).

Grundy, S. (1990) 'Fast and friendly', *Police Review*, 17 August.

Guyomarch, A. (1991) 'Problems of law and order in France in the 1980s: politics and professionalism', *Policing and Society*, 1, pp. 319–32.

Hain, P. (ed.) (1980) *Policing the Police*, Vol.1, (London: John Calder).

Hathaway, J. (1993) 'Harmonizing for whom? The devaluation of of refugee protection in the era of European economic integration', Toronto (mimeo).

Hebenton, B. and Thomas, T. (1992) 'The Rocky path to Europol', *Druglink*, November/December.

Hebenton, B. and Thomas, T. (1993) *Criminal Records: State, Citizen and the Politics of Protection* (Aldershot: Avebury).

Hebenton, B. and Spencer, J. (1994) 'The contribution and limitations of Anglo–American Criminology to understanding crime in Central–Eastern Europe', *European Journal of Crime, Criminal Law and Criminal Justice*, 2 (1), pp. 50–62.

Heidensohn, F. (1991) 'Introduction, in Heidensohn and Farrell (1991).

Heidensohn, F. and Farrell, M. (eds) (1991) *Crime In Europe* (London: Routledge).

Helm, S. (1990) 'British police to seek Council of Europe forces', *The Independent*, 19 June.

Her Majesty's Customs and Excise (1992) *Annual Report 1991–2*, Cm 3054 (London: HMSO).

Herman, E. and O'Sullivan, G. (1989) *The Terrorism Industry: The Experts and Institutions that Shape our View of Terror* (New York: Pantheon).

Hermitage, P. (1989) 'Light on the start of the tunnel', *Policing*, Summer, pp. 121–31.

Hillyard, P. (1993a) *Suspect Community: People's Experience of the Prevention of Terrorism Acts in Britain* (London: Pluto Press).

Hillyard, P. (1993b) 'The Prevention of Terrorism Acts and the new European State', in Bunyan (1993).

Hobsbawm, E. J. (1959) *Primitive Rebels* (Manchester University Press).

Holdaway, S. (1983) *Inside the British Police* (Oxford: Basil Blackwell).

Home Office (1979) *Committee of Inquiry on the Police: Report III. The Structure and Role of Police Staff Associations*, Cmnd 7633 (London: HMSO).

Home Office (1988) *International Mutual Assistance in Criminal Matters* (London: HMSO).

Home Office (1989a) Communication with police forces abroad (Ref. Circular 17/1989).

Home Office (1989b) *Higher Police Training and the Police Staff College – the Government Reply to the Third Report from the Home Affairs Committee Session 1988–9, HC 110–1*. Cmnd 926. London: HMSO.

Home Office (1991a) 'National Criminal Intelligence Service: Appointment of Director Designate', Press Release, 3 June.

Home Office (1991b) *The Government Reply to the Second Report from the Home Affairs Committee Session 1990–1 HC 001. Policing Football Hooliganism*, Cmnd 1539 (London: HMSO).

Home Office (1991c) *The Government Reply to the Seventh Report from the Home Affairs Committee Session 1989–90 HC363–1. Practical Police Cooperation in the European Community*, Cmnd 1367 (London: HMSO).

Home Office (1991d) *The National Collection of Criminal Records: Report of an Efficiency Scrutiny* (London: Home Office).

Home Office (1992a) 'Conclusions of the Meeting of the Ministers responsible for Immigration', Press Release, 30 November.

Home Office (1992b) National Criminal Intelligence Service (NCIS), Note by the Home Office (submitted to AMA Police Committee ref. NCIS/RCS(91)17 as amended).

Home Office (1993) *Police Reform: A Police Service for the Twenty-First Century*, Cmnd 2281 (London: HMSO).

Home Office (1993b) Protection of Children: Disclosure of Criminal Background of those with Access to Children (Ref. HOC 47/93).

Home Office (1993c) *Police Scientific Development Branch, Annual Report 1992/93*.

Home Office Police Department (1993) 'Home Office Police Research Award Scheme 1993 Winners', *Focus*, 2 (August) pp. 15–17.

Hondius, F. (1991) 'Legal aspects of the movement of persons in Greater Europe', *Yearbook of European Law*, 10, pp. 291–307.

House of Commons (1986) *Misuse of Hard Drugs, 1st Report of the Home Affairs Committee Session 1985–6, HC66* (London: HMSO).

House of Commons (1989a) *Drug Trafficking and Related Serious Crime. Home Affairs Committee 7th Report, Session 1988–9. HC 370-1/11* (London: HMSO).

House of Commons (1989b) *Higher Police Training and the Police Staff College. Home Affairs Committee 35d Report, Session 1988–89, HC 110-1/2* (London: HMSO).

House of Commons (1990a) *Policing Football Hooliganism, Second Report of the Home Affairs Committee Session 1990–1, HC 001* (London: HMSO).

House of Commons (1990b) *Practical Police Cooperation in the European Community. Home Affairs Committee (7th Report) Session 1989–90* (London: HMSO). Vol.1 – Report and Proceedings.

House of Commons (1991a) *Fire Safety and Policing of the Channel Tunnel. Home Affairs Committee (1st Report) Session 1991–2,* (London: HMSO). Vol.1 – Report and Proceedings 23–1.

House of Commons (1991b) *Fire Safety and Policing of the Channel Tunnel. Home Affairs Committee (1st Report) Session 1991–2* (London: HMSO), Vol.2 – Minutes of Evidence and Appendices 23–2.

House of Commons (1992) *Migration Control at External Borders of the European Community. Home Affairs Committee, HC 215* (London: HMSO, Minutes of Evidence i, ii and iii.

House of Lords (1989) *1992: Border Control of People. Select Committee on the European Communities, HL 90* (London: HMSO).

House of Lords (1992) *Protection of Personal Data. Select Committee on the European Communities (20th Report) Session 1992–3,* HL paper 75 (London: HMSO).

Iatrides, J. O. (ed.) (1981) *Greece in the 1940's* (Hanover, New Hampshire: University Press of New England).

ICPO – Interpol General Secretariat (1990) 'The European Secretariat', *International Criminal Police Review,* May–June, pp. 10–12.

Interpol (1988) *European Police and Judicial Systems* (Lyons: Interpol).

Jenkins, P. (1988) 'Policing the Cold War: the emergence of new police structures in Europe 1946–1953', *The Historical Journal,* 31, 1, pp. 141–57.

Jensen, R. B. (1981) 'The International Anti-Anarchist Conference of 1898 and the origins of Interpol', *Journal of Contemporary History,* 16, pp. 323–47.

Johnson, R. B. (1992) 'The Story of ACPO', *Police Journal,* LXV, 3 (July–September), pp. 193–9.

Johnston, L. (1992) *The Rebirth of Private Policing* (London: Routledge).

Joutsen, M. (1993) 'The potential for the growth in organized crime in Central and Eastern Europe', *European Journal on Criminal Policy and Research,* 1, 3, pp. 77–87.

Judge, T. (1991) 'Can Soldiers be Bobbies?', *Police,* XXIV, 4 (December).

Kania, R. R. E. (1989) 'The French Municipal Police experiment', *Police Studies,* 12, pp. 125–33.

Kattau, T. (1990)' 1992 – Europe without frontiers', Paper to International Conference on Crime and Policing Islington Borough Council, London, 26–7 November.

Kendall, R. E. (1989) 'Computerisation at the General Secretariat', *International Criminal Police Review*, November–December, pp. 9–16.

Keyser-Ringnalda, F. (1992) 'European integration with regard to the confiscation of the proceeds of crime', *European Law Review*, 17, pp. 499–515.

Killias, M. (1993) 'Will open borders result in more crime? A criminological statement', *European Journal on Criminal Policy and Research*, 1, 3, pp. 7–10.

King, M. (1993) 'The impact of Western European border policies on the control of refugees in Eastern and Central Europe', *New Community*, 19, 2, pp. 183–99.

Kirby, T. (1989) 'Hurd considers plan to form a criminal intelligence unit', *The Independent*, 27 September.

Kirby, T. (1990) 'Chief Constables disagree on FBI-style crime unit', *The Independent*, 19 January.

Kirby, T. (1991) 'Open frontiers "could boost crime"', *The Independent*, 4 April.

Kirby, T. (1992a) 'National drive on top criminals is launched', *The Independent*, 1 April.

Kirby, T. (1992b) 'Pressure grows for an EC-wide detective force', *The Independent*, 20 April.

Kirby, T. (1992c) 'RUC chief proposes national police units', *The Independent*, 22 July.

Klerks, P. (1993) 'Police forces in the EC and EFTA countries, in Bunyan (1993).

Krasner, S. (1983) *International Regimes* (London: Cornell University Press).

Kritz, M., Keely, C. and Tomasi, M. (eds) (1981) *Global Trends in Migration* (New York: Centre for Migration Studies).

Kuhne, H. (1993) 'Control at Internal Borders and National Security', Paper to Public Administration Colloquium Luxembourg, 14–15 October.

Lash, S. and Urry, J. (1987) *The End of Organised Capitalism* (Cambridge: Polity Press).

Latter, R. (1990) 'Crime and the European Community after 1992'. *Wilton Park Papers 31* (London: HMSO).

Lee III, R. W. (1992) 'Dynamics of the Soviet illicit drug market', *Crime, Law and Social Change*, 17, 3, pp. 177–234.

Levi, M. (1993) 'The extent of cross-border crime in Europe', *European Journal on Criminal Policy and Research*, 1, 3, pp. 57–77.

Liang, Hsi-Huey (1970) *The Berlin Police Force in the Weimar Republic* (Berkeley, CA: University of California Press).

Lock, J. (1982) *Tales from Bow Street* (London: Robert Hale).

Lodge, J. (1988) *The Threat of Terrorism* (Brighton: Harvester).

Loescher, G. (1989) 'The European Community and refugees', *International Affairs*, 65, pp. 617–25.

Lowman, J., Menzies, R. and Palys, T. (eds) (1987) *Transcarceration: Essays in the Sociology of Social Control* (Aldershot: Gower).

Lustgarten, L. (1986) *The Governance of the Police* (London: Sweet & Maxwell).

Lyon, D. (1991) 'British identity cards: the unpalatable logic of European membership', *The Political Quarterly*, 62, 3 (July–September), pp. 377–85.

McLaughlin, E. (1992) 'The Democratic Deficit', *British Journal of Criminology*, 32, 4, pp. 473–87.

Maertens, F., Sailas, J., and Joutsen, M. (1992) 'Report on a Joint UNDCP/WHO Mission to Lithuania', 26–28 May 1992, Vienna (unpublished).

Manning, P. (1992) 'Information technologies and the police', in Tonry and Morris (1992).

Marshall, A. (1992) 'Drugs "Marching through Europe's porous borders"', *The Independent* 11 May.

Martin, J. and Romano, A. (1992) *Multinational Crime* (London: Sage).

Mason, G. (1992) 'NCIS is ready to go', *Police Review*, 27 March.

Mawby, R.I. (1990) *Comparative Policing Issues* (London: Unwin Hyman).

Meijers, H., Bolten, J.J., Cruz, A., Steenbergen, J.D.M., Hoogenboom, T., Swart, A.H.J., Verhey, L.F.M. and Boeles, P. (eds) (1991) *Schengen: Internationalisation of central chapters of the law on aliens, refugees, privacy, security and the police* (Deventer: Kluwer).

Miles, R. (1992) 'Europe 1993: l'état, les contradictions de l'immigration et la restructuration de l'exclusion', *Sociologie et Sociétés*, 24, 2, pp. 45–58.

Morgan, R. and Smith, D. (eds) (1989) *Coming to Terms with Policing: Perspectives on Policy* (London: Routledge).

Moskalewicz, J. and Swiatkiewicz, G. (1992), 'Social problems in the Polish political debate', in Simpura, J. and Tigerstedt, C. (eds) *Social Problems Around the Baltic Sea* (Helsinki: Nordic Council for Alochol and Drug Research), No.21 pp. 85–108.

Nadelmann, E. A. (1990) 'The role of the United States in the international enforcement of criminal law', *Harvard International Law Journal*, 31, 1 (Winter), pp. 37–76.

National Criminal Intelligence Service (NCIS) (1993) *Organised Crime Conference: A Threat Assessment, Police Staff College Bramshill, UK*, 24–26 May 1993 (London: NCIS).

Nettl, J. (1968) 'The State as a conceptual variable', *World Politics*, 20, pp. 560–5.

Newing, J. (1990) 'Information technology for the improvement of policing', *International Criminal Police Review*, September–October.

Norton-Taylor, R. and Campbell, D. (1992) 'MI5 wins fight to take on IRA', *The Guardian*, 9 May.

Nugent, N. (1991) *The Government and Politics of the European Community*, 2nd edn (London: Macmillan).

Nundy, J. (1993) 'Corsican who knew too much', *The Independent*, 19 August.

Nundy, J. and Doyle, L. (1993) 'France retains frontier controls', *The Independent*, 1 May.

O'Keefe, D. (1992) 'The Schengen Convention: A suitable model for European integration?', *Yearbook of European Law*, Vol.11, 1991 (Oxford: Clarendon Press).

Organisation for Economic Cooperation and Development (OECD) (1980) *'Guidelines on the Protection of Privacy and Transborder Flows of Personal Data'* (Paris: OECD).

Organisation for Economic Cooperation and Development (OECD) (1989) *OECD Observer* (various) (Paris: OECD).

Pallister, D. (1982) 'Softly, softly approach to new police data link', *The Guardian*, 22 March.

Palmer, J. (1990) 'Why is open Europe so secretive?' *The European*, 2–4 November.

✳Palmer, S. H. (1988) *Police and Protest in England and Ireland 1780–1850* (Cambridge University Press).

Pastore, M. (1991) 'Towards the building of a fortress Europe?', Paper presented at the 19th Annual Conference of the European Group for the Study of Deviance and Social Control, 4–8 September 1991, Potsdam.

Petracca, F. (1993) Intervention in: *Forum on Economia e Criminalita of the Italian Antimafia Commission 14–15 May 1993, Rome, Italy*.

Philips, D. (1977) *Crime and Authority in Victorian England* (London: Croom Helm).

Pope, D. W. and Weiner, N. L. (eds) (1981) *Modern Policing* (London: Croom Helm).

Porter, B. (1987) *The Origins of the Vigilant State* (London: Macmillan).

Porter, B. (1989) *Plots and Paranoia* (London: Routledge).

Programme of Action (1990) *Reinforcement of Police co-operation and of the endeavours to combat terrorism or other forms of organised crime. June* (Dublin: TREVI).

Protocol France No. 1 (1992) *Protocol between the Government of the United Kingdom of Great Britain and Northern Ireland and the Government of the French Republic concerning Frontier Controls and Policing, Cooperation in Criminal Justice, Public Safety and Mutual Assistance relating to the Channel Fixed Link, Cmnd 1802* (London: HMSO).

Punch, M. (ed.) (1983) *Control in the Police Organisation* (Cambridge, MA: MIT Press).

Raab, C. (1994) 'Police Cooperation: the Prospects for Privacy', in Anderson and den Boer (eds) (1994).

Radzinowicz, L. (1948–68) *A History of English Criminal Law and its Administration from 1750*, 4 vols (London: Stevens).

Reiner, R. (1983) 'The politicisation of the police in Britain', in Punch (1983).

Reiner, R. (1992a) 'Policing a Postmodern Society', *Modern Law Review*, 55, 6, pp. 761–81.

Reiner, R. (1992b) *The Politics of the Police*, 2nd edn (Hemel Hempstead: Harvester Wheatsheaf).

Reiner, R. and Spencer, S. (eds) (1993) *Accountable Policing* (London: Institute for Public Policy Research).

Reinke, H. (1991) ' "Armed as if for war": the state, the military and the professionalisation of the Prussian police in Imperial Germany, in Emsley and Weinberger (1991).

Reinke, S. (1992) 'The EC-Commission's anti-fraud activity', in Anderson and den Boer (1992).

Reith, C. (1956) *A New Study of Police History*, London: Oliver & Boyd.

Report of the Royal Commission on Criminal Justice (1993) Cmnd 2263 (London: HMSO).

Reynolds, G. W. and Judge, A. (1968) *The Night the Police went on Strike* (London: Weidenfeld & Nicolson).

Robertson, K. (1992) 'Police Intelligence Co-operation: Problems and Prospects', Paper to European Consortium for Political Research, Joint Sessions, Limerick.

Rose, D. (1993) 'Memo to Sheehy: You're joking', *The Observer*, 25 July.

Ruimschotel, D. (1993) 'Ambiguities between criminal policy and scientific research: the case of fraud against the EC', *European Journal on Criminal Policy and Research*, 1, 3, pp. 101–23.

Russell, S. (1993) 'Cross Border Crime and the Changing Role of Customs in Europe', Paper presented to Police, Crime and Justice in Europe Conference, University of Leicester, 23 September 1993.

Sage, A. (1992) 'European Court should have power over extradition, Delors says', *The Independent*, 5 December.

St Johnston, E. (1978) *One Policeman's Story* (Chichester: Barry Rose).

Salt, J. (1992) 'Current and future international migration trends affecting Europe', in *People on the Move: New Migration Flows in Europe* (Strasbourg: Council of Europe Press).

Saltmarsh, G. (1993) 'Organised/Enterprise Crime', in NCIS (1993).

Savona, E. (1990) 'Social change, organization of crime and criminal justice systems', in *Essays on Crime and Development* (Rome: United Nations Interregional Crime and Justice Research Institute).

Scheller, S. (1992) 'Legal problems of the Schengen Information System', in Anderson and den Boer (1992).

Schengen Convention (1990) 'Applying the Schengen Agreement of 14 June 1985 between the Governments of the Benelux Economic Union, the Federal Republic of Germany and the French Republic on the gradual abolition of checks at their common borders', June, mimeo.

Schermerr, H., C., Kellermann, A., Haersolte, J. and Meent, G. van de (eds), *Free Movement of Persons in Europe* (Asser Institute, Dordrecht: Martinus Nijhoff).

Schmidt-Nothen, R. (1989) 'Police Cooperation in Europe in the context of the abolition of border controls', *International Criminal Police Review*, September–October, pp. 5–9.

Schutte, J. (1990) 'Strafrecht in Europees verband', *Justitiële Verkenningin* No.9, pp. 8–17.

Schutte, J. (1991) 'Schengen: its meaning for the free movement of persons in Europe', *Common Market Law Review*, 28, pp. 549–70.

Scraton, P. (1985) *The State of the Police* (London: Pluto Press).

Sheey, Sir P. (1993) *Inquiry into Police Responsibilities and Rewards* (London: HMSO).

\Sheills, D. (1991) 'The Politics of Policing: Ireland 1919–1923' in Emsley and Weinberger (eds) (1991).

Sherlock, A. and Harding, C. (1991) 'Controlling fraud within the European Community', *European Law Review*, 16, 1, pp. 20–36.

Smart, V. (1993) 'Passport checks to be abolished at last', *The European* 1–4 July.

SOPEMI (1994) *Trends in International Migration* (Paris: OECD).

Southgate, P. (ed.) (1988) *New Directions in Police Training* (London: Home Office Research and Planning Unit, HMSO).

Spencer, M. (1990) *1992 and all that: Civil Liberties in the Balance* (The Civil Liberties Trust: London).

Spitzer, S. (1987) 'Security and Control in Capitalist Societies: The Fetishism of Security and the Secret Thereof', in Lowman, Menzies and Palys (1987).

Standing Conference on Drug Abuse (1992) *Annual Report 1991/ 1992* (London: SCODA).

Stead, P. J. (1957) *The Police of Paris* (London: Staples Press).

Storch, R. (1975) 'The plague of blue locusts: police reform and popular resistance in Northern England 1840–57', *International Review of Social History*, 20.

Sutton, M. and Maynard, A. (1992) *What is the Size and Nature of the 'drug problem' in the U.K.?* Occasional Paper No.3, Yorkshire Addictions Research, Training and Information Consortium, Centre for Health Economics (University of York).

Sutton, M. and Maynard, A. (1994) *Trends in the Cost Effectiveness of Enforcement Activity in the Illicit Heroin Market, 1979–1990*, Occasional Paper No.4, Yorkshire Addictions Research, Training and Information Consortium, Centre for Health Economics (University of York).

Tendler, S. (1992) 'MI5 vies with police for anti-IRA operations', *The Times*, 6 April.

Thompson, E. P. (1968) *The Making of the English Working Class* (London: Penguin).

Tonry, M. and Morris, N. (eds) (1992) *Modern Policing* (Crime and Justice Annual Review of Research Vol. 15) (Chicago University Press).

Townson, N. (1993) 'How Spain broke the Eta Bombers', *The Observer*, 28 November.

Treaty of Canterbury (1986) *Treaty between the United Kingdom of Great Britain and Northern Ireland and the French Republic concerning the Construction and Operation by Private Concessionaires of a Channel Fixed Link with Exchange of Notes*, Cmnd 9745 (London: HMSO).

Treaty on European Union 'Maastricht Treaty' (1992) (Luxembourg: Office for Official Publications of the European Communities).

Tremblay, P. and Rochon, C. (1991) 'Police organizations and their use of knowledge: a grounded research agenda', *Policing and Society*, 1, pp. 269–83.

UNISYS (1991) European Police Seminar, 25–27 November 1991, Unisys International Management Centre, Saint-Paul-de-Vence, France, Unisys Europe-Africa Ltd, Uxbridge, UK.

United Nations (1990) World Ministerial Summit to Reduce the Demand for Drugs and to Combat the Cocaine Threat (text of the London Declaration ref. A/45262), mimeo.

United Nations (1991) *Situation and Trends in Drug Abuse and Illicit Traffic* (Vienna: Commission on Narcotic Drugs, United Nations).

Usborne, D. (1990) 'Clear from Biarritz to Berlin', *The Independent on Sunday*, 17 June.

van Dijk, J. (1993) 'Crime in Europe: trends and prospects', Paper to Crime in Europe: Patterns and Prospects for the 1990s, 23 September 1993, Centre for the Study of Public Order, University of Leicester, UK.

van Dijk, J. and Mayhew, P. (1993) 'Criminal victimization in the industrial world', Report to the NICRI Conference Understanding Crime: Experiences of Crime and Crime Control, 18–20 November 1992.

van Dijk, J., Mayhew, P. and Killias, M. (1990) *Experiences of Crime Across the World* (Deventer: Kluwer).

van Duyne, P. (1993) 'Organized crime markets in a turbulent Europe', *European Journal on Criminal Policy and Research*, 1, 3, pp. 10–30.

van Reenen, P. (1989a) 'Policing Europe after 1992: cooperation and competition', *European Affairs*, 3(2), pp. 45–53

van Reenen, P. (1989b) 'Cooperation and integration of Police throughout the EEC: the alternative of the special police', Seminar paper presented to IPEC, London, September 1989.

van Reenen, P. (1992) 'Today's training: a European Police Institute', in Anderson and Den Boer (1992).

Vergnolle, J.-L. (1992) 'The Mattheus Programme', in Anderson and den Boer (1992).

Verhey, L. F. M. (1991) 'Privacy aspects of the Convention applying the Schengen Agreement', in Meijers *et al.* (1991).

Waddington, P. A. (1984) 'Citizen or Slag?', *Police*, XVI, 6.

Walker, C. (1992) *The Prevention of Terrorism in British Law*, 2nd edn (Manchester University Press).

Walker, N. (1991) 'The United Kingdom Police and European Cooperation' (Dept. of Politics, University of Edinburgh).

Walker, N. (1993) 'The international dimension', in Reiner and Spencer (1993).

Warren, P. (1992) 'Crime sans frontiers or the end of liberty?' *Computer Weekly*, 7 May.

Wasserman, G. (1989) 'Putting crime into context' (interview) *Siemens Magazine*, COM 5/89.

Watts, S. (1991) 'Police computer could be threat to civil rights', *The Independent*, 18 December.

Webber, F. (1993) 'The new Europe: immigration and asylum', in Bunyan (1993).

Weeks, J. (1990a) 'The £1 billion bill for "Europol"', *Police*, April.

Weeks, J. (1990b) 'Seeing eye to eye at both ends of the tunnel', *Police*, May, pp. 10–12.

Wheeler, J. (1993) 'How criminals cross the thin blue line', *The Independent*, 9 February.

Wiebrens, C. (1990) 'Police Personnel Re-allocation: the Dutch case', *Policing and Society*, 1, pp. 57–76.

Wilkitzki, P. (1991) 'Development of an effective international crime and justice programme – A European view', Paper to the International Workshop on Principles and Procedures for a New Transnational Criminal Law, The Society for the Reform of Criminal Law and Max Planck Institute for Foreign and International Criminal Law, 21–25 May, Freiburg, Germany.

Winder, R. (1993) 'Spill the beans, pal, and make it vite', *The Independent*, 17 September.

Woodcock, J. (1991) 'Overturning police culture', *Policing*, 7, 3, pp. 172–82.

World Bank (1991) *World Development Report 1991* (Oxford University Press).

Young, O. (1983) 'Regime dynamics: the rise and fall of international regimes', in Krasner (1983).

Young, O. (1989) *International Co-operation* (London: Cornell University Press).

Zacher, M. W. (1990) 'Toward a theory of international regimes', *Journal of International Affairs*, Spring, pp. 139–57.

Zolberg, A. (1981) 'International migrations in political perspective', in Kritz, Keely and Tomasi (1981).

Index